T0250609

Brian C. Warboys (Ed.)

Software Process Technology

Third European Workshop, EWSPT '94
Villard de Lans, France, February 7-9, 1994
Proceedings

Springer-Verlag

Berlin Heidelberg New York
London Paris Tokyo
Hong Kong Barcelona
Budapest

Series Editors

Gerhard Goos
Universität Karlsruhe
Postfach 69 80
Vincenz-Priessnitz-Straße 1
D-76131 Karlsruhe, Germany

Juris Hartmanis
Cornell University
Department of Computer Science
4130 Upson Hall
Ithaca, NY 14853, USA

Volume Editor

Brian C. Warboys
Department of Computer Science, University of Manchester
Manchester M13 9PL, United Kingdom

CR Subject Classification (1991): D.2, K.6, K.4.2

ISBN 3-540-57739-4 Springer-Verlag Berlin Heidelberg New York
ISBN 0-387-57739-4 Springer-Verlag New York Berlin Heidelberg

This work is subject to copyright. All rights are reserved, whether the whole or part
of the material is concerned, specifically the rights of translation, reprinting, re-use
of illustrations, recitation, broadcasting, reproduction on microfilms or in any other
way, and storage in data banks. Duplication of this publication or parts thereof is
permitted only under the provisions of the German Copyright Law of September 9,
1965, in its current version, and permission for use must always be obtained from
Springer-Verlag. Violations are liable for prosecution under the German Copyright
Law.

© Springer-Verlag Berlin Heidelberg 1994
Printed in Germany

Printing and binding: Druckhaus Beltz, Hemsbach/Bergstr.
Typesetting: Camera-ready by author
45/3140-543210 - Printed on acid-free paper

Lecture Notes in Computer Science 772

Edited by G. Goos and J. Hartmanis

Advisory Board: W. Brauer   D. Gries   J. Stoer

Preface

The software process is the total set of software engineering activities necessary to develop and maintain software products. Software process technology (SPT) deals with methods, formalisms and tools for supporting the software process.

SPT has developed into a key technology in terms of its importance to software engineering environments, systems integration, cooperative working and business process re-engineering. This widespread influence means that it has connections to many disciplines such as product modelling, configuration management, groupware, cooperating transactions, interpretive systems, and rule-based systems.

The field of SPT started some 10 years ago and there are now a number of international workshops, symposia and conferences on SPT. However there was little organised contact in Europe until the European Workshops on Software Process Technology (EWSPT) were initiated.

The first EWSPT was held during May 1991 at Cefriel in Milan. The workshop brought together practitioners working in the field and led an initiative to develop common technology, frameworks and research on models. One result of the workshop was the creation of the Working Group on Software Processes of the ESPRIT III programme in Basic Research (called BRA-WG *Promoter*). This three-year project aims to promote the common activity in the field.

Promoter started in September 1992 and the second EWSPT '92 was held in Trondheim, 7-9 September 1992. The proceedings are available in this series as LNCS 635. The third meeting EWSPT '94 will be held near Grenoble during 7-9 February 1994 and organised by Christer Fernstrom of Cap Gemini Innovation.

We wish to thank Cap Gemini Innovation and all our supporting organisations, as well as Springer-Verlag who once again kindly agreed to publish these proceedings. Thanks also to the programme committee, the reviewers and all of the authors who have provided either full length or position papers.

The six workshop sessions organised around architecture, meta process and methodology, process modelling concepts, PML concepts and paradigms, experiences with SPT and related domains were supported by the papers which form the chapters of these proceedings.

November 1993
Brian Warboys
Programme Committee Chairman

Table of Contents

Architecture session

Jacky Estublier

L.G.I. BP 53X 38041 Grenoble FRANCE

It is a consequence of the Software Process Technology rapid maturation that efficiency, availability, generality, and architectural issues in general, come to the surface.

We are faced with at least three aspects of the problem: 1) identifying the components of a Process centred SEE, or of any process management tool, 2) identifying, adapting and using enabling technology, and 3) define and evaluate the different relationships between these components.

The first issue is be to identify which are the specific components of Process centred SEE, or of any process management tool. In the various prototypes can be found: active data- bases, event managers, inference engines, activity managers, formalisms interpreters, blackboards, GUI, workspace managers, cooperation managers, and much more. Few agreement haver been reached, so far, on which are the specific components, which are their function, which are their relationships. More work needs to be done in order to better identify these components in relation with the different classes of software process manager tools. Furthermore, these components are usual ad-hoc, and their interface not clearly defined. Is it possible to isolate components usable by a large number of Process tool.

Most work identified also a need for interfacing/integrating with network, message servers and tool interoperability support currently available. Clearly network and interop- erability issues are (or will be) central to any process management tool, since one of the goals is to control tools and activities of large teams, thus across a network. Do we require specific services? which one. This is an issue to be addressed in the very near future.

The need for an Object Manager System, DBMS, Product repository, Tools repository and repositories in general, needed for Software Process support, is accepted by most researchers. However it is also a general feeling that the available tools for repository do not provide the services we need. What are these services, what role the repositories have to play in a tool for Process modelling and support?. This is also an open issue.

So far, in most work, there is a single process engine. I do suspect, in the future, different process engine will collaborate. Each process engine being specialized in a kind of task, or supporting a different class of users, or controlling the processes on a given machine/ machine-cluster. These process engines could be homogeneous, i.e interpreting the same formalism and/or the same model or not. In a more general way, interoperability between the different process engines present in the same PSEE, will have to be addressed.

In this session, different aspects have been addressed: networking is addressed by Spade paper and "PMIPS" position paper, parts of the repositories by Oikos, interoperability by the ICL position paper. However, so far, architecture have been addressed essentially from a given project perspective. A general work on architecture is still to be done.

The Oikos Services for Object Management in the Software Process*

Vincenzo Ambriola, Giovanni A. Cignoni and Carlo Montangero

Dipartimento di Informatica, Università di Pisa

Corso Italia 40, 56125 Pisa, Italy

Abstract. A software development process is strictly related to the representation and the management of the involved objects. Software products, tools, and computational resources are typical objects. It is convenient to distinguish the definition of software process activities and the issues that pertain to object management. Standard services have been introduced in Oikos to provide process activities with a set of primitive functionalities for object management. These standard services present the Object Management System functionalities at an abstraction level that well matches the definition of the process activities.

1 Introduction

A *software development process* is usually described as a set of concurrent activities [12, 13]; its *performance* is the interpretation of these activities by human people and machines [18]. Each activity has an associated set of *agents* and a set of *objects*. The first set consists of the agents in the software process: automatic components of the process and people participating to its performance. The set of objects includes development products, tools in use, computational resources, and the representation of the components of the process themselves. For instance, the objects of an edit-compile cycle are the modules under development and the tools in use; the objects related to a task assignment are the representations of the task and of the technician who will carry it out.

In this perspective it is important to define a model that takes into account the representation and the management of all the objects involved in the software process. Such a model must allow a clear distinction among the peculiarities of object management and the description of process activities. In other words, the model must introduce a set of primitive operations on objects, thereby defining an abstraction layer on top of which the activities of the software process can be defined.

In Oikos, a software process is described as a set of co-operative *entities*. The idea of defining a number of basic concepts for the software process is currently widely accepted [13]: a specific software process is thus obtained by specialising and

---

* This work is funded by Progetto Finalizzato Sistemi Informatici e Calcolo Parallelo del CNR, MURST 60%, and ESPRIT BRA Promoter WG.

composing these concepts. In Oikos the following entities are introduced, one for each software process concept: *processes*, *environments*, *offices*, *desks*, and *services* [1]. Typically an entity is defined in terms of simpler entities according to a composition strategy that introduces several abstraction levels [2]. The leaves of the resulting hierarchy are simple entities, ie entities that are not decomposed and that constitute the base of the software process description. Among these simple entities, services are introduced to manage the resources exploited in the software development. Resources are naturally grouped in classes and a different service is introduced for each class. Moreover, each service defines the interface used by software process activities to access the resources, ie the objects.

The need of encapsulating object management functionalities in a well identified component of the run time support is commonly addressed in the literature related to software process representation and enactment. For this purpose, Arcadia [24] and Odin [10] introduce *object managers*; EPOS [11], Marvel [17] and Spade [4] exploit *databases*; Merlin [20] relies on a *knowledge base*. In Oikos, objects are managed by an *Object Management System* in a peculiar way: management functionalities are indirectly presented to software process activities by services. The major advantage of this approach is that it leads naturally to a modular definition of the specific resource model of a given process.

The next section describes object management from the viewpoint of the software process introducing the concept of Oikos service. Section 3 presents the core of the model for the management of products and tools, ie the basic objects and the operations shared by any process enacted in Oikos. Section 4 describes the architecture of the Oikos OMS and Section 5 points to the evolution of the current implementation.

2 The Service Concept

The idea of services as resource managers is largely used in concurrent programming and operating systems. Similar concepts are found in *monitors* [15] and *client-server* architectures [23]. The main objective in applying these concepts to process-centred development environments is to achieve a better structure and more modularity both in the process description and in the architecture of its enactment support.

In this context, a *resource* is any element needed to the software process for which the notions of access, sharing, and arbitration are meaningful. The service monitors the accesses to a shared resource and solves the related concurrency conflicts. Different classes of resources are managed by different services each one defining the relevant access protocols.

A *protocol* defines an access mode to a resource of a given class: it defines a set of functionalities that act on the resource and the policies that rule their invocation. A service is characterised by the whole set of functionalities offered by its protocols. As an example, consider a service that manages a resource consisting of a document repository: its functionalities include creation and deletion of a document, and access controlled by read or write rights. The service protocols define the available functionalities in terms of the resource state. For instance, a protocol will control concurrent write accesses to a document and the rights to deposit or delete a document.

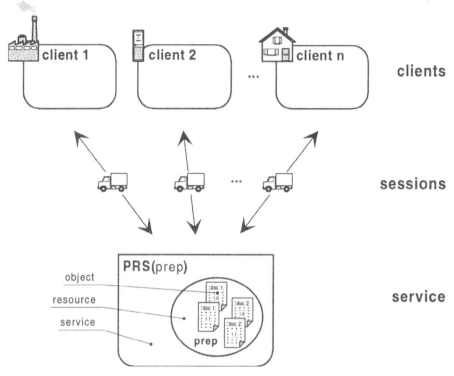

Fig. 1. Relations between *clients*, *sessions*, and *services*.

The notion of service is general and each specific service depends on the class of the managed resource. A service *instance* manages a specific, concrete resource of the class for which the service has been defined. *Clients* may use the functionalities offered by a service instance via a mechanism based on *sessions*. A client issues a request to open a private session; the client can then use the service functionalities until the session is closed either by an explicit request or because of a service decision. Each session has an associated protocol; only one protocol can be associated to a session. Clients and service instances interact only via sessions. A client can request multiple private sessions with each service instance: more than one session can be simultaneously open, even with different protocols for the same client.

The request to open a session is a functionality common to all services. Like any other functionality, this request must follow a *login* protocol associated to a login session. The login session is a public session automatically opened when a service instance is created and available to its clients as long as the service instance is active.

In Oikos, a service instance is meaningful only as a component of a more complex entity [1]. Each service instance is *activated* as a component of a unique entity, called its *mother*. On the other side, a service instance is *available* to its mother and to all the entities in the hierarchy rooted in the mother. This set of entities constitutes *the set of clients* of the service instance. Access to a service instance is granted to its clients by the login session. Availability does not necessarily mean that a session request will be satisfied: in general the service makes a decision according to its state.

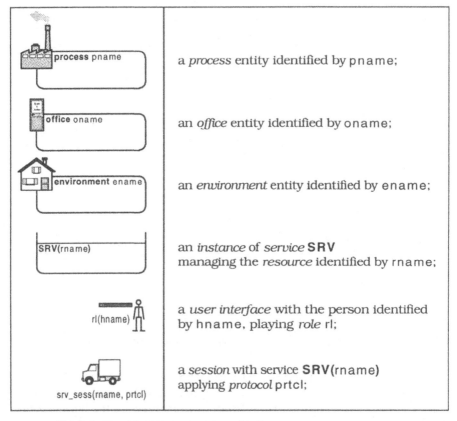

process pname	a *process* entity identified by pname;
office oname	an *office* entity identified by oname;
environment ename	an *environment* entity identified by ename;
SRV(rname)	an *instance* of *service* **SRV** managing the *resource* identified by rname;
rl(hname)	a *user interface* with the person identified by hname, playing *role* rl;
srv_sess(rname, prtcl)	a *session* with service **SRV(rname)** applying *protocol* prtcl;

Table 1. Graphical representation of software process components.

Figure 1 sketches the relations between clients, sessions, services, and the managed resources. The graphical notation is explained in Table 1. Figure 2 graphically presents an example of the use of services in a simple software process. The whole process corresponds to the composed entity named development. This entity consists of the manager office and of several environments. A developer performs his task in each environment. Moreover, process development consists of two service instances, namely PRS(main), as an instance of the *Product Repository Server* (PRS), and TRS(main), as an instance of the *Tool Repository Server* (TRS). Since they have been activated in the external entity they are also available to the internal components, ie to the office manage and to the environments develop_i. Another service, the *Workspace Server* (WS), is also used in the process. Its instances are labelled with the name of the managed workspaces: WS(manage) in the office manage, and WS(develop_i) in each develop_i environment. The manager accesses WS by session ws_sess(manage, access) and PRS functionalities by session prs_sess(main, management). The arguments in the session name define the resource and the protocol. The manager can deposit development products in the product repository main since the *management* protocol allows him to do so. Each developer has a session with each of the service instances WS(develop_i), TRS(main), and PRS(main). Session prs_sess(main, access) allows the developer, via the *access* protocol, to check-out and check-in the products belonging to the main product repository. The same protocol forbids the developer to destroy or deposit products, leaving this responsibility to the manager.

The nature of the sample resources, product repository, tool repository, and workspaces will be discussed in detail in the next section.

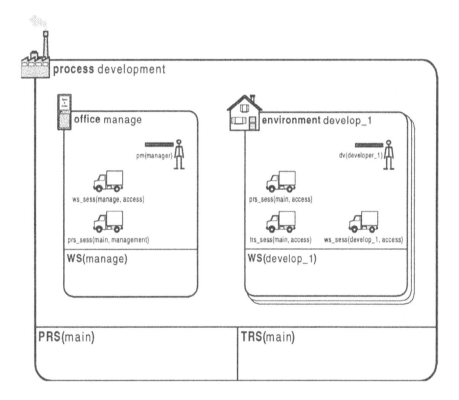

Fig. 2. Representation of a software process in Oikos.

3 Modelling Products and Tools

Most policies for the management of objects like products and tools are common to all software processes. In Oikos, in order to foster reuse and standardisation, a set of *standard services* are predefined to offer functionalities to access the process objects. Among these, the already mentioned standard services PRS, TRS, and WS offer access protocols that guarantee consistent access with respect to the basic model for products and tool management. Each standard service supports the management of a specific class of objects or of a facet of the model: for instance, service WS allows tthe application of tools to products.

The main characteristic of the product model in Oikos is the distinction between *deposited documents* and *working documents.* Deposited documents are the real products of the software process, ie those documents that in their development have reached a consistent state, even if not necessarily the ultimate one. A *product repository*, ie the resource managed by an instance of PRS, holds a set of deposited documents. The protocols of service PRS define the concurrency control of the access to deposited documents, according to a policy based on the *check-out/check-in* mechanism: a deposited document can be locked, therefore ensuring that it can be modified in just a workspace at a time. Moreover, it is possible to constrain access to selected documents exploiting access keys. Documents held in repositories may have *revisions* and *releases* according to the SCCS/RCS model for version control [21, 25].

Many approaches to software process modelling provide a specific representation of the environment where documents are operated on. For instance, Adele2 [6] has the notion of *working environment* and Merlin [22] that of *working context*. In Oikos a *workspace* is a set of computational and memory resources allocated to a given task to hold the products currently under development, namely the *working documents*, and the tools to work on them. Standard service WS defines the access protocols to a workspace, ie how it is possible to manage working documents and to apply tools to them.

Finally, both deposited and working documents have a type used to control tool application. The set of document types of a given software process can be partially ordered in such a way that tools can be applied to documents of different types in a controlled way. For instance, given the partial order shown in Figure 3, and given that an editor is applicable to documents of type *text*, the same editor can be applied also to documents of types *source*, *c_module*, and so on.

The tool model has three main facets: tool *representation*, *installation*, and *application*. A *signature* is associated to each tool. The signature specifies the number and the types of input working documents, the number and the types of output working documents, and the parameters for tool application. As shown in Figure 4, the output working documents are grouped in two classes: those that are created by the tool application and that are not in the workspace before, and those modified which are a subset of the input documents already in the workspace and that are changed by the tool application.

A *tool repository*, ie the resource managed by an instance of TRS, holds a set of signatures. The protocols of service TRS have the functionalities to modify the set of signatures in the resource and to install the tools in a workspace. Installing a tool in a workspace amounts to defining its application environment, ie the set of documents on which the tool can work and the physical resources used by the tool (the machine that will run it and the X display that will be used to interact with the user, whenever the tool needs one).

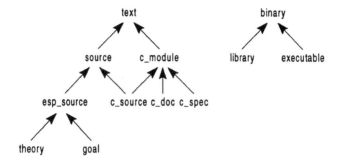

Fig. 3. An example of document types ordering.

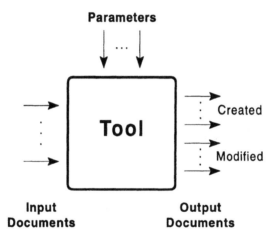

Fig. 4. Tool signature.

Finally, the details of tool application are defined in the tool model. There are three phases:

- **check**: the correctness of the application request is verified with respect to the tool signature, the availability of the tool and of the input working documents in the workspace;
- **execution**: the tool is run on the resources associated to the workspace;
- **update**: the set of working documents in the workspace where the tool has been applied is updated according to the outcome of the execution.

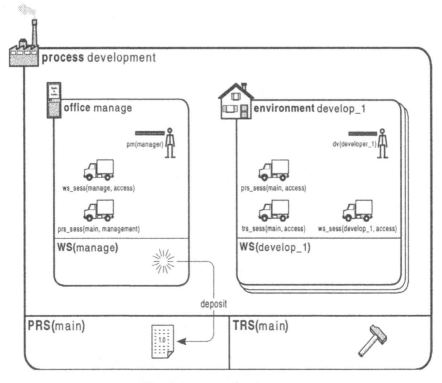

Fig. 5. *Deposit* of a document.

A fourth important facet of tool management is related to tool integration. Oikos fulfills the requirements of *Rapid Tool Integration* [19]: any tool which is considered useful to the software development can be easily integrated, without the need of modifying the tool. The approach is the same of Marvel [14], where tools are wrapped in an *envelope* that redefines the tool interface to suit the environment needs [3].

As an example of use of standard services in object management we describe a fragment of the life of a source module in the process introduced in Figure 2. Figure 5 shows how the first version of the source, which has been created by the manager in his own workspace, is deposited in the product repository associated to the PRS(main). The document is deposited via session prs_sess(main, management). This deposited document then makes the source available to all the developers involved in the process.

Figure 6 shows the state of the process after a developer has copied the source module, as a working document, in his own workspace. The copy is done by a check-out operation via session prs_sess(main, access). After this check-out operation, the document in the repository is locked so that no other developer can modify it. Moreover, developer dv(developer_1) accessed the tool repository managed by TRS(main) and installed the needed tools, eg an editor and a compiler.

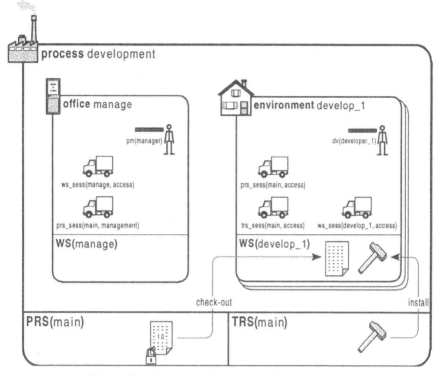

Fig. 6. *Check-out* of a document and *install* of a tool.

The developer then applies the tools to the working document in the workspace via session **ws_sess(develop_1, access)**. Finally, once the module has been completely coded, the developer will check-in the document, always via session **prs_sess(main, access)**: a new version has been created and the lock on the previous one has been released, as shown in Figure 7.

Different typical development policies, with respect to tool access in the development context and to documents visibility at different stages of the process, can be represented in Oikos by suitable tailoring of service instances availability to the process entities.

4 OMS Architecture

Standard services are responsible for the presentation of the operations on objects to the software process. Besides presentation, object representation must also be considered, as well as the management of their physical components. Several approaches consider an object as a set of *attributes* and a *contents* [5, 7]. The set of attributes characterises the object representation, ie the form of its presentation to the software process; the contents correspond to the objects substance, ie its physical nature as it exists in the real world of the development. Accordingly, the Oikos OMS is structured in three abstraction levels, as depicted in Figure 8.

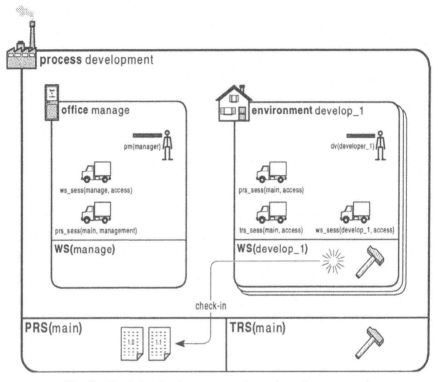

Fig. 7. *Check-in* of a document and creation of a new version.

- *Service level*: this level is in charge of object presentation to the software process entities. The Oikos standard services define the protocols used by the entities to access the objects under development. The services, being entities themselves, belong naturally to the description of the software process: in fact they provide the basic functionalities in the description of the process. To this purpose, the interfaces of the services toward the process are defined in Patè, the Oikos enactment language.
- *Object Level*: this level is in charge of the management of the object form, ie of the objects representation with respect to the process description which has the property of being independent of its physical nature. Goals of this level are the persistency of the object representation and the availability of a logical global view of the objects. In this way, it is possible to manage the relations among different classes of objects such as the link between a working document and the original deposited document in a repository or the link between a tool installed in a workspace and the tool signature in the tool repository. This global view of the objects defines an essential part of the process state upon which it is possible to make queries and verify properties.
- *Item Level*: this level is in charge of the substance of the objects. Most classes of objects represented at the object level have a corresponding substance in the

real world: the item level interfaces the OMS to the operating system supporting the Oikos environment. Therefore the item level represents also the portability level of Oikos.

In the OMS implementation, the above level are layered virtual machines each devoted to support a specific facet of the object nature. The object level plays a central role, while the other two are interfaces.

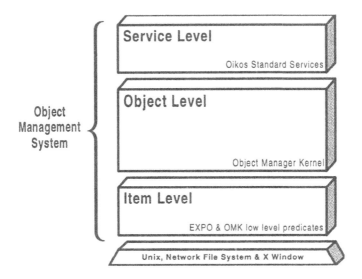

Fig. 8. Structure of the Oikos OMS.

The *Object Manager Kernel* (OMK) is the OMS component that implements the functionalities of the object level. The OMK manages the set of resources, ie repositories and workspaces. It supports resource allocation and deallocation and implements the operations on objects. Currently the OMK is implemented as a logic database defined in LDL [9]. Operations on objects are implemented as transactions on the database.

With respect to the integration of the OMK and the Item Level we adopted an approach like the one introduced in [16]: the Item Level consists of several components each one in charge of the management of a specific class of objects. This approach naturally matches the diversity of the physical objects to be considered: the OMK is then viewed as a means to integrate specialised lower level managers. As a consequence, there is a great flexibility to choose the mechanism for the physical object management at this level. The current implementation interfaces the underlying file system via a set of external predicates written in C and imported in LDL. On the other hand, tool integration and execution exploit the functionalities offered to this purpose by EXPO [3].

5 Future Development

A first foreseen extension of the OMS is related to the process representation and its enactment state. Two new standard services, *Process Model Server* and *Process State Server*, are being designed together with the definition of the relevant object classes, namely the objects capturing the entities in the process model and their states.

A number of operations related to the management of computation resources and of the envelopes to integrate tools are now performed, at low level, outside Oikos. It is foreseen that these operations will be presented to the software process entities via new protocols of the relevant standard services, therefore providing a more uniform environment for process enactment.

An independent extension is related to the document model as a whole. The software process definer needs to introduce structured types in order to tailor the document model to a specific software process. This entails the introduction of a more sophisticated approach to concurrency control in the access to documents and to the related merging and versioning policies.

Acknowledgements

We want to thank our users Cristina Iorio, Silvana Fantoni, Alessandra Tesauro, and Stefano Tirabassi for their constructive criticisms. Tito Flagella and Mauro Gaspari developed the first version of the Oikos Run-time Support.

References

1. V. Ambriola, C. Montangero, "Hierarchical Specification of Software Processes in Oikos", Proceedings of the 7th International Software Process Workshop, Yountsville, October 1991.
2. V. Ambriola, C. Montangero, "Oikos at the age of three", Proceedings of the 2nd European Workshop on Software Process Technology, Trondheim, 1992.
3. V. Ambriola, C. Montangero, M. Gaspari, T. Flagella, "EXPO: a Framework for Process Centered Environments", Technical Report 21/92, Dipartimento di Informatica, Università di Pisa, August 1992.
4. S. Bandinelli, A. Fuggetta, C. Ghezzi, S. Grigolli, "Process Enactment in SPADE", Proceedings of the 2nd European Workshop on Software Process Technology, Trondheim, September 1992.
5. P. Baumann, D. Köhler, "Archiving Versions and Configurations in a Database System for System Engineering Environments", Proceedings of the International Workshop on Software Version and Configuration Control, Grassau, January 1988.
6. N. Belkatir, J. Estublier, W. Melo, "A Support to Large Software Development Process", Proceedings of the First International Conference on the Software Process, Redondo Beach, June 1991.
7. L. Bendix, "Automatic Configuration Management in a General Object Based Environment", Proceedings of the 4th International Conference on Software Engineering and Knowlwdge Engineering, Capri, June 1992.

8. A. Bucci, P. Ciancarini, C. Montangero, "A Distributed Logic Language Based on Multiple Tuple Spaces", Proceedings of the Logic Programming Conference, Tokyo, July 1991.

9. D. Chimenti, R. Gamboa, R. Krishnamurthy, S. Naqvi, S. Tsur, C. Zaniolo, "The LDL System Prototype", *IEEE Transactions on Knowledge and Data Engineering*, Vol. 2, No. 1, March 1990.

10. G. Clemm, L. Osterweil, "A Mechanism for Environment Integration", *ACM Transactions on Programming Languages and Systems*, Vol. 12, No. 1, 1990.

11. R. Conradi, Ola Heensåsen, Svein-Olaf Hvasshovd, "EPOS DB Data model", EPOS Project Report, Division of Computer Science Norwegian Institute of Technology, Trondheim, June 1987.

12. B. Curtis, M.I. Kellner, J. Over, "Process Modeling" *Communications of ACM*, Vol. 35, No. 9, September 1992.

13. M.Dowson, B. Nejmeh, W. Riddle, "Fundamental Software Process Concepts", Proceedings of the First European Workshop on Software Process Modeling, Milano, May 1991.

14. M.A. Gisi, G.E. Kaiser, "Extending a Tool Integration Language", Proceedings of the First International Conference on the Software Process, Redondo Beach, 1991.

15. C.A.R. Hoare, "Monitors: An Operating Systems Structuring Concept", *Communications of ACM*, Vol. 17, No. 10, October 1974.

16. B. Holtkamp, H. Weber, "Object-Management Machines: Concept and Implementation", *Journal of Systems Integration*, Vol. 1, No. 3/4, 1991.

17. G.E. Kaiser, N.S. Barghouti, "Database Support for Knowledge-Based Engineering Environments", *IEEE Expert*, Summer 1988.

18. C. Liu, R. Conradi, "Process Modeling Paradigms: An Evaluation", Proceedings of the First European Workshop on Software Process Modeling, Milano, May 1991.

19. A. Mahler, A. Lampen, "Integrating Configuration Management into a Generic Environment", Proceedings of ACM SIGSOFT '90, 4th Symposium on Software Development Environments, Irvine, December 1990.

20. B. Peuschel, W. Schäfer, S. Wolf, "A Knowledge-Based Software Development Environment Supporting Cooperative Work", *International Journal of Software Engineering and Knowledge Engineering*, Vol. 2, No. 1, 1992.

21. M.J. Rochkind, "The Source Code Control System", *IEEE Transactions on Software Engineering*, Vol. SE-1, No. 4, December 1975.

22. W. Schäfer, S. Wolf, "Multi-User Support in the Process-Centered Software Engineering Environment Merlin", Position Paper, Workshop on "Process Sensitive Software Development Environment Architectures", Boulder, 1992.

23. A. Sinha, "Client Server Computing", *Communications of ACM*, Vol. 35, No. 7, July 1992.

24. R.N. Taylor et al., "Next Generation Software Environments: Principles, Problems and Research Directions", COINS Technical Report 87-63, University of Massachusetts at Amherst, July 1987.

25. W.F. Tichy, "RCS - A System for Version Control", *Software–Practice & Experience*, Vol. 15, No. 7, July 1985.

The Architecture of the SPADE-1 Process-Centered SEE

S. Bandinelli (1&2), M. Braga (2), A. Fuggetta (1&3), L. Lavazza (1)

CEFRIEL (1), DEC (2), Politecnico di Milano (3)

ABSTRACT

SPADE is a project carried out at CEFRIEL and Politecnico di Milano. It aims at defining a process modeling language (called SLANG) and a Process-centered Software Engineering Environment (PSEE) based on this language. PSEEs support software activities through the execution of the model of the software process. Such a model integrates the description of human activities and of the interaction between humans and software development tools. Moreover, PSEEs must provide the means to manage and persistently store the artifacts developed within the process. SPADE-1 is an implementation of the SPADE concept. In particular, it includes a SLANG interpreter and facilities to store process artifacts in an object-oriented database (O_2), and to interface the process interpreter with an integrated tool environment (DEC FUSE). This paper summarizes the architectural requirements derived from SPADE and provides a description of the SPADE-1 prototype.[1]

1 Introduction

Recently, much research and industrial effort has been devoted to study software processes. In particular, it has been argued that processes need to be analyzed and carefully modeled. An explicit process representation makes process understanding easier and improves communication among people. Moreover, by using formal executable notations to model the process, it is also possible to formally reason on processes, to automate parts of them, and to provide guidance and support to users during process execution.

Software Engineering Environments (SEE) based on the above idea are called Process-centered Software Engineering Environments (PSEEs). In a PSEE, the process model plays the role of the "code" to be executed to provide support to process agents. There are several PSEEs that have been developed and are

---

[1] Authors can be contacted at the following address: Luigi Lavazza, CEFRIEL, Via Emanueli 15, 20126 Milano (Italy). E-mail: `lavazza@mailer.cefriel.it`, Tel. +39-2-66100083, Fax +39-2-66100448.

being used in trial sites. There are also a few products that are being marketed [12].

SPADE [2, 5, 3] is a PSEE that has been designed at Politecnico di Milano and CEFRIEL. SPADE goals are to support Software Process Analysis, Design, and Enactment. A process model is specified in SPADE using SLANG (Spade LANGuage [4]), which is a process modeling language based on an extension of a high-level Petri net formalism, called ER nets [14]. In SLANG, a software process is described as a hierarchy of Petri net fragments called *activities*. Each activity may include user/tool interactions and accesses to process data.

The SPADE environment provides multiuser support and exploits parallelism among activities by associating different activities with different concurrent process engines, i.e. instances of the SLANG interpreter. These process engines may be distributed over a net of workstations. Tools are integrated in the environment and their invocation can be described in the process model. Process data (including the process model itself) is contained in an object-oriented repository.

This paper presents the architecture of the first prototype implementation of the SPADE concept, called SPADE-1. SPADE-1 features a reduced set of functionalities with respect to the goals of SPADE, namely it concentrates on process enactment. The design of SPADE-1 has been centered on the principle of separation of concerns between process model interpretation and user interaction. In particular, SPADE-1 is structured in three different layers: the process enactment environment, the user interaction environment, and the filter.

The process enactment environment includes facilities to execute a SLANG specification, by creating and modifying process artifacts. These process artifacts are stored and managed using the object-oriented DBMS O_2 [15, 7].

The user interaction environment manages the interaction between users and tools in the environment, and SPADE-1. It is based on an enhanced version of DEC FUSE [9], a product that provides service-based tool integration. In DEC FUSE, a tool is viewed as a set of services that can be invoked through a programmatic interface. This programmatic interface defines a protocol to manage tool cooperation. The protocol is based on a standard set of messages that are exchanged using a multicast mechanism.

The filter manages the communications between the two aforementioned environments. In particular, it converts messages generated by tools into tokens to be managed by the SLANG process model being executed. In the same way, operations accomplished by the SLANG interpreter that affect the user interaction environment are converted by the filter into messages to specific tools.

The partitioning in the three layer mentioned above constitutes one of the main features of SPADE-1. The basic underlying idea is that the paradigm used to model the process and support its enactment, and the paradigm used to guide the interaction with the user can be reasonably kept distinct. This is useful to support distribution, evolution and improvement of the environments, and the integration of different types of paradigms in the same PSEE. In particular, different types of user interaction environment can be simultaneously supported by providing suitable filtering mechanisms to/from the process enactment environment.

A second important feature of the design of SPADE-1 is that it is based on the integration of advanced, commercially available technologies. In order to obtain a fully functional PSEE without building it from scratch, we used DEC FUSE as an integrated tool environment and the O_2 object-oriented DBMS as a repository.

The paper is organized as follows. Section 2 provides a brief description of the SPADE environment. Section 3 discusses the problem of tool integration in SLANG. Section 4 presents and describes the architecture of SPADE-1. Section 5 discusses related work. Finally, Section 6 draws some conclusions and describes the state of implementation.

2 The SPADE environment

This section briefly introduces the SPADE environment. In particular, we show SLANG main features and its execution model. More details on process enactment and process evolution of SLANG models can be found in [2], while problems related to process modularization are discussed in [5].

2.1 Overview of SLANG

A SLANG process specification is composed of a set of activities. An activity encapsulates a set of logically related process operations and may include invocations to other activities.

Tokens in the net may be arbitrarily complex object structures that model documents, tools, resources, data, programs, plans, etc. Places are viewed as distributed persistent object containers. Places are typed and every place may contain only tokens of its associated type.

A transition firing represents the occurrence of an event taking a negligible amount of time. The net topology describes precedence relations among events; it also describes parallelism and conflict situations. Each transition is associated with a *guard* and an *action*. The guard is a condition on the transition input places, that indicates whether the event may occur in a given state. The action represents the reaction to the event.

An activity definition has an interface part and an implementation part. The activity interface includes a set of *starting transitions* and a set of *ending transitions*, that represent respectively the starting and ending events of the activity. It also includes two sets of places, namely *input* and *output places*. The activity begins its execution when one of its starting events occurs, and terminates with the occurrence of one of its ending events. Activities may share places, that can be used for communication and synchronization during activity execution.

Figure 1 presents the SLANG specification of an activity to modify a program unit, according to the requirements contained in a change request document. The example is intentionally kept simple, since the goal is to quickly introduce SLANG features and to make it possible a deeper discussion of architectural issues. The part inside the dashed box corresponds to the activity implementation, while external places and transitions represent the activity interface. The description of the activity is completed by a textual part (not shown here) with guard and action specifications. The activity shows an edit-save-compile cycle that is terminated when no compilation errors are obtained. At that point the file being edited is closed and the activity finishes.

SLANG provides a special kind of transitions and places, called respectively *black transitions* and *user interface places*, to manage interaction with the external environment (see Section 3). A black transition represents the execution of any external program (i.e. not coded in SLANG). In Figure 1, "cc" is an example of a black transition invoking the C compiler. The notification to the process enactment environment of relevant events that occur in the external environment, generated by users or by tools, are accomplished in SLANG through *user interface* places —depicted with a double circle. These events are communicated to the process enaction environment by "translating" them into tokens that are stored in appropriate user interface places. Based on these features, the semantics of the interaction among tools and human beings can be described in SLANG, as part of the process model. Black transitions and user interface places are SLANG basic mechanisms to *delegate* tasks to tools and human agents, and to *trigger* any request or significant event occurring outside the control of process engines.

2.2 SPADE execution model

The *SLANG interpreter* is responsible for the enaction of SLANG activities. Each activity is executed by one *process engine*, i.e., an instance of the SLANG interpreter.

When a starting event of an activity occurs, a new process engine is dynamically bound to the activity definition, and activity execution starts. The process engine evaluates the guards associated with transitions and analyzes their time constraints (in SLANG it is possible to specify the time interval during which a transition may or must be fired). A transition is enabled to fire when both the guard and the time constraint are satisfied. The SLANG interpreter cyclically selects one enabled transition (automatically or with user intervention) and fires it. The firing removes tokens from the input places, executes the corresponding action, and inserts the produced tokens in the output places. Transition firing is an atomic action, i.e., no intermediate state of the firing is made visible to other process engines. Black transitions are an exception to this rule: since the execution of a tool invoked by a black transition could take a long time, it would be unacceptable to stop the activity enactment waiting for the tool to terminate. Therefore, black transitions are not fired atomically: once the external tool has been started, the activity execution is resumed. The same black transition could even be fired again before the first firing terminates. This means that black transitions execution is *asynchronous* with respect to process engines evolution. This means also that output places of a black transition are not filled when the

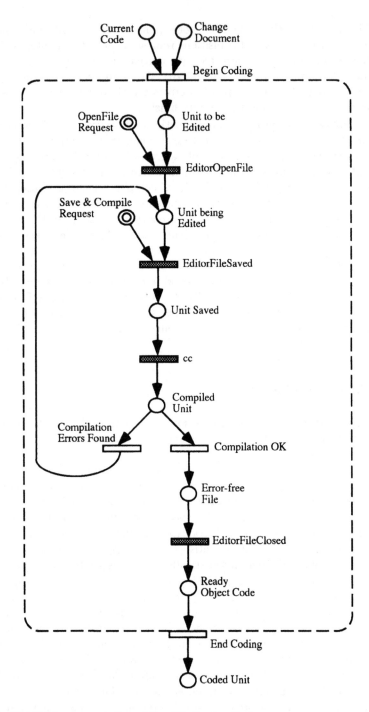

Fig. 1. SLANG implementation of the "Coding" activity.

transition is fired (this corresponds just to tool invocation). They receive output tokens when the tool terminates its execution.

The occurrence of the event (the transition firing) produces a state change that may enable new firings. Eventually, one of the ending events of the activity is fired. When this occurs, the process engine execution terminates and the output tokens are made available to the calling activity.

Activities are organized in a hierarchy described by the relation "invokes". An activity A "invokes" an activity B iff A's implementation part contains an invocation of B. This hierarchy has one *root activity* that is not invoked by any other activity. The (unique) instance of the root activity is created by a specialized boot program when SPADE is started. Note that this schema makes it possible to have multiple process engines that concurrently execute instances of process activities. Activity invocation is accomplished by spawning new process engines that are concurrently executed.

3 Tool integration in SPADE-1

In building the first prototype of the SPADE environment, it was clear from the very beginning that a powerful mechanism to support the integration of tools with the process enactment facility was necessary. In SPADE-1 this integration is achieved through DEC FUSE. In this section, this choice is motivated both considering the general issue of tool integration and the characteristics of DEC FUSE. Moreover, the strategy adopted to integrate DEC FUSE and SLANG is described and discussed.

3.1 Tool integration in PSEE

A PSEE should be able to invoke and control a variety of tools supporting software development and management activities. From the tool integration perspective, tools may be classified into two classes: *black-box tools* and *structured tools*. Black-box tools are viewed by the PSEE as a function performed on an input and producing some output. No interaction between the PSEE and the tool can occur during tool execution. Moreover, from the PSEE perspective, it is not relevant whether the function is performed automatically by the tool or with user intervention. Examples of black-box tools are UNIX tools such as *vi* and *cc*.

Structured tools provide a programmatic interface that can be used to integrate the functionalities offered by the tool in an environment. One way to achieve tool integration is by message passing. Messages may represent either notifications that the internal state of the tool has changed, or service requests [19]. Therefore, these tools provide means for a tighter integration with the PSEE, since they enable the invocation of every single service offered by the tool. The features offered by this class of tools can be exploited by the PSEE, that can specify how tools have to interact, when service invocations have to be pursued, etc.

In general, structured tools provide a significant advantage to PSEE developers. In particular, process knowledge can be removed from individual tools, and the policy concerning the use of tools can be made explicit in the process model.

3.2 DEC FUSE

DEC FUSE (DEC Friendly Unified Software Environment) is an integrated tool environment for software development [9]. DEC FUSE offers a set of integrated tools and provides an utility called EnCASE to add other tools to the environment [8]. Tools already integrated in DEC FUSE implement a large set of functions (editing, compiling, configuration building, etc.). Each DEC FUSE tool exports a set of services, that can be invoked by other tools by issuing the appropriate message. In a forthcoming release, DEC FUSE will support also a set of messages for tool integration that has been submitted for standardization[2]. The already integrated tools include an Editor/Browser, a Builder (based on the Unix and GNU *make*), a C++ Class Browser, a Call graph browser, a Cross Referencer, a Debugger, a Code Manager (based on SCCS or RCS), and a Profiler.

The integration of a new tool in the environment is accomplished by specifying the interface and the set of services provided by the tool. Such an interface contains the declaration of the services imported from other tools, the possible states of the tool, and the services that are exported by the tool in each state.

Figure 2 shows DEC FUSE architecture. DEC FUSE supports tool integration by means of a multicast mechanism. A message encodes both the service name and the parameters. A tool can invoke another tool service by sending a message to the *message server*. The message server determines the set of tools that are enabled to receive the message. This information is contained in a table, called *schema*, that specifies for each tool, the states in which it can receive a message. If there are no running instances of the tool that should provide a required service, the message server first starts an instance of the tool and then forwards the message to it. A tool can also send messages to communicate its internal state to the message server or to notify to other tools that it has terminated a specific operation.

3.3 DEC FUSE and SLANG

To support the integration of SPADE-1 and DEC FUSE it is necessary to define how significant events in the user interaction and process enactment environments are managed and communicated between the two layers. Each message sent by a DEC FUSE tool represents a significant event occurring in the user interaction environment. This event will normally require some reaction of the PSEE that depends on the process model being interpreted. This means that DEC FUSE messages must be made visible in some way to the process engine(s). In the same way, when a process engine needs to communicate with the

---

[2] A standard set of messages was submitted by DEC, Silicon Graphics and SunSoft to the ANSI X3H6 Tool Integration Models Committee, Tool Integration Subcommitte.

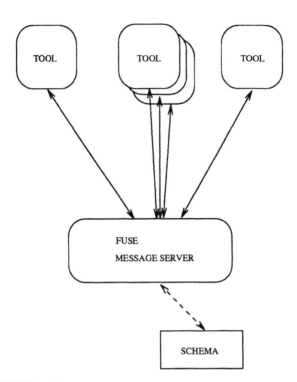

Fig. 2. DEC FUSE architecture.

user interaction environment, it is necessary to provide means to support the generation of messages from the process enactment environment towards the user interaction environment.

In SPADE-1, any relevant event that occurs in the user interaction environment, including each message issued by DEC FUSE tools, is captured by the filter. It then creates a token that is stored in some user interface place of the SLANG net being interpreted. The filter contains the information to determine the place where the token has to be stored (this place is independent on the state of the net, instead it depends on the type of the message and on the identity of the tool that generated it). The new token corresponding to the received message will, in general, enable one or more transitions in the process model being executed.

Conversely, it is possible to send a message to a tool using a black transition. As discussed in section 2, this SLANG construct makes it possible to asynchronously invoke any Unix executable file. In particular SPADE-1 includes a very simple tool, called *SendMessage*, that receives as input parameter a string representing a FUSE message, and forwards it to the filter. Messages can be composed by some other transition of the activity being executed, possibly taking into consideration user interface places and, thus, messages previously sent by FUSE to the process enactment environment.

It is important to notice that the above strategy to handle the communication between the process enactment environment (i.e., process engines) and the user interaction environment is only known by the filter and by the *SendMessage* tool. Thus, the SLANG interpreter is not aware of the presence of DEC FUSE. A process engine sees new tokens in user interface places, but it does not know that they correspond to DEC FUSE messages. In the same way, it invokes the *SendMessage* tool as any other tool. This means that the communication between the two environments is completely specified in the process model and supported by components that are independent of the SLANG language. This means also that the semantics of the process modeling language is independent of the user interaction paradigm.

4 SPADE-1 architecture

This section describes the SPADE-1 architecture. First a static description of the architecture components is provided. Then we discuss how the presented architecture may be distributed. Finally, we describe the dynamic behavior of the environment during enaction.

4.1 Architecture components

The SPADE-1 architecture has been designed to support multiple users who work concurrently using workstations interconnected over a local area network.

As already mentioned in previous sections, SPADE-1 architecture has three main components: the *user interaction environment*, the *process enactment environment*, and the *filter* (see Figure 3).

- The user interaction environment is composed of instances of DEC FUSE.
- The filter, called SCI (SPADE Communication Interface), is the communication subsystem and connects the process engines with the instances of DEC FUSE. In the current prototype architecture there is only one SCI.
- The process enactment environment contains the process engines (i.e. the instances of the SLANG interpreter) and the object-oriented repository of the process-centered environment.

The message server used by DEC FUSE to support communication among the different tools in the environment has been modified so that all the messages sent by the tools are forwarded to the SCI (and not locally forwarded to some other tool). Conversely, tools receive messages (through the message server) only from the process engines via the SCI. The SCI maintains a map describing the correspondence among process engines, messages and tools: for example, when a reply to message M is received by the SCI, it looks in the map to find which process engine originated message M. This process engine is the recipient of the reply. We may view the process enactment environment as taking the place of the schema table in the original DEC FUSE architecture. The process enactment environment drives FUSE message servers through the enactment of

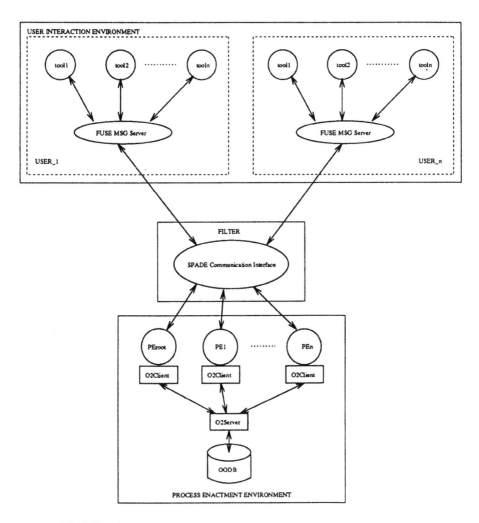

Fig. 3. SPADE architecture.

the process model. The schema provides a primitive and static process control, by telling a FUSE message server which tools are enabled to receive a message. The process enactment environment, instead, provides sophisticated process control mechanisms to model any desired process behavior.

As discussed above, the SCI converts each message from the DEC FUSE format to the format that we have defined to support communication between DEC FUSE and process engines. In addition, it acts as a router among each instance of DEC FUSE and process engines.

The implementation of the SPADE repository is based on O_2 [15, 7]. The process model and the process data are both stored in the repository. The benefits of using O_2 as database support for SPADE can be summarized as follows:

- The object-oriented data model is particularly suited to support SLANG types: for example, inheritance can be used to specialize the generic class "Token", obtaining user-defined process data types.
- The process artifacts (i.e. code, documents, reports, etc.) can be stored in the database, where security and access control are guaranteed.
- O_2 is based on a client-server architecture. Each process engine is a database client that may reside on different machines. The database server, instead, is centralized in one machine.
- O_2 provides basic concurrency control mechanisms, that are required to ensure atomicity of transition firings.
- Some features of O_2, such as the query language $O_2 SQL$ and the *Metaschema*, support SLANG process evolution capabilities [1].

The decision of storing all SPADE data (including every software artifact) in the O_2 database, has also a drawback: since in general DEC FUSE and Unix tools work on data that are stored in Unix files, it is not possible to achieve a high degree of data integration; instead, it is necessary to copy data from and to the database. This can be accomplished in the action part of any transition in the model. The development of a set of tools directly integrated on O_2 is accomplished in the ESPRIT project GoodStep [21]. The results of this project will provide useful insights on the pros and cons of the approach.

4.2 Distribution issues

The current SPADE-1 architecture supports multiple users that may be distributed over a network.

In general, the architecture depicted in Figure 3 can be distributed in different ways (see for example the solution presented in Figure 4). In particular any machine of the network can run one or more instances of the user interaction environment, according to the number of connected users. In the current implementation, however, the filter and all process engines run on the same machine. This is not a limitation from a functional point of view, but just a possible source of performance degradation.

The current architecture can evolve to provide a higher degree of distribution. On one hand, process engines executing different activities may be distributed over different machines. In such a case, in order to keep the message traffic low, it would be preferable that each machine were equipped with an instance of the SCI filter. This scenario can be obtained by means of a different configuration of SPADE-1, and does not require any relevant change in the components of the system.

4.3 The architecture at work

When a new user is logged into the system, a new message server is started and it is connected to the SCI. The user is presented with the FUSE Control Panel

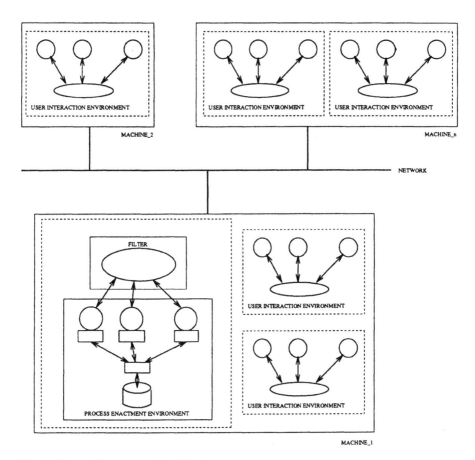

Fig. 4. Currently supported architecture.

which allows him/her to launch tools, to configure his/her FUSE instance, and to monitor the FUSE tools that have been activated so far.

As an example, consider again Figure 1. Assume that a user has issued the "Save" command in his/her editor. Following the procedure described above, a token is placed in "Save & Compile Request", enabling transition "Editor-FileSaved". When this transition fires, the *SendMessage* tool is invoked and a message to save the file (with the corresponding parameters) is sent to filter, which, in turn, forwards the message to the specified message server. As soon as the message has been sent, a token appears in the place "Unit Saved". Now, transition "cc" is enabled and fired. The firing of this transition provokes the invocation of the C compiler as a black-box tool. The invocation of black-box tools may be done directly by the process engine (by forking a UNIX process launching the tool), or via DEC FUSE if the tool has been previously integrated in the environment using EnCASE. A token containing the compiled code appears in place "Compiled Unit" when the compiler finishes its execution.

5 Related Work

The architecture of process-centered environments is a hot topic that is being intensively debated. There is no general agreement on what the architectural requirements to support tool integration in PSEEs should be. Contributions on this issue can be gained both by considering general works on the subject and by looking at significant PSEEs developed during the last years. An important survey of problems and open issues is contained in [16]. In [17], some general requirements and architecture schemes supporting them are proposed.

MARVEL [6] is a ruled-based PSEE that supports invocation of external tools through *activation rules*. Each tool is encapsulated in a tool envelope (written in an extension of the C-shell language) that is responsible for setting the tool parameters and invoking the tool. This mechanism is adequate only to support the invocation of black-box tools. The level of granularity of tool integration offered by MARVEL is not appropriate if the process model needs to take control during tool execution [11].

A similar approach is taken in the rule-based PSEE MERLIN [18], where tools are also invoked via an encapsulator or tool envelope. A MERLIN rule may contain the built-in *CALL* statement that, when executed, performs the tool invocation. MERLIN suffers from the same drawbacks as MARVEL, since the process model looses control of the tool during its execution.

Process WEAVER [10] implements process activities by describing the control flow with a Petri net like notation. A precondition and an action are associated with each transition in the net. The precondition or action may specify a procedure to be executed. These procedures are expressed in the *Co-shell* language, which is similar to the UNIX shell, and provides the means to operate on tools and services of the environment. An interesting feature of Process WEAVER is that the mapping from the tool class (e.g. *TextEditor*) to the particular tool (e.g. *vi*) is accomplished dynamically, allowing users to work on different platforms and using each time the appropriate tool. Process WEAVER does not provide a structured data repository and thus data is managed as byte streams (i.e. UNIX files).

Forest [13] is an extension of FIELD in which all the policies to invoke and control tools are described using a set of conditions-actions rules. In this way, Forest provides a simple and effective "process description language" to easily specify the "process" to be followed in controlling tools. However, even if it is quite easy to specify and implement a policy using the policy description language, Forest is severely limited with respect to full-fledged process modeling languages and environments, since it is quite difficult to express complex tool interaction policies and integrate them within a complete process model.

An important dimension of the problem is related to process evolution. In fact, processes are evolving entities that are subject to changes during their execution. In particular, changes may be applied to the user interaction environment, for example by adding new tools to the environment or changing the way a tool is used. This aspect is addressed in [20], that reviews existing integration environments and presents *mediators*, a tool integration mechanism to support environment evolution. In SPADE-1, evolution is accomplished through the dynamic modification of the process model [3].

In conclusion, the SPADE-1 architecture introduces the following ideas: independence of the user interface environment from the process enactment environment (through the filter); integration at a service level of tools within a full-fledged process-centered environment.

6 Conclusions

This paper has presented the architecture of the SPADE-1 PSEE. It is based on DEC FUSE to support user/tool interaction and uses the object-oriented database O_2 to store process artifacts.

The main features of SPADE-1 can be summarized as follows:

- The paradigms used in the user interaction environment and in the process enactment environment are kept separate. There is a filter that is able to convert messages and events from one environment to the other one.
- Tools are controlled at a service level. The only constrain is that tools have to be built in such a way that they notify the "external world" of the actions they want to accomplish.
- The SPADE-1 components can be distributed on a network.

The first prototype of the SPADE-1 environment has been developed and it is under testing at CEFRIEL. The main limitation of the current implementation is that it supports only one process engine at a time. This is due to the currently used version of O_2 that supports only single user applications. The multiuser version of O_2 is being integrated in SPADE-1 and will support multiple process engines accessing the same process data base.

Acknowledgments

The authors wish to thank the people of the DEC Laboratories in Varese for their continuous support, and in particular P. Rivera and F.V. Bagatin, for their useful suggestions. Luciano Baresi provided a valuable contribution in the development of the O_2 based repository. The first prototype implementation of SPADE was made possible by the enthusiastic work of P. Battiston, M. Signori, and G. Galli de' Paratesi.

DEC FUSE and DEC EnCASE are trademarks of Digital Equipment Corporation, O_2 and O_2SQL are trademarks of O_2 Technology.

References

1. Sergio Bandinelli, Luciano Baresi, Alfonso Fuggetta, and Luigi Lavazza. Requirements and Early Experiences in the Implementation of the SPADE Repository using Object-Oriented Technology. In *Proceedings of the International Symposium on Object Technologies for Advanced Software*, Kanazawa, Japan, November 1993.

2. Sergio Bandinelli and Alfonso Fuggetta. Computational Reflection in Software Process Modeling: the SLANG Approach. In *Proceedings of the 15th. International Conference on Software Engineering*, Baltimore, Maryland (USA), May 1993.

3. Sergio Bandinelli, Alfonso Fuggetta, and Carlo Ghezzi. Software Process Model Evolution in the SPADE Environment. *IEEE Transactions on Software Engineering - Special Issue on Process Evolution*, to appear.

4. Sergio Bandinelli, Alfonso Fuggetta, Carlo Ghezzi, and Luigi Lavazza. The SLANG 1.0 Process Modeling Language Reference Manual. Technical Report RT93032, CEFRIEL, Via Emanueli, 15 - 20126 Milano (Italy), September 1993.

5. Sergio Bandinelli, Alfonso Fuggetta, and Sandro Grigolli. Process Modeling-in-the-large with SLANG. In *Proceedings of the 2nd International Conference on the Software Process*, Berlin (Germany), February 1993. IEEE.

6. Naser S. Barghouti and Gail E. Kaiser. Scaling up rule-based software development environments. In Axel van Lamsweerde and Alfonso Fuggetta, editors, *Proceedings of ESEC 91-Thrid European Software Engineering Conference*, volume 550 of *Lecture Notes on Computer Science*, Milano (Italy), October 1991. Springer-Verlag.

7. O. Deux. The O_2 System. *Communications of the ACM*, 34(10), October 1991.

8. Digital Equipment Corporation, Maynard, Massachusetts. *DEC FUSE EnCASE Manual*, December 1991. Version 1.1.

9. Digital Equipment Corporation, Maynard, Massachusetts. *DEC FUSE Handbook*, December 1991. Version 1.1.

10. Christer Fernstrom. PROCESS WEAVER: Adding Process Support to UNIX. In *Proceedings of the 2nd International Conference on the Software Process*, Berlin (Germany), February 1993. IEEE.

11. A. Finkelstein, J. Kramer, and M. Hales. Process Modelling: a critical analysis. In P. Walton and N. Maiden, editors, *Integrated Software Reuse: management and techniques*, 1992.

12. Alfonso Fuggetta. A classification of CASE technology. *Computer*, to appear.

13. David Garlan and Ehsan Ilias. Low-cost, Adaptable Tool Integration Policies for Integrated Environments. In *Proceedings of Fourth Symposium on Software Development Environments*. ACM, 1990.

14. Carlo Ghezzi, Dino Mandrioli, Sandro Morasca, and Mauro Pezzé. A Unified High-level Petri Net Formalism for Time-critical Systems. *IEEE Transactions on Software Engineering*, February 1991.

15. C. Lecluse, P. Richard, and F. Velez. O2, an object-oriented data model. In *Proceedings of SIGMOD '89 - Int. Conf. on the Management of Data*, pages 424–433, Portland, OR, 1989. ACM.

16. Maria Penedo and William Riddle. Process-sensitive SEE Architecture, Workshop Summary. In *Proceedings of the 2nd International Conference on the Software Process*, Berlin (Germany), February 1993. IEEE.

17. B. Peuschel and S. Wolf. Architectural Support for Distributed Process Centered Software Development Environments.

18. Burkhard Peuschel, Wilhelm Schäfer, and Stefan Wolf. A Knowledge-Based Software Development Environment Supporting Cooperative Work. *International Journal of Software Engineering and Knowledge Engineering*, 2(1):79–106, 1992.
19. S. Reiss. Connecting Tools using Message Passing in the FIELD Program Development Environment. *IEEE Software*, pages 57–67, July 1990.
20. Kevin J. Sullivan and David Notkin. Reconciling Environment Integration and Software Evolution. *ACM Transactions on Software Engineering and Methodology*, 1(2):229–268, July 1992.
21. The GoodStep team. Description of software engineering applications and requirements for an object-oriented repository. Deliverable 1, ESPRIT project 6115 GoodStep - General Object-Oriented Databases for Software Processes, March 1993.

The Nature of the Software Process Modelling Problem is Evolving

Mike Anderson and Phil Griffiths

ICL Enterprises, Eskdale Road, Winnersh, Wokingham, Berks. U.K.

Abstract. Research work on Software Process Modelling in which ICL has been involved has focussed on the use of specially designed process modelling languages such as MASP [Gri92] from the ALF Project [Old92] or PML [B+] from the IPSE 2.5 Project [War89], which are used to construct the "glue" that binds software development tools together to create "process centred environments" (PCEs). A problem common to all PCEs is that of dealing with the processes that are enshrined inside large, functionally rich software development tools that users may require them to host. In this position paper we look at the implications of some recent developments and standards and how we perceive they are changing the nature of the software process modelling problem.

1. Introduction

In recent years there have been a number of prototype software development environments constructed, many of which have been described, with varying degrees of accuracy, as being process centred. The tendency to demonstrate these prototypes using compile/edit/test scenarios (although the ISPW 6 example [Ref90] has become more prevalent over the last 2 years) implies that to use these environments you have to work with tools at that level of granularity.

There are a number of explanations for this particular phenomenon, including:

convenience - editors and compilers were tools freely available to software developers working on these projects;

cost - anything more sophisticated would probably have to be paid for (money is always a problem in research projects of the size required to do this type of work);

adequacy - by just dealing with this set of tools it was possible to show something meaningful (i.e. cause and effect) without getting overly complicated;

prejudice - the assumption that the so called software-crisis is a programming problem.

This approach has resulted in a number of problems which have impeded the uptake of software development environment technology. During a period when CASE tools were becoming increasingly sophisticated in offering integrated capabilities, the work done on prototype IPSEs was increasingly seen as dealing with technologies of the past [Som93]. There was a growing confusion between the roles of IPSEs and big integrated CASE tools which the CASE tools were winning (at least in the market place) [BEM92]. The issues arising from the need to handle process models which were protected by being inside large multi-functional CASE tools remained unresolved.

Claims in the late 1980s that the big integrated CASE tools would eventually deal with all aspects of the software lifecycle have come to be recognised as fallacious. The reasons for this are that such tools are method based and therefore are entirely satisfactory only as long as their capabilities fit the requirements of the problem domain. Such tools are closed worlds, having no concept of integrating external tools and thus having fixed capabilities. The inability to extend the capabilities of these tools has led to demand from users to be able to "plug and play" by adding tools to an environment as needs dictate and to share data between tools to facilitate the software design process. Users have expressed frustration with the rigid process models that have been enacted through these tools [B$^+$93], a problem that has led to the tendency to look for ways to extract the process support aspects of such tools[PR93].

2. Recent Developments

The development of open systems and integration mechanisms, such as CDIF [Ass91], PCTE [LW93], ESF software bus [FO90], and message server protocols, allows disparate tools to be integrated in ways which add value. However none of these approaches is without disadvantage, nor are they, despite some claims to the contrary, able to integrate tools without some cost. A further problem is that many require the participation of the tool vendor.

CDIF supports data integration of tools by defining a common data exchange format that can be used by import/export tools that have been written to be CDIF compliant. CDIF uses abstract data schemas to define exchange data, but the structure, content and interpretation of that data is left to the tool developer to work out and how this is done remains undefined.

HP-Softbench has achieved notable success in providing message passing mechanisms to support the control integration of tools. A software tool registers with a message server the messages that it can respond to or that it can send. To date more than 70 tool vendors have ported their products to the Softbench framework. The integration of simple tools such as text editors and compilers in this way is quite feasible as shown in the Forest environment [GI90]. However it is not clear that more complex tools will necessarily be interoperable given that to achieve interoperability of such tools requires close collaboration between two or more tool vendors. This is a recognised problem and as a first step to solving it, the CASE Interoperability Alliance and CASE Communiqué have submitted a joint proposal for a messaging architecture to X3H6 [AC93]. This proposal will only be a partial solution however, as for CDIF, the content and interpretation of messages will remain undefined.

PCTE supports data integration through a shared data repository and the use of published schemas which allow other software tools to have access to "public data". The schemas describe the structure and nature of the data, but PCTE does not say anything about standard formats for data interchange. In this sense, the PCTE and CDIF standards can be seen as being complementary. PCTE also provides mechanisms to support inter-tool communication in the form of pipes and message queues in addition to supporting controlled access to shared objects. The ideas underpinning PCTE's data integration mechanisms have been amply proven by commercial CASE products that achieve degrees of data integration through use of a shared relational database. These tools frequently use SQL interfaces to interwork with the underlying database and thus achieve a degree of portability at the same time. In essence it can be argued that these tools are clients and that the database is a server and thus that the architecture of such systems is essentially a client-server model. The Eureka Software Factory offers a broader client-server approach in which tools provide services to each other in response to messages passed along a "Software Bus".

3. What is needed

These developments will, we believe, collectively contribute to greater degrees of integration and interoperability of CASE tools than has hither to been possible. The highly integrated CASE tools, that emerged at the end of the last decade, were only possible because they were designed as a complete system to give presentation, control and data integration. If we are to achieve open integratable CASE technology, there will need to be a recognised way of cataloguing the capabilities and requirements of such tools.

Central repository technologies, such as PCTE or the use of a Client-Server database, require that the tool vendors actively participate in integrating tools. To do this they must be convinced that there is a benefit for them in porting their tools and collaborating to achieve added value for users.

Issues such as ownership of data objects still pose problems. Tools own objects and are required to share them, either by handing them on, or by acting as servers to other tools. Any new tool that requires an object or service cannot a priori assume that some other tool will provide it, unless that tool already exists in a stable form when the new tool is being designed.

Thus, whilst it is beginning to be possible to integrate tools at a lower level, it is not clear what this will mean in practice. One possible scenario is that environment vendors will be motivated to gather "families" of tool vendors around them for mutual commercial advantage. Another is that tool vendors "see the light" and start publishing APIs that allow process invasion of their tools, at least on a client/server basis. For this to be a viable scenario, there is a need for some hard work by the standards bodies.

Standards such as CDIF and the proposals on message passing only deal with how data and control integration can be effected. The problem of defining at what level integration occurs and publishing specifications of what data is used to effect such integration remains unresolved.

There is a need to be able in some way to capture the behavioural characteristics of large software development tools, to identify/model possible interconnection/interaction points in their functional profiles and describe the data and control information that are required to effect the functional integration of tools.

Addressing these issues is the next challenge, not just for the vendors of CASE tools, but also for the software process technology community, if we are to finally deal with the requirement to manage small processes in order to have control over large processes.

References

[AC93]   CASE Interoperability Alliance and CASE Communique. *Proposed Messaging Architecture - A Joint Proposal.* X3H6/93-008, 1993.

[Ass91]   Electronic Industries Association. Eia interim standard - cdif standardized case interchange meta-model. EIA/IS-83, July 1991.

[B$^+$]   R Bruynooghe et al. *PSS: A System for Process Enactment.* Presented to 1st International Conference on Software Process, Los Angeles.

[B$^+$93]   D Budgen et al. *CASE Tools: Masters or Servants?* In *Proceedings of the Software Engineering Environments 1993 Conference, Reading, England.* IEEE, 1993.

[BEM92]   A Brown, A.N. Earl, and J.A. McDermid. *SOFTWARE ENGINEERING ENVIRONMENTS - Automated Support for Software Engineering.* McGraw-Hill, ISBN: 0-07-707432-7, 1992.

[FO90]   C Fernstrom and L Ohlsson. *The ESF Approach to Factory Style Software Production.* In *Proceedings of the First International Conference on System Development Environments and Factories.* Pitman, ISBN 0-273-08829-7, 1990.

[GI90]   D Garlan and E Ilias. *Low-cost, Adaptable Tool Integration Policies for Integrated Environments,* December 1990.

[Gri92]   P Griffiths. *MASP/DL:The ALF Language for Process Modelling. ICL Technical Journal (v8:1), ISSN 0142-1557,* May 1992.

[LW93]   J Jowett L Wakeman. *PCTE - The Standard for Open Repositories.* Prentice-Hall, ISBN 0-13-065566-X, 1993.

[Old92]   D Oldfield. *ALF: A Third Generation Environment for Systems Engineering. ICL Technical Journal (v8:1), ISSN 0142-1557,* May 1992.

[PR93]   M Penedo and W Riddle. *Process-sensitive SEE Architecture (PSEEA) Workshop Summary,* April 1993.

[Ref90]   *Proceedings of the Sixth International Software Processing Workshop.* Tokyo, Japan, 1990.

[Som93]   I. Sommerville. *Environments for Cooperative Systems Developent.* In *Proceedings of the Software Engineering Environments 1993 Conference, Reading, England.* IEEE, 1993.

[War89]   B Warboys. *The IPSE 2.5 Project: A Process Model Based Architecture.* In K Bennett, editor, *Software Engineering Environments.* Ellis Horwood, ISBN: 0-74-580665-1, 1989.

The Authors

Mike Anderson and Phil Griffiths worked on the ALF Project (ESPRIT Project no. 1520) and are currently engaged in the development of a PCTE based SDE under the EUREKA OPERA Project. Mike Anderson convenes the ICL Process Modelling Special Interest Group.

Searching for PMIPS: Process Model Instructions Per Second

Mario Baldi, Silvano Gai,
Maria Letizia Jaccheri, Patricia Lago

Dipartimento di Automatica e Informatica
Politecnico di Torino
10129 Torino, Italy

Possible Architectures

The architecture of a generic process support environment (PSE) can be viewed as composed of communication services, operating system (o.s.), tools, workspaces (WSes), data base management system (DBMS), process engine (PrE), and user interface (UI) service. The PrE interprets and executes process models. The DBMS stores and manages both software products and process models. The communication service supports UI protocol (e.g. the protocol exploited by X-Windows), data transfer (e.g. ftp), tool integration, and inter-process communication. A distributed PSE architecture will encompass many machines ranging from terminals to mainframes.

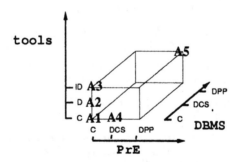

Fig. 1. Distribution possibilities of the main architecture components.

As exemplified in figure 1, there are three main distribution axes. Both the PrE and the DBMS can be either centralized (located on a server that serves the whole configuration)(C), or distributed over the sites of the PSE in either a client server (DCS) or peer-to-peer (DPP) fashion. Analogously, tools may be executed and WSes created and handled either on the process server (C) or on the client sites. In the latter case, tool execution can be either integrated (ID) or not integrated (D).

Five architectures are considered: in the mainframe architecture (A1 in fig. 1), all the components except the UIs run on a server machine. Each user is connected on a client site through a UI that communicates with the PrE by a UI protocol, e.g. that provided by X-Windows.

Architecture A2 is still client server. Tools and WSes reside on client machines, but are not controlled by the PrE, which resides on the server. Tool invocation can only be suggested (not enforced) by the PrE and is the user's responsibility. Data are transferred into and from WSes during the user working session.

Architecture A3 extends A2 concerning tool integration. The process thus enforces tool invocation and manages tool results, e.g. failure management.

In architecture A4, the PrE is distributed. It is assumed that the DBMS resides on the process server, the process model lies on the server, and the PrE manages the model and delegates the single instructions to each client. The differences and enhancements with respect to A3 solution are that UIs are completely managed on the client site, thus avoiding the UI protocol overhead.

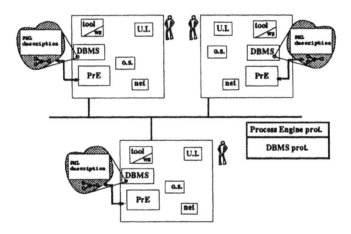

Fig. 2. A5: Distributed process and DBMS architecture

Architecture A5 is depicted in figure 2: the DBMS is distributed. Both software products and process model fragments are managed by peer PrEs. The enactable process model fragments are split among the different sites, while for simplicity a customized process model is assumed to be replicated on each site.

Further, client PrEs communicate with each other, and synchronize the process between sites. There is a process protocol which uses the functionalities provided by the underlying DBMS protocol.

Process Model Instructions

The process model instructions composing a generic process model, can be classified as follows: (1) communication (user-to-user or task-to-task), (2) workspace checkin and checkout, (3) tool invocation, (4) tool execution, and (5) data access.

Our goal is to develop a method to assess a PSE architecture with respect to the process models that will be enacted. Each model is characterized by a mixing of the above listed process model instructions. Architecture may be assessed measuring the average process model instruction execution time according to the given mixing.

We will describe what can be usefully measured as process model instruction execution time. Experimental ways of measuring are omitted here, for space reason.

The cost of a user-to-user communication is regarded as the cost of exchanging e-mail messages. For task-to-task communication we assume that the enacting process model resides on the server machine in all architectures but A5, and hence its cost is that of an inter-process communication on a single machine in all architectures but A5.

The cost of WS checkout is determined by the cost of reading a set of files from the DBMS and storing them in the appropriate WS. It will depend on the number of files, their dimension, DBMS performance, and DBMS/WS coupling.

The cost of tool invocation can be calculated from a weighted average of both interactive and non-interactive tool invocation costs.

The costs of tool execution depend on both machine load and the underlying hardware, while those for interactive tools also on coupling between the tool and its interface. If tool and UI are loosely coupled, i.e. they do not reside on the same machine, the costs are affected by network type and load.

Single data access can be measured from the DBMS access time to an object. Data access can be local data to either a centralized DBMS or a distributed DBMS, and thus may involve data transfers between machines. These data transfers are managed by the DBMS.

Conclusions

We have presented a taxonomy for PSE architectures and process model instructions. A method for measuring the performance of PSE architectures is given w.r.t. process models.

We would have liked to categorize existing PSEs according to the architectures we have presented, but papers about these PSEs always refer to out-of-date versions and it could have been easy to make mistakes or underestimations. An ambitious objective of our work is to yield benchmarks for PSE evaluation.

Further, the different architectures do not only influence execution time, but many other parameters such as change management, transaction management, etc. Work has to be done in those directions.

Meta-Process / Methodology Session

Reidar Conradi

Norwegian Institute of Technology (NTH), Trondheim, Norway

A process in an application (software production, banking etc.) has two parts: a production process and a **meta-process**, that can change all parts of the process including itself.

The meta-process "operands" are both **external** process elements (like production tools, human resources, or company procedures) and **internal**, computer-supported process model fragments, that have to be drafted, refined and customised, executed, and later evolved. Since processes are carried out in applications with humans as active agents, change is inevitable, frequent, and often desirable.

The meta-activities to evolve the process model has conventional life-cycle phases, such as acquisition, definition, analysis, design, implementation, execution, assessment, and maintenance (later evolution). All these phases should be supported by (meta-)process methods, formalisms, and tools.

However, not every PM Support Environment (PSE) allows the distinction or formalisation of all these meta-activities. And in PSEs with late/dynamic binding, the sequence of and boundaries between these phases may be diffuse. That is, model definition, refinement, customisation, execution, and change are part of an incremental and never-ending meta-process.

This dynamic situation necessitates a process modelling language (PML) and related support architecture with *reflective* facilities, so that the entire process model can be adequately described and managed.

Then, what structuring and binding facilities should such a PML offer? What are the process *parameters*? How, when and by whom are they going to change – i.e. binding and rebinding? And what is the relationship to configuration management, regarding the process model as a versioned, composite object? Proper access control is of course needed, as for general database operations. There are also well-known problems in changing executing process models ("pulling the rug").

And what is the **methodology** to guide process development, and later customisation and general evolution? For normal software development there is a plethora of development technology covering the whole life-cycle, e.g. SADT or SA/SD supported by CASE tools, normal programming languages etc. etc. For process modelling, most PMLs have been at the implementation level, and we need more high-level approaches and associated methodologies.

For more concrete evolution of process models, we can sketch the following meta-activities: 1) submit a request for model change; 2) assess (validate, simulate etc.) the request; 3) reject or accept a possibly adjusted change request; 4) carry out the accepted change; 5) propagate it to a subset of the affected internal fragments and possibly to their external process elements; 6) re-establish internal and external consistency. To facilitate precise impact analysis and later change propagation and to preserve backward traceability, the external process elements and their dependencies must be explicitly represented in an internal process model.

The papers in this session covers many aspects of the above, and are as follows:

Jin Sa and Brian C. Warboys: "Modelling Processes Using a Stepwise Refinement Technique". This reports the concrete modelling of the ISPW7 example.

Tom Roden et al.: "Process Programming and Development Practice". This relates the process modelling field to practice.

Keith Phalp: "A Pragmatic Approach to Process Modelling". This proposes a rather low-tech approach to the problem.

Gerald Junkerman and Wilhelm Schäfer: "A Design Methodology for Process Programming". This is intended to guide development using the MERLIN PML.

The first one is a full paper, the remaining are position papers.

Modelling Processes Using a Stepwise Refinement Technique

Jin Sa and Brian C. Warboys

Department of Computer Science,
University of Manchester,
Manchester M13 9PL, England.
emails: {jsa@cs.man.ac.uk, brian@cs.man.ac.uk}

Abstract. In many existing process modelling approaches, the emphasis is on the *representations* of process models, but not so much on the *development* of them. In this paper we present a method, called *OBM*, for developing such representations using a stepwise refinement technique. An example is used to show how a model may be gradually refined.

1 Background and Introduction

In EWSPT'92 [10], we reported a small case study [24] which we undertook to investigate the application of an existing concurrent formal specification method, Base Model (BM) [23], to process modelling. The case study showed that although BM could be used as a specification method for some applications, particularly those targeted by the process modelling language PML [5], there was still a wide scope for improvement so that BM could be a more suitable technique for process modelling.

Our subsequent work mainly concentrated on specifying[1] the ISPW-6 software process problem example (ISPW-6 example for short) [15]. As a result of this work, BM was specialised with some constructs specific to modelling software process. The details of this work have been described in [21].

Since the ISPW-6 example was clearly described, the emphasis of the modelling exercise as reported in [21] was mainly on the *representation* of a model, but not so much on the *development* of a model. This emphasis is in fact also true with many existing process modelling techniques. However, in reality, processes are often unclear to the process participants and to the process modeller. This is especially true in organisations, where the same process may be viewed from different angles or at different levels of abstraction by different people or at different times. This makes it very difficult for the process modeller to model all the details of a process. In this paper, we present an approach, called Organisational Base Model (OBM), which provides a means to gradually identify the details of a process in an organisation and develop the detailed representation of the organisational process by a stepwise refinement technique.

OBM is based on BM. The specification constructs are defined using a temporal logic as it is a widely accepted formal tool for the specification and verification of concurrent systems [17].

---

[1] The words "specify", "define" and "model" are often used interchangeably in this paper.

2 Brief Overview of OBM

In OBM, a system is considered to be composed of components which may be executed concurrently. Each component provides a number of operations and contains some variables which can only be accessed by the operations. An operation may call other operations in other components. An *active* operation of a component is invoked by the component itself, and a *passive* operation is invoked by another operation in another component (or by an agent).

The model of a system is developed at different levels. Each level specifies the system at a certain level of abstraction. The specification at each level contains a collection of component specifications. Each component specification defines the operations and the pattern to which its operations, when executed, conform. Such patterns are called *operation patterns*.

In developing a model, *abstract objects* are used to define components which may be refined in the subsequent levels. *Agent objects* and *step objects* are used to define components which will no longer be refined. *Boxed objects* are used to compose a number of components. The process for developing a model using OBM is as follows:

1. Define the top level as an abstract object or a collection of abstract objects.
2. At each level, e.g. level i, for each abstract object A in level i, a level i+1 refinement may be carried out to produce level i+1 specification for component A. The level i+1 specification contains a number of components. Each component is defined as either an abstract object, an agent object or a step object.
3. Check the consistency of each level i+1 refinement
4. Repeat 2 to 3.

The rest of this paper describes two OBM constructs and illustrates the above development process with an example.

3 Abstract Object

Representation

An abstract object may have two types of operation: *compound operations* and *simple operations*. A compound operation may be refined into several operations which may themselves be compound operations. In the rest of this paper the term operation denotes simple operation and the term *coperation* denotes both compound operation and operation. An abstract object provides coperations and may require coperations provided by other components. The definition of an abstract object is divided into two parts: the interface part and the body part.

The **interface part** consists of:

− a list of provided coperations
− a list of required coperations
− an operation pattern defined in terms of the provided coperations.

The provided coperations are further divided into three categories: supply, receive and action.

supply: supply artifacts to other components, e.g. send scheduled tasks. Supply operations are usually active operations.

receive: receive artifacts from other components, e.g. receive progress reports. Receive operations are usually passive operations.

action: perform activities, e.g. schedule and monitor. Action operations may be either active or passive.

Supply coperations are matched with receive coperations, for example, to send an artifact d from component P to component Q, P needs to have a supply coperation $dtoQ$ and Q needs to have a receive coperation $dfrP$. The artifact d is passed from P to Q after $dtoQ$ has completed the call to $dfrP$. Each supply coperation may be matched with a number of receive coperations.

Operation patterns are defined using *ordering expressions*. Section 6.6 describes a subset of ordering expressions. The full definition can be found in [23, 22]. Operation patterns are defined in terms of coperation names.

The **body part** consists of

- a *call template* for each required coperation
- a definition for each provided coperation, which contains
  - the type of this coperation, i.e. active or passive
  - the order of the operation calls made by this coperation
  - the pre- and the post-conditions of the coperation

Each call template is in the form

!name	
prop	*func*
obj	*another*
apar	v

where *name* is the name of the coperation being called; by our convention, the name of the call template is always the name of the called coperation prefixed with "!"; "prop" defines the type of the call, e.g. a functional call sends a call request and receives a result, a procedural call sends a call request and does not expect any result; "obj" states the name of the component providing the required coperation and "apar" specifies the actual parameter.

The order of the operation calls is defined using ordering expressions.

The pre- and the post-conditions of a compound operation are defined in terms of the parameter, the result and the values received from the calls made to the required coperations.

Semantics

The execution of an abstract object is determined by its operation pattern. The following six types of events may be used to define the behaviour of an abstract object.

- *start*: start the execution of an active coperation.
- *end*: finish the execution of an active coperation.
- *accept*: accept a call request and start the execution of a passive coperation.

- *return*: return the result of a passive coperation to the caller and finish its execution.
- *send*: send a request to a component to call one of its coperations.
- *receive*: receive the result returned from the called coperation.

Call Templates: Each functional call template specifies a set of sequences. Each sequence contains a *send* event, followed by a number of idle steps, followed by a *receive* event. Each procedural call template specifies a set of sequences. Each sequence contains a *send* event and followed by a number of idle steps.

The temporal semantics of call templates are described in sub-section 6.5.

Order of Calls: The ordering expression defining the order of the operation calls made by a coperation specifies a set of sequences. Each sequence is concatenated from the sequences specified by the call templates of this coperation.

The temporal semantics of ordering expression are defined in sub-section 6.6.

Coperations: Each coperation specifies a set of sequences. Each sequence of an active coperation contains a *start* event, followed by a sequence determined by the order of the operation calls, followed by a *finish* event. The pre-condition of the coperation must be true in the step that the *start* event is taking place, and the post-condition must be true in the step immediately after the *finish* event. The sequences of passive coperations are similar to those of active ones with the exception that the *start* and *finish* events are replaced by the *accept* and *return* events respectively.

The temporal semantics of coperations are defined in sub-section 6.4.

Operation Pattern: An operation pattern specifies a set of sequences. Each sequence is a combination of the sequences specified by its coperations. The ordering of the combination must conform to the operation pattern.

The temporal semantics of operation patterns are defined in sub-section 6.6.

Abstract Object: An abstract object specifies a set of sequences. Each sequence is specified by its operation pattern.

The temporal semantics of abstract objects are given in section 6.2.

4 Refinement

The level i+1 refinement of a level i abstract object consists of the following:

Component Refinement
Replacing the level i abstract object by a number of level i+1 components. Each component may be either an abstract object, an agent object or a step object.

Coperation Refinement
Replacing the sub-patterns of the level i operation pattern by operation patterns defined in terms of level i+1 coperations. A single coperation can also be regarded as a sub-operation pattern.

The consistency checking of refinements is described in section 7.

5 Boxed Object

Given a level i+1 refinement of a level i abstract object, in order to justify the refinement, it is necessary to show that the composition of the sub-components is consistent with the abstract object. A boxed object is used to compose the sub-components.

Internal Coperations: Given a level i+1 refinement of a level i component, a level i+1 coperation is *internal* if it is not used in the **Coperation Refinement** part.

Interleavings: In OBM, parallelism is defined by interleaving the events of different components. As mentioned in section 3, each specified sequence of a component contains idle steps as well as events. Each idle step can be viewed as a slot for another component to perform an event.

Synchronisations: The executions of two components are synchronised if one is performing a *send* (or *receive*) event and the other is performing the corresponding *accept* (or *return*) event.

Representation

A boxed object contains a number of components and a list of internal coperations.

Semantics

A boxed object specifies a set of sequences. Each sequence is merged from the sequences of its sub-components according to the following two constraints:

- there is at most one sub-component performing a non-synchronising event at any time;
- if a sub-component is performing a synchronising event, the corresponding sub-component must be performing the matching event at the same time.

In the merged sequence, internal events are replaced with idle steps. All synchronising events are internal, they become idle steps in the merged sequence. Therefore each step of the merged sequence contains at most one (non-internal) event.

The temporal semantics of boxed objects are defined in section 6.3.

6 Temporal Semantics

Long before temporal logic was used to reason about programs, there was substantial work on temporal logic in philosophy for reasoning about time, e.g. [19, 20]. The application of temporal logic in computer science was first introduced in [6]. A logic framework for reasoning about properties of concurrent programs was later developed by Pnueli [18]. Although that framework provided very powerful specification and verification tools for global programs, it did not provide much support for decomposition and composition of components. In [4], a compositional temporal logic proof system for specification and verification of concurrent program was introduced. This approach offered support for *development* of concurrent systems. In this paper, we will use the temporal logic described in [4] to define the semantics of OBM.

6.1 Temporal Operators

The following temporal operators are used in the semantic definitions in this paper. Their intuitive meanings are described below:

fin: end of the sequence.
$\bigcirc P$: P is true at the next moment.
$\square P$: P is true always.
$P \; \mathcal{C} \; Q$: P is true, and then Q is true.
$P \; \mathcal{C}^* \; Q$: P is true for a number of times, and then Q is true.
$P \; \mathcal{U} \; Q$: P is true until Q is true.

6.2 Temporal Semantics of Abstract Objects

The semantics of an abstract object is determined by the semantics of its operation pattern with the constraint that at most one event may take place at any time. This constraint is to ensure that parallel activities are interleaved. Let

- *Abs* denote the name of an abstract object;
- *X* denote the context in which the semantics of *Abs* is defined; a context of a component contains all the information required to define its semantics, for instance, the component name, names of all the provided coperation, names of all the required coperations and names of all the variables;
- *op.pattern* denote the operation pattern of *Abs*;
- *atmostone*(*X*) denote the formula stating that at most one event may take place;
- $[Abs]_X$ denote the semantics of *Abs* in context *X*;

The semantics of *Abs* is

$$[Abs]_X \triangleq [op.pattern]_X \; \wedge \; \square atmostone(X)$$

where *op.pattern* is defined using an ordering expression. The semantics of a subset of the ordering expression is defined in section 6.6. Due to lack of space, *atmostone*(*X*) is not defined in this paper. Its definition can be found in [22].

6.3 Temporal Semantics of Boxed Objects

Let

- *Bobj* denote the name of a boxed object containing two sub-components *C*1 and *C*2;
- *W*, *W*1 and *W*2 denote the contexts of *Bobj*, *C*1 and *C*2 respectively;
- *Iops* denote the internal coperations of *Bobj*;
- *interleave*(*W*, *W*1, *W*2) denote the temporal formula stating that events from *W*1 and *W*2 are interleaved;
- *synchronise*(*W*1, *W*2) denote the temporal formula stating that there exists an event in *W*1 which is synchronised with an event in *W*2;
- *hide*({*C*1, *C*2}, *Iops*) denote the temporal formula stating that all the events made by coperations in *Iops* are hidden.

The semantics of *Bobj* is

$$[Bobj]_W \triangleq$$
$$([C1]_{W1} \; C \; (idle(W1)\,\mathcal{U}\,fin)) \; \wedge \; ([C2]_{W2} \; C \; (idle(W2)\,\mathcal{U}\,fin)) \; \wedge$$
$$\Box(interleave(W, W1, W2) \; \vee \; synchronise(W1, W2)) \; \wedge$$
$$\Box hide(\{C1, C2\}, Iops)$$

In the above formula, $C1$ and $C2$ are extended with idle steps so that their sequences have the same length. The definitions of *idle*, *interleave*, *synchronise* and *hide* are given in [22].

6.4 Temporal Semantics of Coperations

The semantics of the different types of coperations are slightly different. To save space, only the semantics of passive compound operations are defined here. Let

- *cop* denote a passive compound operation;
- *Abs* denote the name of the abstract object providing *cop*;
- X denote the context in which the semantics of *Abs* is defined;
- *callorder* denote the ordering expression defining the order of the calls made by *cop*;
- *precond* and *postcond* denote the pre- and the post-conditions of *cop*;

The semantics is

$$[cop]_X \triangleq$$
$$accepting(X, cop, precond) \; C \; [callorder]_X \; C \; returning(X, cop, postcond)$$

cop is defined as an *accept* event, followed by a sequence of operation calls, followed by a *return* event.

$$accepting(X, cop, precond) \triangleq$$
$$idle(X)\,\mathcal{U}$$
$$(\pi_{abs} \; \wedge \; acc\text{-}abs\text{-}cop \; \wedge$$
$$reset.history(X) \; \wedge$$
$$precond(fpar\text{-}abs\text{-}cop) \; \wedge \; fin)$$

Due to lack of space we shall not explain all the details of the formula. Briefly speaking, the *accept* event is defined as a number of idle steps following by a step in which some flags and variables are set to indicate the event and the pre-condition must be true. Note how the pre-condition is embedded in the temporal formula in the definitions of the *accept* event. The *return* event is defined similarly.

6.5 Temporal Semantics of Call Templates

Due to lack of space, only the semantics of functional call templates are defined here. Let

- *op1* denote the coperation being called by *cop*;
- *O1* denote the name of the component providing *op1*;

Given the call template,

!op1	
prop	*func*
obj	*O1*
apar	*v*

The semantics is

$$[\![!op1]\!]_X \triangleq$$
$$sending(X, O1, op1, v) \, \mathcal{C} \, receiving(X, O1, op1)$$

$$sending(X, O1, op1, v) \triangleq$$
$$(idle(X) \wedge \exists n \cdot occno\text{-}O1\text{-}op1 = n) \, \mathcal{U}$$
$$(\pi_{abs} \wedge send\text{-}O1\text{-}op1 \wedge$$
$$apar\text{-}O1\text{-}op1(n) = v) \wedge fin)$$

Briefly speaking, the *send* event may be preceded by a number of idle steps. In the *send* event, the parameter of this call is put in the variable *apar-O1-op1*. When the executions of the calling component and the called component are synchronised on the *send* event and the corresponding *accept* event of *op1*, the value of *apar-O1-op1* is passed on to the formal parameter of *op1*. This property is defined by the predicate *synchronise* in [22]. The definition of the *receive* event is similar.

6.6 Temporal Semantics of Ordering Expression

In this section, only a subset of the ordering expression is defined. The full definition can be found in [22].

$$[\![\circ]\!]_C \triangleq fin$$

∘ indicates the end.

$$[\![P1; P2]\!]_C \triangleq [\![P1]\!]_C \, \mathcal{C} \, [\![P2]\!]_C$$

$P; Q$ means that P is followed by Q.

$$[\![P1 \parallel P2]\!]_C \triangleq$$
$$([\![P1]\!]_{C1} \, \mathcal{C} \, (idle(C1) \, \mathcal{U} \, fin)) \wedge ([\![P2]\!]_{C2} \, \mathcal{C} \, (idle(C2) \, \mathcal{U} \, fin))$$

$P1 \parallel P2$ means that $P1$ is in parallel with $P2$.

$$[\![P^+; Q]\!]_C \triangleq [\![P]\!]_C \, \mathcal{C}^* \, [\![Q]\!]_C$$

$P^+; Q$ means that there is one or more occurrence of P before Q happens.

$$[\![[P]; Q]\!]_C \triangleq ([\![P]\!]_C \, \mathcal{C} \, [\![Q]\!]_C) \oplus [\![Q]\!]_C$$

$[P]; Q$ means that P may happen before Q. $\oplus$ denotes the exclusive "or" operator.

7 Consistency of Refinement

Given a level i abstract object A and its level i+1 refinement, the consistency of the level i+1 refinement is validated by the following stages:

1. Identify the internal coperations.
   Let *Iops* denote the set of internal coperations.
2. Define the boxed object of the level i+1 refinement.

   <u>Boxed Object</u> *B*
   contains
       $r1, r2, ..., rn$
   hidden coperations
       Iops

3. Replace the operation pattern of *A* with level i+1 coperations.
   Let *A'* denote the same specification as *A* except that the operation pattern
   is replaced according to the operation patterns as defined in the **Coperation
   Refinement** part.
4. Hide calls made to internal coperations.
   After replacing the coperations of *A* with level i+1 coperations, *A'* may then
   contain calls made to the internal coperations. Let $hidecall(Iops, \{r1, r2, ..., rn\})$
   denote the formula stating that the internal calls are hidden.
5. Extend the variables of *A'* so that *A'* and *B* contain the same variables.
   Let *vars* denote the set of variables in $r1, r2, ..., rn$, but not in A'; $anyvalue(vars)$
   denote the formula stating that variables in *vars* can have any value.

Let *Ca* and *Cb* denote the contexts of *A'* and *B* respectively; we define that the
level i+1 refinement is consistent with *A* if

$$[\![B]\!]_{Cb} \Rightarrow ([\![A']\!]_{Ca} \wedge \Box hidecalls(Iops, \{r1, r2, ..., rn\}) \wedge \Box anyvalue(vars))$$

Due to lack of space, *hidecalls* and *anyvalue* are not defined here. The above
formula states that all the sequences specified by the left hand side are specified by
the right hand side, i.e. the refinement does not violate the abstract specification.

8 Example

As mentioned before, the ISPW-6 example describes a clearly defined software process, although it may not be necessary to develop a model for this example using
a stepwise refinement technique, due to the fact that it is a well known example
within the software process community, in this paper, we will still use this example
to illustrate how to gradually develop a model using our approach.

8.1 Brief Description of the ISPW-6 Example

A full description of the example is given in [15]. The core problem focuses on the
designing, coding, unit testing, and management of a rather localized change to a
software system. This is prompted by a change in requirements, and can be thought
of as occurring either late in the development phase or during the support phase
of the life-cycle. In order to confine the problem, it is assumed that the proposed
requirements change has already been analyzed and approved by the configuration
control board and only a single code unit is to be affected. The problem begins with

the project manager scheduling the change and assigning the work to appropriate staff. The example problem ends when the new version of the code has successfully passed the new unit tests. During the software process, the following steps may be taken by various personnel: Schedule and Assign Tasks, Modify Design, Review Design, Modify Code, Modify Test Plans, Modify Unit Test Package, Test Unit and Monitor Progress.

8.2 Top Level

At the top level, one may view the ISPW-6 example as one component which responses to requirements issued by the configuration control board (CCB); it then repeatedly carries out some activities to produce the required changes until either that the changes are completed or a cancellation is received from CCB.

In OBM, this component can be specified as an abstract object as follows:

Abstract Object *ISPW6-top* <u>The Interface Part:</u>

provides

>   *supply* : *none*
>   *receive* : *reqfrCCB*, *canfrCCB*
>   *action* : *produce*

requires

>   **ObjName** : **OpNames**
>   *none*   : *none*

operation pattern

$$reqfrCCB; produce^+; [canfrCCB]; \circ$$

In the above specification, *ISPW6-top* does not provide any operation to supply artifact. In reality, the produced software should be supplied to some clients. Since this is not mentioned in [15], it is not modelled here. *ISPW6-top* provides two cooperations for receiving information from CCB: *reqfrCCB* receives the requirements; *canfrCCB* receives cancellation. It also provides one action operation, *produce*, which produces the changes required.

The operation pattern specifies that first of all *ISPW6-top* is allowed to receive the requirements from CCB, and then it will repeatedly produce the required changes until either that the process is finished or a cancellation is received from CCB, and the process is then finished.

The body part of *ISPW6-top* is trivial and hence not defined here due to lack of space.

8.3 Level 1 Refinement

ISPW6-top can be refined as follows:

Component Refinement

$ISPW6\text{-}top$ is replaced by two level 1 components: $MTeam$ and $TTeam$. $MTeam$ is responsible for management issues and $TTeam$ is responsible for technical issues. $MTeam$ and $TTeam$ are defined as follows:

Abstract Object $MTeam$ The Interface Part:

provides

> $supply : tasktoTTeam_1$
> $receive : reqfrCCB_1, canfrCCB_1, repfrTTeam_1$
> $action : schedule_1, monitor_1$

requires

> **ObjName : OpNames**
> $TTeam \qquad : taskfrMTeam_1$

operation pattern

> $reqfrCCB_1; schedule_1; tasktoTTeam_1;$
> $((schedule_1; tasktoTTeam_1) \oplus monitor_1 \oplus repfrTTeam_1)^+;$
> $[canfrCCB_1]; \circ$

where the subscripts are used to indicate the level numbers. Subscripts may be omitted if the level numbers are obvious. The operations are used for the following purposes:

$tasktoTTeam_1$: supply the scheduled tasks to the technical team.

$reqfrCCB_1$: receive the requirements from CCB.

$canfrCCB_1$,: receive the cancellation from CCB.

$repfrTTeam_1$: receive the progress report from the technical team.

$schedule_1$: schedule and assign tasks.

$monitor_1$: monitor the progress.

The operation pattern of $MTeam$ states that after receiving the requirements from CCB, $MTeam$ is allowed to do some scheduling and send the scheduled task to $TTeam$. After that $MTeam$ is allowed to repeatedly perform its main process until either that it is finished or a cancellation is received from CCB. The main process of $MTeam$ is either performing more scheduling or monitoring the progress or receiving report from $TTeam$.

Abstract Object $MTeam$ The Body Part:

call templates

$!taskfrMTeam_1$	
prop	$func$
obj	$TTeam$
apar	t

coperation definitions

> $tasktoTTeam_1$ is active
> $tasktoTTeam_1$'s **call order**
>
> > $!taskfrMTeam_1; \circ$

> *taskto TTeam*$_1$'s pre- and post-conditions
> trivial

In the above, the body part of *MTeam* contains one call template. The name of the call template is *!taskfrMTeam*. Its type is a function call. The called object is *TTeam*. The parameter of the call is t.

Due to lack of space, only one coperation, *tasktoTTeam*, is defined. It is an active coperation; the order of the call is simply *!taskfrMTeam* because this is the only operation call; the pre- and the post-conditions are trivial.

Abstract Object *TTeam* The Interface Part:

provides

> *supply* : *reptoMTeam*$_1$
> *receive* : *taskfrMTeam*$_1$
> *action* : *workonchange*$_1$

requires

> *MTeam* : *repfrTTeam*$_1$

operation pattern

> *taskfrMTeam*$_1$; *workonchange*$_1$; (*workonchange*$_1$ $\oplus$ *reptoMTeam*$_1$)$^+$; $\circ$

In the above definition, the coperations are used for the following purposes:

reptoMTeam$_1$: supply the progress report to *MTeam*.
taskfrMTeam$_1$: receive the scheduled task from *MTeam*.
workonchange$_1$: work on the required changes.

The operation pattern of *TTeam* states that after receiving an assigned task from *MTeam*, *TTeam* is allowed to do some work on the required changes, and subsequently, it is allowed to either perform more work or report its progress to *MTeam* repeatedly.

The body part is trivial, and not included here due to lack of space.

Coperation Refinement

The following sub-operation patterns of *ISPW6-top* are replaced with the level 1 coperations as follows:

> *reqfrCCB* $\triangleq$ *reqfrCCB*$_1$

> *canfrCCB* $\triangleq$ *canfrCCB*$_1$

> *produce*$^+$; [*canfrCCB*]; $\circ$ $\triangleq$
> *schedule*$_1$;
> (((*schedule*$_1$ $\oplus$ *monitor*$_1$)$^+$; [*canfrCCB*$_1$]; $\circ$) || (*workonchange*$_1^+$; $\circ$))

8.4 Consistency of the Level 1 Refinement

1. Let *intops* denote the set of internal operations, *intops* contains

$$\{ tasktoTTeam_1, taskfrMTeam_1, reptoMTeam_1, repfrTTeam_1 \}$$

2. Let *ISPW6-level1* denote the boxed object containing *MTeam* and *TTeam*,

Boxed Object *ISPW6-level1*
contains
    MTeam, TTeam
hidden coperations
    intops

3. Let *ISPW6-top'* denote the same specification as *ISPW6-top* except that the sub-operation patterns are replaced according to the level 1 **Coperation Refinement** part. The resulting operation pattern of *ISPW6-top'* is

$$reqfrCCB_1; schedule_1;$$
$$(((schedule_1 \oplus monitor_1)^+; [canfrCCB_1]; \circ) \parallel (workonchange_1^+; \circ))$$

4. Let $hidecalls(intops, \{MTeam, TTeam\})$ denote the formula for hiding the internal calls.

5. Let $anyvalue(vars)$ denote the formula for extending the variables of *ISPW6-top'*.

Let $C1$ and $C0$ denote the contexts of *ISPW6-level1* and *ISPW6-top'* respectively, according to section 7, the aim is to prove

$$[\![ISPW6\text{-}level1]\!]_{C1} \Rightarrow$$
$$([\![ISPW6\text{-}top']\!]_{C0} \wedge$$
$$\Box hidecalls(intops, \{MTeam, TTeam\}) \wedge$$
$$\Box anyvalue(vars))$$

Let Cm and Ct denote the contexts of *MTeam* and *TTeam* respectively; according to section 6.3, the semantics of the boxed object *ISPW6-level1* can be expanded as follows:

$$[\![ISPW6\text{-}level1]\!]_{C1} \triangleq$$
$$([\![MTeam]\!]_{Cm} \mathcal{C} (idle(Cm) \mathcal{U} fin)) \wedge$$
$$([\![TTeam]\!]_{Ct} \mathcal{C} (idle(Ct) \mathcal{U} fin)) \wedge$$
$$\Box(interleave(C1, Cm, Ct) \vee synchronise(Cm, Ct)) \wedge$$
$$\Box hide(\{MTeam, TTeam\}, intops)$$

Expand the semantic definitions of the abstract objects *MTeam* and *TTeam* according to the definition in section 6.2, the above formula becomes:

$$[\![ISPW6\text{-}level1]\!]_{C1} \triangleq$$
$$(([\![MTeam.pattern]\!]_{Cm} \wedge \Box atmostone(Cm)) \mathcal{C} (idle(Cm) \mathcal{U} fin)) \wedge$$
$$(([\![TTeam.pattern]\!]_{Ct} \wedge \Box atmostone(Ct)) \mathcal{C} (idle(Ct) \mathcal{U} fin)) \wedge$$
$$\Box(interleave(C1, Cm, Ct) \vee synchronise(Cm, Ct)) \wedge$$
$$\Box hide(\{MTeam, TTeam\}, intops)$$

We then further expand the semantics of the operation patterns according to the definitions in section 6.6 to give:

$$[ISPW6\text{-}level1]_{C1} \triangleq$$
$$((([reqfrCCB_1]_{Cm}\ C\ [schedule_1]_{Cm}\ C\ [taskto\,TTeam_1]_{Cm}\ C$$
$$(([schedule_1]_{Cm}\ C\ [taskto\,TTeam_1]_{Cm}\ \oplus\ [monitor_1]_{Cm}\ \oplus$$
$$[repfrTTeam_1])\,C^*$$
$$(fin\ \oplus\ [canfrCCB_1]_{Cm}\ C\ fin)))\ \wedge$$
$$\Box atmostone(Cm))\ C\ (idle(Cm)\ \mathcal{U}\ fin))$$
$$\wedge$$
$$((([taskfrMTeam_1]_{Ct}\ C\ [workonchange_1]_{Ct}\ C$$
$$([workonchange_1]_{Ct}\ \oplus\ [reptoMTeam_1]_{Ct})\,C^*\ fin)\ \wedge$$
$$\Box atmostone(Ct))\ C\ (idle(Ct)\ \mathcal{U}\ fin))$$
$$\wedge$$
$$\Box(interleave(C1, Cm, Ct)\ \vee\ synchronise(Cm, Ct))\ \wedge$$
$$\Box hide(\{MTeam, TTeam\}, intops)$$

Each sequence specified by the above formula is merged from the following two:

MTeam: $reqfrCCB_1$ followed by $schedule_1$ followed by $taskto\,TTeam$ followed by an iteration of either $schedule_1$ followed by $taskto\,TTeam$ or $monitor_1$ or $repfrTTeam$ until either $canfrCCB_1$ or the end;

TTeam: $taskfrMTeam$ followed by $workonchange_1$ followed by an iteration of either $workonchange_1$ or $reptoMTeam$;

with the constraints that

1. the events between the two sets are either interleaved or synchronised,
2. all events of the internal coperations are hidden.

Since $taskto\,TTeam_1$ and $taskfrMTeam_1$ are synchronised coperations, it means that TTeam cannot start its execution until MTeam has done $reqfrCCB_1$ and the first $schedule_1$, see the illustration below:

MTeam: $reqfrCCB_1$, $schedule_1$ $taskto\,TTeam_1$, ...
TTeam: $taskfrMTeam_1$, $workonchange_1$,...

In addition, according to the second constraint, events of $taskto\,TTeam_1$, $taskfrMTeam_1$, $repfrTTeam_1$ and $reptoMTeam_1$ are hidden because they are internal coperations. Therefore each sequence specified by the above formula is as follows:

ISPW6-level1: $reqfrCCB_1$ followed by $schedule_1$ followed by a sequence merged from the following two:

1. an iteration of either $schedule_1$ or $monitor_1$ until either $canfrCCB_1$ or the end;
2. $workonchange_1$ followed by an iteration of $workonchange_1$.

Now consider the right hand side of the proof, if we expand $[ISPW6\text{-}top']$ according to the semantic definition of the abstract objects, we get the following formula,

$$[reqfrCCB_1; schedule_1;$$
$$(((schedule_1 \oplus monitor_1)^+; [canfrCCB_1]; \circ) \parallel$$
$$(workonchange_1^+; \circ))]_{C0} \land$$
$$\Box atmostone(C0) \land$$
$$\Box hidecalls(intops, \{MTeam, TTeam\}) \land$$
$$\Box anyvalue(vars))$$

Again expanding the semantics of the operation pattern, we get,

$$[reqfrCCB_1]_{C0} \, C \, [schedule_1]_{C0} \, C$$
$$(((([schedule_1]_{C0} \oplus [monitor_1]_{C0}) \, C^*$$
$$(fin \oplus \cdot [canfrCCB_1]_{C0} \, C \, fin)) \, C \, (idle(C0) \, U \, fin))$$
$$\land$$
$$([workonchange_1]_{Ct} \, C^* \, fin \, C \, (idle(Ct) \, U \, fin))) \land$$
$$\Box atmostone(C0) \land$$
$$\Box hidecalls(intops, \{MTeam, TTeam\}) \land$$
$$\Box anyvalue(vars))$$

Each sequence specified by the above formula contains a $reqfrCCB_1$ followed by a $schedule_1$ followed by a sequence merged from the following two:

1. an iteration of either $schedule_1$ or $monitor_1$ until either $canfrCCB_1$ or the end;
2. an iteration of $workonchange_1$.

It is not difficult to see that the behaviour specified by $ISPW6\text{-}level1$ satisfies the behaviour specified by $ISPW6\text{-}top'$.

9 Discussion, Related Work and Future Work

9.1 Information Flow

In many existing process modelling approaches, activities are modelled as operations. Inputs and outputs of activities are treated as parameters and results of the operations. However we found that problems exist with this type of modelling if the results of an operation are not needed by the caller of this operation, but by some others, and similarly if the inputs of an operation are not supplied by the caller of this activity. In our approach, there is a clear distinction between operations regarding information flow and operations regarding activities. Information flow is explicitly modelled with the supply and receive operations. We believe this gives better control to where the information is going and when the information may be transferred.

9.2 Multiple Levels of Abstractions

The need for modelling processes in multiple levels of abstraction has been clearly recognised. Dowson pointed out in [9] that modelling formalism should accommodate a wide range of model granularity, and allow the refinement of initially large-grain models to address increasing details. The example above has shown that OBM has achieved this requirement.

In OBM, multiple levels of abstraction can be reflected in two ways. One is that a model is refined with increasing details as illustrated by the example above. The other is that different parts of the model may be represented at different levels of abstraction. For example, one may decide to refine *TTeam*, but not *MTeam*, in the next level of refinement.

Several existing approaches also provide means to represent a model in multiple levels of abstraction. Some of these are based on hybrid formalisms that use different notations for large-grain and small-grain aspects of process. An example of this type of approach is Process Weaver [11]. Another type of approach is incremental definitions. Examples of this type of approach include: tasks in Epos [8], activities in Slang [3], blackboard in Oikos [2]. However there is no support for formal reasoning between different levels of abstraction. Since Slang is based on Petri-net, it should be possible to perform formal reasoning, however, it is not clear to the authors whether such a facility is provided by [3]. Work on consistency proof for refinement in Oikos is in development [2, 7].

In [16], a method based on data flow diagram (DFD) for modelling process interface is defined. Although the method has a formal basis for process decomposition, it provides very limited expressive power.

9.3 Alternative Refinement

In OBM, it is possible to have different refinements for the same abstract object. For instance, in the above example, one possible refinement for *TTeam* is to decompose it into two components: Design Team and Implementation Team, where Design Team is responsible for modify design, review design etc. and the Implementation Team is responsible for modify code and testing. Alternatively it can be decompose into three components: Design, Coding and Testing. The consistency of both refinements can be checked against *TTeam*.

This facility allows us to refine sub-processes according to the different needs. For instance, for different projects, in which there will be different resources and different requirements, it is possible to refine a part of a process to suit the specific need without affecting the behaviour of the overall process. This is particularly useful in process modification.

9.4 Verification and Validation

In [12], the concepts of verification of a software process model and validation of a software process model are defined. Verification means to prove the correctness of a model. Validation means to test if a model behaves as expected using simulation. If a model can be verified to have a certain property, it means that all processes of that model have that property. In contrast, validation only tests individual process, and in general, it is not possible to test all processes.

Ideally, one would like to verify a model. However, verifications can be complicated, and sometimes theoretically impossible. Although validation does not test all the possibilities, it does give valuable feedbacks so that confidence in the model can be built up.

We are aiming to support both verification and validation facilities so that they can be used in a complementary way.

9.5 BM Stepper

Currently we are working with the Southampton University to develop a simulation tool, called BM stepper, for stepping through the operation patterns. The BM stepper is implemented using the object-oriented proto-typing language *Enact* [13]. Our experience has shown that the BM stepper has proved to be useful with identifying errors and gaining confidences [21].

At the moment, the BM stepper only covers a sub-set of the operators used in OBM operation patterns. More work will be done to extend the BM stepper to include all the operators.

9.6 Tool Support

OBM was first used in a case study reported in [25]. The details of the proofs for the example described above and the one in [25] are very similar. In fact, for most part of the proof, it is only necessary to substitute the names. This similarity suggests that tools may be built to assist the proofs.

9.7 Executable Specifications

The BM stepper allows us to simulate simple operation patterns. Investigation on supporting executable OBM with *Enact* is underway. This involves defining the semantics of the OBM constructs in *Enact*. A case study, called "Integrated Store Solution" (ISS400) [1], is being undertaken to illustrate both the development process of OBM and the use of the executable OBM.

9.8 Data Refinement

In this paper, we have described component refinement and coperation refinement. What remains to be studied is data refinement. One aspect of our future work is to investigate how to reason about the consistency between the refinement and its abstract object if data refinement is included. A possible solution is to use the data reification technique as described in [14].

The work on OBM is ongoing. There is still a wide scope for improvement. However, we believe the concepts and features offered by OBM can play an important part in the area of process modelling.

Acknowledgements

The authors would like to thank Professor P. Henderson for the detailed discussions and suggestions on the ideas for the executable OBM, Mark Greenwood for his comments on the earlier drafts and all members of IPG for the useful discussions through out this work.

References

1. ISS400 Technical Introduction. Technical Report 53423/001, Internationl Computer Limited, June 1993.
2. V. Ambriola and Carlo Montangero. Oikos at the Age of Three. In *Proceedings EWSPT'92*, volume 635 of *Lecture Notes in Computer Science*. Springer Verlag, 1992.
3. S. Bandinelli, A. Fuggetta, and S. Grigolli. Sprocess Modelling In-the-Large with SLANG. In *Proceedings of the Second International Conference on the Software Process*, Berlin, 1993.
4. H. Barringer, R. Kuiper, and A. Pnueli. Now you may compose temporal logic specifications. In *Proceedings of the 16th A.C.M. Symposium on Theory of Computing*, 1984.
5. R.F. Bruynoghe, J.M. Parker, and J.S. Rowles. PSS: A system for Process Enactment. In *Proceedings of the first International Conference on the Software Process, Manufacturing Complex Systems*. IEEE Computer Society Press, 1991.
6. R.M. Burstall. Program Proving as Hand Simulation with a Little Induction. In *Information Processing 74*, Pages 308-312, North-Holland Pub. Co., 1974.
7. X.J. Chen and C. Montangero. Compositional Refinement in Multiple Blackboard Systems. In *ESOP'92 European Symposium on Programming*, February.
8. R. Conradi et al. Design, Use and Implementation of SPELL, a Language for Software Process Modeling and Evolution. In *Proceedings EWSPT'92*, volume 635 of *Lecture Notes in Computer Science*. Springer Verlag, 1992.
9. Mark Dowson. Software Process Themes and Issues. In *Proceedings of the Second International Conference on the Software Process*. IEEE Computer Society Press, 1993.
10. J. C. Derniame (Editor). *Lecture Notes in Computer Science 635: Software Process Technology*. Springer-Verlag, 1992.
11. C. Fernström. PROCESS WEAVER: Adding Process Support to UNIX. In *Proceedings of the Second International Conference on the Software Process*, Berlin, 1993.
12. V. Gruhn and A. Saalmann. Software Process Validation Based on FUNSOFT Net. In *Proceedings EWSPT'92*, volume 635 of *Lecture Notes in Computer Science*. Springer Verlag, 1992.
13. P. Henderson. *Object-Oriented Specification and Design with C++*. International Series in Software Engineering. McGraw-Hill, 1993.
14. C.B. Jones. *Systematic Software Development Using VDM*. Computer Science. Prentice-Hall International, 1986.
15. M. Kellner, P. Feiler, A. Finkelstein, T. Katayama, L. Osterweil, M. Penedo, and H.D.Rombach. ISPW-6 Software Process Example. In *Proceedings of the First International Conference on Software Process*, Washington, DC, 1991. IEEE Computer Society Press.
16. C. Kung. Process Interface Modelling and Consistency Checking. *Journal of System and Software*, 15:185-191, 1991.
17. L. Lamport. What Good is Temporal Logic? In R.E.A. Mason, editor, *Information Processing 83*, pages 657-668, IFIP, 1983.

18. A. Pnueli. The Temporal Semantics of Concurrent Programs. *Theoretical Computer Science*, 13:45–60, 1981.
19. A.N. Prior. Time and Modality. Oxford University Press, 1957.
20. N. Rescher and A. Urquhart. Temporal Logic. Springer-Verlag Wien New York 1971.
21. I. Robertson J. Sa R.A. Snowdon R.F. Bruynooghe, R.M. Greenwood and B.C. Warboys. *Towards a Total Process Modelling System: A Case Study Using ISPW-6.* A Chapter in "Advances in Software Process Technology", to be published by Research Studies Press, J. Wiley, In Preparation, 1993.
22. J. Sa. OBM: A Tutorial. Project Report, March 1993.
23. J. Sa and B.C. Warboys. Specifying Concurrent Object-based Systems using Combined Specification Notations. Technical Report UMCS-91-9-2, Department of Computer Science, University of Manchester, July 1991.
24. J. Sa and B.C. Warboys. Integrating a Formal Specification Method with PML: A Case Study. In *Proceedings EWSPT'92*, volume 635 of *Lecture Notes in Computer Science*, pages 106–123. Springer Verlag, 1992.
25. J. Sa, B.C. Warboys and J.A. Keane. OBM: A Specification Method for Modelling Organisational Process. *Proceeding of Workshop on Constraint Processing at CSAM'93*, St. Petersburg, July 1993.

Process Modelling and Development Practice

Tom Rodden, Val King, John Hughes, Ian Sommerville

Departments of Computing and Sociology,
Lancaster University,
Lancaster LA1 4YR,
United Kingdom.
telephone: +44 524 593823
e-mail: tam@comp.lancs.ac.uk

1 Introduction

Software development is complex and time consuming. It involves a considerable investment of people, resources and time. Severe problems exist in understanding the activities involved in software development and in effective management of the process. Given the risks involved in the construction of software and previous errors in development and procurement it is not surprising that considerable research effort has been invested in understanding and supporting the software development process. We wish to complement this body of existing work on process modelling by a consideration of the experiences of the software process in practice.

The intent of much of process modelling investigation is to develop appropriate ways of managing the software development process. This has resulted in the construction of generic models of the software process that provide a framework for understanding and managing software development. These process models have traditionally considered the activities involved in software development in isolation of the application domain and as abstract tasks that need to be completed to realise a software system. The most notable of these models included the Waterfall Model, Exploratory Prototyping and the Spiral Model of software development.

A historical focus of the software process highlights the development of an abstract statement of how things should be done to manage the software development process effectively [13, 11, 1]. Many of these models included either an implicit or explicit understanding that some from of development method such as Structured Development was been applied. The assumption is that developers followed a set of prescribed activities to realise the finished software system. However, in actuality while certain aspects of these methods were used studies have highlighted that the methods were seldom followed by developers in any prescriptive manner[3].

The current trend in software process technology has seen the development of technological support for abstract representations of the software process. The focus of this work has been a consideration of the software process as a set of procedures [12] which could be used to control software development. Generally, the software process has been consider in terms of an abstract model that is instantiated for a particular setting before being enacted to manage the use of tools within an environment.

A wide range of formalisms have been used to describe process models, including Petri Nets [2], CSP[8] and logic based systems[1]. These models have tended to consider the software process purely as communicating functions undertaking independent activities to realise effective software development. Common description of the software process used within the literature highlight the procedural nature of these models:-

"A software process is a complex net of interacting objects" [9]
"Software Processes are software too" [12]
"A software process model defines the activities performed in a software engineering environment in order to produce a software product." [2]

The description of the software process adopted by these different formalisms have reflected a generic view of the software process. Many projects within the process modelling community can be characterised as fulfilling one of a number of goals

– Adopting an abstract representation of the software process.
– Developing formalisms to express this representations.
– Constructing environments to enact an abstract model of the process

Underpinning all of this work is an acceptance that a procedural abstraction of the software process effectively describes software development. We readily accept the view within process modelling that software development is a form of work susceptible to problems of scale and needing to be managed and controlled. However, in contrast to previous abstract considerations of the software process we want to pay service to the "real world" needs of development. As part of an on-going project we have undertaken a series of field studies of software development at different sites. The intent of these studies is to gain an insight into the nature of software development as it actually occurs in practice and to inform the development of effective support for the software development process.

2   A study of software development

We have been studying the development of a new aircraft within a military avionics company. By necessity, the focus of software development is concerned with issues of safety and development relies on a well defined and enforced model of development. Many of the current processes are paper based and exploit strict control on the generation and handling of software control reports to manage the process. In essence, the management view of the model reflects the prescriptive and abstract consideration of the software process prevalent within many process modelling systems.

The approach we have adopted is to make use of an ethnographic form of investigation. The tradition of ethnographic enquiry is well-established within sociology. Ethnography is an observational technique that uses a naturalistic perspective. That is, it seeks to understand settings as they naturally occur, rather than in artificial or experimental conditions, from the point of view of the people who inhabit those settings, and usually involves quite lengthy periods of time at the study site. However where ethnographers have historically concerned themselves with issues that might be described as quintessentially "sociological", more recently they have been used as a means of informing design and change- management processes at work. Such studies have included investigations of domains such as Air Traffic Control; Police work; Architects; the International Monetary Fund; Stock Exchange dealing rooms; the London Underground, among others. The rationale for this is that such descriptions not only provide a base line but also a detailed understanding of work practices as currently constituted, in such a way as to provide resources for understanding change.

Ethnographic studies take place over an extended period and are extensive in nature. Rather than consider the emerging results of our studies in detail it is worth highlighting a number of effects that have been observed within our particular setting. We believe that the observed effects highlight a mismatch between the nature of software development as it is carried out by systems engineers and the abstract representations embodied in process modelling. Two particular areas of importance are the implications of over prescription and the importance of professional practice.

2.1 The danger of over prescription

The software process we are studying is concerned with the development of a software product where errors are potentially life threatening. Consequently, software development focuses on the need to development safe software and much of the focus on strict process management is intended to reinforce the development of safe software systems. The approach adopted is prescriptive and detailed in nature.

However, overly prescriptive processes and management styles also serve to problematise the "normal" ad-hocing that engineers do when problems arise. All organisational life involves "cutting corners", informal "bending of rules" and so forth. In most instances, organisational managements are aware that such work goes on, if not in detail, and allow it precisely because it is a means by which the work can be done. However, with routine day by day work what is allowable can change because of the adopted process and particular informal strategies can become very different when procedures are strictly enforced.

Problems can be created when engineers do the sorts of thing they have always done, but where strict following of procedures mean that such practices have consequences outside their own domain. Thus in the case of our study when code changes are made within a sub- system, the need for strict overall monitoring across the process meant that the formal notification of such changes was strongly encouraged.

Rather than rely purely on the prescribed formal testing process engineers often made use of local "engineers testing" which allowed them to informally test code by recording it as still been under development. Everyone in an organisation is generally aware that such practices as the use of informal testing are commonplace. Examples within the project under review include the testing of code written before it comes to a formal release, by such means as the debugging tool for syntax error testing and "engineers' tests" for functionality. This use of informal testing often resulted in a tension between the needs of the process model and the actual practice of the engineers.

> "Have you told X.... about all your code changes ... there was a cock-up yesterday ... some were missed off the database ... if you leave them in development you need to give him a ring ...."

Thus, the perceived need for an overview across the development process compromises a practice that is endemic in development. It is not unreasonable to view such practices as "trustworthy" in that local and unofficial use of some form of informal "engineers testing" is a perfectly normal practice, and indeed necessary. However, overly prescriptive adoption of a process can create a climate of uncertainty for engineers wherein the limits of their rule bending become more difficult to identify and consequently acceptance of the process itself is threatened.

2.2 The role of professional practice

An important part of software development is the use of professional practices across a development team. The effect of professional practice was also evident in adoption of informal testing within the process we observed. The status of "engineers testing" of code is clear given that they are not acceptable as any formal proof of the quality of the code. The testing process required code to be formally realised for testing and for SPRs (System Problem Reports) to be raised against this code. These formal report where then logged and developers were actioned to carried out the actions necessary to correct the reported problem. When it comes to formal release, the amount of SPRs was used as an indication of "how good the work is ..." That is, subsystems have an interest in minimising the number of SPRs that are generated. The use of informal "engineers' tests" combined with an acceptance of good professional practice across the software developers allowed the development team to achieve this.

However within the process we studied it was quite apparent that one of the fundamental problems was that the SPRs were "out of control ...." . The response in this case was understandably to create pressures for effectively and speedily dealing with SPRs to improve "quality control" by the adoption of a set of managed procedures. Attempts of this sort to speed processes have immediate consequences for accountability. Thus, where informal processes are habitually used as a first quality test, the security of engineers in their own practices is undermined by these external demands, precisely because their decisions are formed out of a tension between the need to have addressed actions promptly and their habitual use of informal methods of testing.

In other words, the professional character of their work is compromised by the pressing need to 'sort out' a whole gamut of problems in a timely way. Engineers who are taken aback by vigorous injunctions to complete work are not unusual in this context:

> "Something's been actioned for you to do, and you haven't been able to do it, and you're getting told to 'get your arse into gear ..' " .

This is not to say that pressures for action and control are not necessary for effective product development, for there is every indication that they often are, but the tension created represents a way in which uncertainties are generated. The implication is that a strong impedance to the acceptance of a process model is its limited consideration of the substantial professional practices used by software engineers. Given, the resources invested in the training of software engineers and the establishment of a set of professional practices it is likely that this impedance will need to be addressed in the adoption and enactment of any formal model of the development process.

3 Conclusions

The view of software development as a set of procedural activities has a striking similarity to the view of office work adopted by the office automation community[7]. As in the case of process modelling the office automation tradition followed a perspective of constructing abstract models that could be instantiated and enacted to automate much of the work within offices. Many of the adopted formalisms were similar to those used by the process modelling community. These included Petri Nets[5, 10], Information Control Nets[6] and production systems [4].

These models considered office work as a series of abstract process in which clerical workers reacted to some stimuli to undertake particular activities based on a given procedure. It was argued that much of office work was routine and procedural in nature and offices were characterised as different types reflecting different levels of routine work. Researchers suggested that different levels of automated support were appropriate for each office type. The development of these office types is analogous to the classification of process levels prominent within process modelling.

In practice, office automation systems made little headway within office environment and were generally not adopted. Empirical studies suggested that in contrast to the view inherent in most office automation models a great deal of office work requires judgement that is situated and dependent on circumstances. Early studies of office work[14] highlighted the use within work setting of situated judgement. For example, plans do not instantiate themselves but are applied by persons within work settings. This application is dependent upon the skills, knowledge and understanding of the person within the domain-at-hand. In this sense rather than being procedural instructions to be literally interpreted plans were resources to be used by users to co-ordinate and manage their work in conjunction with their experience and expertise.

We would argue that a similar situation to office automation exists with software process models and that process modelling systems should pay considerable attentions to lessons learned from the poor uptake of office automation. The reliance of these systems on a purely abstract consideration of software development rather than software development as it actually occurs within a given domain is problematic. As a result, existing process models pay little attention to the kind of day to day problems posed in software development (for example, taking into account skills of users and developers). In many ways the price of their generality is an abstraction that removes them from the actual nature of software development.

In addition, to acting as a warning for the future of software process modelling a comparison with office automation allows us to consider the contrast between software development as it is perceived within the models of the process and as it actually occurs. Continuing from the initial findings of our studies a consideration of how best to support the software process is essential. In contrast to the approach of developing richer models of the software process we advocate the construction of appropriate lightweight mechanisms to support the central features of the process, for example, communication between software developers. These mechanisms should be augment with facilities that allow process models to be referred to as a common resource for the work taking place.

References

1. Ambriola V, Montangero C. 'OIKOS at the Age of Three' in J.C.Derniame (Ed.): Software Process Technology: Second European Workshop, Springer-Verlag, ISBN 3-540-55928-0, pp 84- 94
2. Bandinelli S., Fuggetta A., Ghezzi C., Grigolli S. 'Process Enactment in Spade', in J.C.Derniame (Ed.): Software Process Technology: Second European Workshop, Springer-Verlag, ISBN 3-540- 55928-0, pp 67-98
3. Bansler J., Bodker K. 'A Reapprraisel of Structured Analysis: Design in an Organisational Context', ACMTransactions on Information Systems, Vol 11 No 2, April 1993, pp 165-193
4. Broverman C., Huff K., Lesser V. 'The role of plan recognition in the design of an intelligent user interface', Proceedings of the IEEE Conference on Man,Machine and Cybernetics, pp836-868, 1986
5. De Cindio F., De Michelis G.,et al 'CHAOS as a Coordinating Technology', in proceedings of CSCW 86, Austin, Texas, December 1986
6. Ellis C.A. 'Information Control Nets: A mathematical Model of Office Information Systems' Proceedings of the 1979 ACM Conference on Simulation, Measurement and Modeling of Computer Systems, August 1979, pp 225-239
7. Ellis C A., Nutt G. 'Office Information Systems and Computer Science', ACM Computing Surveys, March 1980
8. Greenwood M. 'Using CSP and System Dynamics as Process Engineering Tools', in J.C.Derniame (Ed.): Software Process Technology: Second European Workshop, Springer- Verlag, ISBN 3-540-55928-0, pp 138-145
9. Jaccheri L., Gai S. 'Initial Requirements for E3 : An environment for Experimenting and Evolving software processess' in J.C.Derniame (Ed.): Software Process Technology: Second European Workshop, Springer-Verlag, ISBN 3-540-55928-0, pp 99-101
10. Kreifelts T., Woetzel T. ' Distribution and error handling in an office procedure system' Proceedings IFIP WG 8.4 Working Conference on Office Systems Methods and Tools, Pisa, Italy, 1986, p 197-208
11. Krzanik L. 'Enactable Models for Quantitive Evolutionary Software Processes' proceedings of the 4th International Software Process Workshop, ACM SIGSOFT Software Engineering Notes, Vol 14 No 4, June 1989, ACMPress, pp 103-111
12. Osterweil L. 'Software Processes are software too' in the 9th International Conference on Software Engineering, 1987
13. Osterweil L.'Automated support for the enactment of rigorously described software processess' proceedings of the 4th International Software Process Workshop, ACM SIGSOFT Software Engineering Notes, Vol 14 No 4, June 1989, ACMPress, pp 122-126
14. Suchman, L. 'Office procedures as practical action', ACMTransactions on Office Information Systems, Vol 1, 1983, pp 320-328

A Pragmatic Approach to Process Modelling

Keith Phalp   Martin Shepperd

School of Computing and Cognition, Bournemouth University
Talbot Campus, Poole, BH12 5BB

Abstract: Many current process modelling approaches are notationally complex, and therefore inappropriate within relatively small software development environments. What is needed is a more pragmatic approach. This paper describes some process modelling work, based upon data flow techniques, conducted at a small software development organization. Our findings suggest that significant benefits can accrue from even a low cost approach. We also discuss some practical lessons learnt for the would-be process modeller.
Keywords: process model, software metrics, goals, reference model, process instance, data flow diagram.

1. Introduction

Process modelling is a method of capturing and describing the software process that promises benefits in a number of areas essential to software engineering. A key feature of process modelling that distinguishes it from other types of modelling in computer science is that "many of the phenomena encountered must be enacted by a human rather than a machine" [1]. Much work has been carried out in this area, particularly since the First International Software Process Workshop in 1984 [2]. However, there has been little acceptance of this technology by the 'smaller' organization. These organizations are typified by a shortage of dedicated resources for process modelling study, often stemming from the fact that staff play many roles, e.g. process group members are also engineers or project managers. The problems for the small developer are exacerbated by the following trends within the process modelling community.

1) Many Notations:
The quest for models to more accurately reflect the realities of the software development process has already led to the production of a multitude of representation schemes. In one classification scheme for process modelling notations no fewer than 11 categories were needed [3]. Despite this proliferation of notation, the search for the perfect scheme, or the perfect model continues. The consequence is a confusing situation for the novice or potential modeller.

2) Complex Models:
A phenomenon that seems to have arisen is the large-scale, large-effort, complex process model [4]. Such models may use a number of notations, and often rely upon their users being given automated support. These may be appropriate for large

software developers, but the overhead and cost is likely to be less attractive to smaller organizations.

3) Evidence:
Lack of evidence for the worth of process modelling, although a general problem is even more pertinent to small organizations, for whom a process modelling programme may be a significant part of their budget. While the academic community has given many assurances of the value of modelling, there is relatively little 'hard' evidence to support this proposition, particularly when one considers the length of time such work has been on-going. In addition many of the objections to process modelling may be political rather than technical. We believe that one way that more software developers can be persuaded of the worth of process modelling, is by providing 'local' evidence in the form of case studies. Despite its theoretical limitations — for example, the inability to have equivalent conditions, control groups or replication — a single local case study may be far more influential than a great deal of 'hard' evidence.

1.1) What is needed

We suggest that what many organizations actually need is a model which though it may be imperfect, is usable and useful. Furthermore, we suggest that sufficient notations already exist, and that the real problem is that not enough work is being done in applying them to real world problems. Such work needs to take account of the characteristics and needs of the organization in order to identify appropriate notation(s) and modelling strategy. It is this lack of appropriate modelling notations and strategies which we believe is the major barrier to acceptance of process modelling within the smaller organization.

This note describes the results of a case study that uses some simple process modelling ideas which have been usefully applied by a smaller software development organization. The next section outlines the work which we carried out. We then discuss the benefits of such work, before finally drawing some conclusions.

2. Our Study

Work was carried out at Schlumberger Technologies - Board Test, in the UK, a site which manufactures products with high software content and complexity, and where the distinctions between hardware and software engineers are often blurred. There are about 50 full time software engineers.

The area of process which we chose to investigate is termed product 'launch'. This covers the stage from the identification of a project or product need, through business and technical feasibility stages to requirements. These requirements are intended to be sufficient for the commencement of design work. The choice of this area was driven by the needs of the organization, primarily because they were keen to better understand the way the process was used, and because they were aware that there was an opportunity to improve it, so that it better catered for a wide range of project sizes and complexities.

Our approach was to tie the modelling notation used to the goal of the work. This is similar to the way in which Goal Question Metric (GQM) measurement paradigm [5] ties metrics to goals. We have adopted a check-list which we call GUIDE (Goal, Use, Investment, Deliverables, Experience) in order to help us do this. We illustrate this by reference to our study.

Goal: To understand (passive purpose) the launch process (object) at Schlumberger Technologies - Board Test (environment) from the view point (perspective) of the actors in that process.

Use: Senior managers and other actors in the process (audience) will use the models in order to enhance their understanding (use1) of the existing process, to aid discussion of it (use2) , and to suggest and communicate (use3) improvements. The model will be used by a guide for enaction by people. There is no need for an enactable model (enaction).

Investment: The initial modelling pilot is allowed only five person days (effort). There will be no additional funding for automated support (other resource) .

Deliverables: Model of procedures(d1). Models of actual process(d2). Report(d3) and presentation(d4) on discrepancies between procedures and reality.

Experience/Environment : Existing procedures focus on activities and products. The engineers and managers are comfortable with procedural notations.

Since communicating the models was essential, we wanted a graphical notation, also we still wished to take into account both the notational experience, and priorities of potential users. There was no need for enaction nor for the detail of a process program. We decided to adopt data-flow diagrams as our modelling technique. This had additional benefits for us, in that we had experience of using data flow diagrams and access to a suitable CASE tool.

3. Use of Models

We believe that there is merit in trying to understand the existing process before any making any attempt at improvement. Furthermore we believe that understanding what is good or bad about the current process leads to the identification of many possible improvements. In this respect our study was successful. The main benefit of this work so far is that it has highlighted five key discrepancies, and many minor discrepancies between the documented and actual process. It is clear that the view of the process which its designers have, and the view of the process its users have are very different, and we have been able to use models to highlight such discrepancies, and suggest improvements.

As a result of this initial success we are now using instance or project models to investigate the relationship between adherence to a process, and project success.The data-flow notation has been extended in order to graphically show the resource, schedule and effort of project activities. The data-flow diagrams thus have time and resource axes, where the area of activity is the amount of effort the activity took (or the percentage of project effort). Thus we can compare projects not only by their 'shape' in terms their constituent activities, but also by looking at the effort expended on activities.

4. Conclusions

The following is a list of the some of the lessons learnt from working on a low budget within an industrial environment.

* Concentrate on the goals and characteristics of the organization.
  Start by letting the organization suggest the problem or opportunity.
  Choose a feasible goal.
* Have a champion of your cause within the organization.
* Don't criticize any individuals: simply assess the process.
* It is a huge benefit to be seen as independent.
* Explain what you are doing and why.
* Be honest. Confess your ignorance.
* Make the organization take decisions.
* Get process users involved in discussion about the process.
* Be prepared to be flexible. Many people have tremendous demands on their time. You may not always be the highest priority.

To date we have carried out a small scale, low-cost pilot, and have produced one instance model. Despite the modest resources — approximately ten person days — the work has resulted in significant benefits to the organisation. These include the identification of discrepancies between documented and actual processes and an increased sense of process ownership and understanding by staff involved. From the evidence of this industrial process modelling exercise, we would argue that there are many benefits to be derived from even the modest application of existing process modelling technology and such work is entirely appropriate for the smaller software development organisation.

Acknowledgements

The authors would like to thank the staff of Schlumberger Technologies - Board Test, for their time, patience and many insights.

References

[1]   Curtis, B., M.I. Kellner, and J. Over, Process Modelling. *Communications of the ACM*, **35**(9): pp75-90, 1992.

[2]   Potts, C., ed. *Proceedings of the First International Software Process Workshop*. IEEE Computer Society Press: Egham, Surrey, England, 1984.

[3]   Madhavji, N.H., The Process Cycle. *Software Engineering Journal*, (Sep): pp234-242, 1991.

[4]   Krasner, H., *et al.*, Lessons Learned from a Software Process Modelling System. *Communications of the ACM*, **35**(9): pp91, 1992.

[5]   Basili, V.R. and H.D. Rombach. Tailoring the Software Process to Project Goals and Environments. in *Proceedings 9th International Conference on Software Engineering*. Monterey: 1987.

A Design Methodology for Process-Programming *

Gerald Junkermann and Wilhelm Schäfer

University of Dortmund, Informatik X, D-44221 Dortmund, Germany

Abstract. An examination of existing process programming-languages has shown, that none of them explicitly supports the design of software processes. Most of the process programming-languages are on the same level as "traditional" programming-languages and, therefore, are difficult to understand and unsuitable for explaining the process defined. A promising starting point for an intuitive representation of the process is to apply the concepts of already well known and accepted graphical languages, which have been used successfully for the design of databases and complex reactive systems.

1 Process Design Issues

In [5], Lee Osterweil compares software processes with software and states, that the development of both requires similar disciplines and methods. This quotation let us focus our interest on the design of software and how we can profit from the knowledge available when developing a language for process design.

The result of a "traditional" software design process is a set of modules, each encapsulating an abstract data-type, related by uses-relationships. The encapsulated data-type is represented by the specification of the type and the specification of the methods. The methods are most important, because they specify the semantics of the data-type, and its dynamic behaviour together with the constraints which must hold. Consider for example a data-type *person* with an attribute *street*. If the attribute *street* is used within the methods as a placeholder for the *family status*, the semantic of this attribute is, to store the *family status* and not the street, even though the attribute name is *street*. A constraint on that attribute might be, that the value *separated* can only be assigned, if the value *married* has been assigned to this attribute in a former state. The instances to be managed by the encapsulated data-types only appear at runtime and can be ignored on the design level.

This tripartition into types, behavioural description together with constraints, and instances is also true for process programs. The counterpart for the data-types are the object types of a process program, e.g. document types, tool types, roles and relationship types. The behavioural part is represented by the control structures and statements of the process modeling language (e.g. rules in Merlin

---

* This work has been supported by the Provincial Ministry for Research (MWF) of the state of Northrhine Westphalia

or Marvel, PML-code in IPSE2.5) and instances are only created when executing the software process.

An important difference between software systems and process programs is the frequency of changes. Software systems are designed, implemented and changes may occur in the future. In contrast to this process programs have to be adapted to the needs of every company and can not be specified completely in advance. This results in many changes, e.g. a new document type has to be specified or an existing document type has to be deleted. A further requirement is, that these changes also may occur during the execution of the process (i.e. on the fly), because the work of many people is coordinated by the process program and therefore the system must not be stopped.

Rule-based systems are good candidates to fulfil this requirement. They offer a comprehensive technique for the description of complex process-programs and a high degree of flexibility by offering the possibility to performing changes on the fly, which is only possible by using an interpretive approach.

Process design in contrast to process enaction should however take into account a clear separation of concerns between the three levels of description as mentioned above, namely type definitions, behavioural and constraint definition and the instance level. This makes processes highly understandable and maintainable. If this separation of concerns is supported by using appropriate languages and a precise definition of how, those possibly somewhat different, languages are integrated, then a process design and its corresponding development process no longer follow the "traditional" programming-like approach.

As an example of such a process design approach we sketch the Merlin process design approach which is based on a combination of Extended Entity Relationship-diagrams [1] and statecharts [2].

2 The Merlin Example

In Merlin, the enactable process programming language is a Prolog-like rule-language [4]. An examination of existing Merlin process-programs has shown, that the process programs can be divided into independent parts according to the above mentioned tripartition. One part, describing the dynamic behaviour of the programs (represented by rules) and another two parts, used to handle the objects and their types which the process-program deals with (represented by facts). In more detail this structure is described as follows:

- **Process:** contains those facts used to specify: the type of objects and relationships between types, the process-program deals with, ,and constraints on the dynamic behaviour of value assignment to attributes specifying the state of an object. These constraints are an essential part of the process-program, because they are used to specify the inter-object dependencies, i.e. how a change to other objects may influence the object of interest.
- **Project:** contains those facts which are instances of types introduced in the process-description. There may exist several different project-descriptions for one process, because they represent a concrete project under development.

- **Kernel:** specifies the semantics of the facts which are part of the process and project by defining the dynamic behaviour of the process through rules which are interpreted by the process-engine.

Further examinations of the trisection have shown, that the Kernel is the invariant part of the process-program which is changed very rarely. The Kernel encapsulates the rules representing the Merlin philosophy and acts as the inference machine for software processes, using Process and Project facts as input. The Kernel defines for example how to interpret the basic entity-types (e.g. roles, tools, documents) concerning how to build a customized working-context for any user, how to deal with a client/server architecture and how to realize multi-user support through a sophisticated transaction concept ([6], [4]). The Kernel only has to be changed when incorporating new concepts like for example a new transaction mechanism, configuration management or if new types of facts are defined and their semantics have to be specified by new rules. This does not affect process-design itself. The Project concerns the management of instances during process enactment and therefore can also be ignored during process-design. The part of a Merlin process-program describing the process is the Process. This lets us focus our design-concepts exclusively on this part. Nevertheless, a support for specifying the Project (e.g. by a browser) or to write and test the process-kernel (e.g. by a syntax-directed editor and a debugger) may be helpful to a process-engineer.

A main part of the process-description is the specification of object-types and relationship-types. Therefore the EER-model which was initially developed for the design of data-models is a suitable expedient for the specification of the document, role and tool types. This model is well accepted, uses a graphical representation and incorporates structuring concepts. For the design of process programs it lacks concepts for the specification of constraints on the dynamic behaviour for value assignment, and for specifying the inter-object dependencies (i.e. how a change of state of one object may trigger a change of state of another object). For that reason we propose to enhance the EER-model with statecharts which can be used to specify the behavioural aspect of processes. Statecharts support the specification of conditions for transitions between the states specified for a document. A transition could be triggered by the invocation of a tool, or by the change of state of a related document.

The example in figure 1 shows how a document hierarchy is specified using EER-diagrams.

The EER-model offers as modeling concepts entities, attributes and relationships as well as refinement (not shown in the example) and inheritance for structuring purposes. For every document type, a predefined set of attributes exists, used to specify its properties (e.g. the underlying structure, its visual representation). These attributes are inherited from the abstract document type *document*, can only be further specified and correspond to the predicates used within the Process.

As an example for the specification of the behavioural part, the corresponding statechart for the document type *c_module* is given in figure 2.

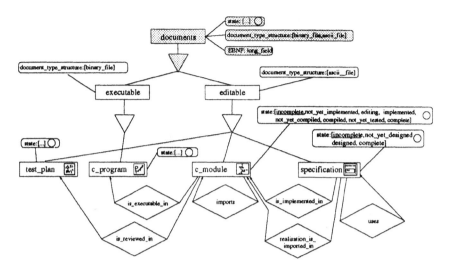

Fig. 1. Example of a document hierarchy

States are represented by ovals and transitions by directed edges. A transition can fire, if a tool is invoked (e.g. transition between *not_yet_implemented* and *editing*) or a condition becomes true. Two kinds of conditions are distinguished. Consistency conditions which are used to preserve the consistency of the process and automation conditions which change the state of a document if the preceding activity is completed correctly.

More details about the design language developed for Merlin can be found in [3].

References

1. Engels, G., Gogolla, M., Hohenstein, U., Hülsmann, K., Löhr-Richter, P., Saake G., Ehrich H.-D.: Conceptual modelling of database applications using an extended ER model. Data & Knowledge Engineering **9/2** 157–204 (1992/1993)
2. Harel, David: Statecharts: A visual formalism for complex systems. Science of Computer Programming **8** 231–274 (1987)
3. Junkermann, G.: How to improve process-programming in Merlin. Technical report: Memorandum des Lehrstuhls Software Technologie, University of Dortmund (1993)
4. Junkermann, G., Peuschel, B., Schäfer, W., Wolf, S.: Merlin: Supporting Cooperation in Software Development through a Knowledge-based Environment. John Wiley & Sons in: em Advances in Software Process Technology (to appear) (1993)
5. Osterweil, L.: Software Processes are Software Too. Proceedings of the 9th International Conference on Software Engineering (1987)
6. Peuschel, B., Schäfer, W., Wolf, S.: A Knowledge-based Software Development Environment Supporting Cooperative Work. International Journal on Software Engineering and Knowledge Engineering **1/2** 79–106 (1992)

73

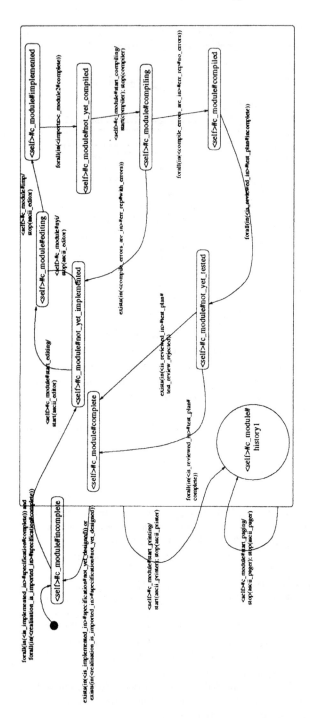

Fig. 2. Example of a statechart

Process Modelling Concepts Session

Jean Claude Derniame

Institut Polytechnique de Nancy and CRIN

This session is focussed on the issues and requirements for the support required in PM environments, not from a language perspective, as in "PML concepts and paradigms" session, but in the context of a general framework for process modelling. The papers in this session raise some of these issues.

- Can we delay decisions about the specific sequence in which individual sub-activities of a process should be performed and how can we use navigation facilities in process models?
- What should we formalise in a software process and what should we not?
- Do we need underlying paradigms which rely mainly on control or can we introduce some flexibility in models? Ian Sommerville's paper contains a plea for supporting informal activities and an analysis of corresponding requirements.
- Could we provide tools for informal information capture, processing and retrieval?
- Software development is a team activity with different roles to be played. How to describe them in terms of goals, interactions, exchanges,... raises many problems in the PM definition , enactment and framework domains. What kind of support mechanism could we provide ? Do we have adequate transaction mechanisms and coordination rules? Is it sufficient to have correct behaviour?
- Could we provide generalised tools for supporting cooperation as CSCW?
- The concept of view can be used to support these cooperative descriptions . When associated with merging facilities it could also be useful for progressively building comprehensive software process models.We need to provide support to (statically or dynamically?) merge them? Could it be done with informal components?
- Are we satisfied with two levels of domains, definition and enactment, or do we need an additional stage, as in the M Dowson and C Fernstrom 's paper? Beside process definition and process enactment (encompassing all that happens in the environment during run-time of a process definition) process performance encompasses all the actual actions conducted by human and non-human agents in the project. Separating these two concerns allows us to better capture the relationships between the PM centered environment and the project. The functionalities which should be provided (guidance,control, enforcement, feedback) can also be expressed in these terms.
- Requirements on the support for dynamic change , dynamic binding,enactment time events and exceptions handling are also discussed.

Obviously, this list of issues is not exhaustive. The selected papers for this session provide a valuable basis for active and intensive workshop discussions.

Process Modelling with Cooperative Agents

George T. Heineman[*]

Columbia University, New York NY 10027, USA

Abstract. Concurrency Control is the ability to allow concurrent access of multiple *independent* agents while still maintaining the overall consistency of the database. We discuss the notion of Cooperation Control, which gives a DBMS, the ability to allow cooperation of multiple *cooperating* agents, without corrupting the consistency of the database. Specifically, there is the need for allowing cooperating agents to cooperate while preventing independent agents from interfering with each other. In this paper, we use the MARVEL system to construct and investigate cooperative scenarios.

1 Introduction

Concurrency Control in database management systems allows multiple independent agents to concurrently access the database while maintaining its consistency. *Cooperation Control* extends this concept by considering situations with *cooperating* agents. To realize cooperation we need to have semantic information about how the agents will act. Our research on Process Centered Environments (PCEs) has shown that these systems have a rich body of semantic information available. In such environments, a process is formally specified in a Process Modeling Language (PML). As part of this specification, the cooperation between agents needs to be defined.

There are several reasons why multiple agents might need to cooperate:

1. Uniqueness of agents – There might be certain tasks which can only be carried out by a particular agent; consider a task which can only be performed by a database administrator.
2. Encapsulation of tasks – The process might be designed such that there are clusters of tasks which are separated from other tasks. This hierarchical organization of tasks becomes necessary as the size and number of tasks grows.
3. Group tasks – There are tasks which need multiple agents to work in concert with each other; consider a conference phone call between three parties.

The MARVEL project is an example of a PCE applied to software development. In this PCE, the process of software development is formally encoded in terms of rules, and the concurrency control of the database is tailored to provide specific

---

[*] Heineman is supported in part by IBM Canada, Ltd.

behavior. In this paper we explore how to use MARVEL to produce a cooperative environment. We start with a simple example of cooperating agents in a "Blocks World" environment, and then apply our results to a fragment of the ISPW-7 [4] sample problem. We conclude with a discussion of the limitations and benefits of this approach.

2 Example problem

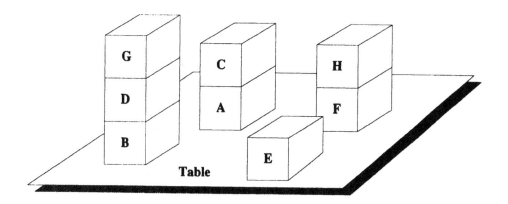

Fig. 1. Blocks World

Consider the "Blocks World" example, as shown in Fig. 1. Blocks can either sit on the table or on top of another block (the table is large enough to accommodate all blocks). A block **X** is *clear* if no block is sitting on top of **X**. Only clear blocks may be moved and a block cannot have two blocks sitting directly on it. To move **A** on top of **E**, for example, **C** must first be moved to the table; then both **A** and **E** are clear and the move can take place.

The PROLOG program in Fig. 3 is a goal-directed process which solves the problem of putting block **X** on top of **Y** by first making sure that both **X** and **Y** are clear, thus allowing the move to take place. Note that the **Table** may not be moved but blocks may be moved onto it. This particular process achieves the put_on(X,Y) goal by first achieving two sub-goals clear_space(X) and clear_space(Y). Figure 2 shows the solution for the request put_on(d,a). Note how put_on and clear_space are recursively defined to invoke each other.

We now introduce multiple agents to this example problem. Assume, in the blocks world, that there are two agents, *Placer* and *Clearer*. These agents cooperate in the following way:

1. When Placer moves block **X** to sit on object **Y**, Clearer is invoked to clear both **X** and **Y**. Note that **Y** may be a block or the **Table**.
2. When Clearer clears block **X**, Placer is invoked to move block **Y**, sitting on **X**, onto the **Table**.

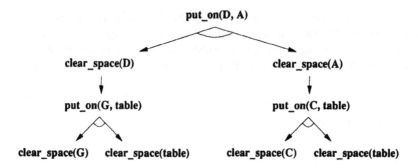

Fig. 2. Goal Tree for put_on(d,a)

```
on_top_of(c,a).              %% Which blocks are on other blocks
on_top_of(d,b).
on_top_of(g,d).
on_top_of(h,f).

                             %% When a block is on the table
on_top_of(BLOCK,table) :- not (on_top_of(BLOCK, X)).
clear_space(table).
clear_space(UNDER)     :- not (on_top_of(TOP, UNDER)).
clear_space(UNDER)     :- on_top_of(TOP, UNDER), put_on(TOP, table).
put_on(SRC,DST)        :- clear_space(SRC), clear_space(DST),
                          write('move '), write(SRC),
                          write(' to '), write(DST), nl.
```

Fig. 3. PROLOG solution for blocks

The responsibilities of each agent are disjoint and each has private tasks. Placer, for example, has no mechanism for knowing if block **X** is clear; it must blindly invoke Clearer. In similar fashion, Clearer knows how to clear a block only by requesting Placer to move other blocks. This scenario cannot be modeled in a single-process PROLOG environment, so we turn to the MARVEL system to design a multiple agent process.

3 Marvel

A MARVEL environment is defined by a data model, process model, tool envelopes, and coordination model for a specific project. The data model is object-oriented and uses classes to define an objectbase. The process is specified by MARVEL's process modeling language, MSL (MARVEL strategy language). Each process step is encapsulated by a *rule*, which has a name and typed parameters.

An MSL rule has four parts, a query, condition, activitym and effects. When a rule is requested, a query is made on the database and the rule's condition is checked. If it is satisfied, the activity is carried out and the assertions are made.

A rule's activity is a shell envelope [3] which allows an administrator to integrate conventional tools into the process. There is a rule engine which employs chaining to drive the process. Backward chaining is initiated to satisfy the failed condition of a user's rule request. Forward chaining carries out the implications of a rule's assertions by firing those rules whose condition has become satisfied by the assertion. Backward and forward chaining are both recursive procedures.

Each rule is encapsulated by a transaction by which the rule accesses the objects it needs. Once the rule's query has determined the necessary objects, the rule processor acquires locks for these objects with lock modes based upon how the rule will access the objects. For example, as seen in Fig. 4, only those those objects being updated in the effects need to be locked in **X** exclusive mode. This table is the *mapping table* which maps rules to transactions.

A lock conflict situation occurs when a rule attempts to acquire a lock on an object which conflicts with an existing lock held by another rule. The conflicts are determined by a lock compatibility matrix supplied by the administrator. Figure 4 contains a sample table of four particular lock modes: *Shared, Exclusive, Shared Write,* and *Weak Read*. The matrix defines the compatibility of two lock modes; for example, **ShW** and **X** conflict, while **WR** is compatible with each lock mode.

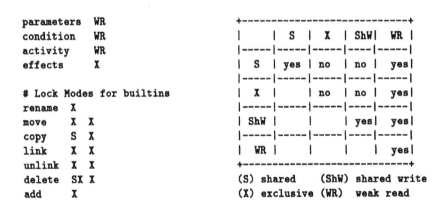

```
parameters   WR            +--------------------------------+
condition    WR            |     |  S  |  X  | ShW|  WR |
activity     WR            |-----|-----|-----|----|-----|
effects      X             |  S  | yes | no  | no | yes |
                           |-----|-----|-----|----|-----|
# Lock Modes for builtins  |  X  |     | no  | no | yes |
rename  X                  |-----|-----|-----|----|-----|
move    X X                | ShW |     |     | yes| yes |
copy    S X                |-----|-----|-----|----|-----|
link    X X                | WR  |     |     |    | yes |
unlink  X X                +--------------------------------+
delete  SX X               (S) shared    (ShW) shared write
add     X                  (X) exclusive (WR) weak read
```

Fig. 4. Transaction Table and Lock Compatibility Matrix

In response to a particular locking conflict, MARVEL turns to the specified coordination model to determine an appropriate response. This model contains a set of CORD (Coordination Rule Language) rules which outlines the prescribed actions to take. If a rule matches a situation, a set of actions are carried out and the conflict is resolved, otherwise the transaction is aborted, and its rule is stopped. We now present a MARVEL environment which solves the multiple agent blocks world.

```
OBJECT_CLASS :: superclass ENTITY;
  clear     : boolean = true;
  on_top_of : set_of OBJECT;
end

OBJECT :: superclass OBJECT_CLASS;
  Movable : boolean = true;
end

TABLE :: superclass OBJECT_CLASS;
  Movable : boolean = false;
end
```

Fig. 5. MSL data schema

3.1 Multiple Agent Solution

The data model, shown in Fig. 5, is comprised of three classes, OBJECT_CLASS, OBJECT, and TABLE. The *clear* attribute of an object tells whether it is clear or not, and the *movable* attribute determines if an object can be moved. The *on_top_of* attribute is a composition attribute which contains the block (if it exists), which is sitting on a given object. Figure 6 shows an objectbase which models the blocks world example from Fig. 1. The block **B**, for example, has its *clear* attribute equal to **false**, and its *on_top_of* attribute would be equal to the block {**D**}.

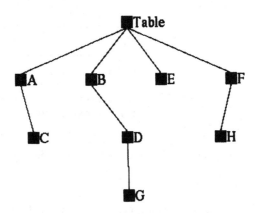

Fig. 6. MARVEL blocks representation

The process model has four rules. There are two PUT_ON rules, to handle different cases, and an AUTO_MOVE rule which automatically sets the *clear* attribute of a block X to `false` when a block is placed on X. There is one CLEAR_SPACE rule which makes a particular block clear. The rules are shown in Fig. 7.

In order to separate tasks belonging to different agents, the PUT_ON and CLEAR_SPACE rules have no logical condition associated with them. The rule PUT_ON[X,Y], for example, must invoke an agent to clear both X and Y to perform its operation. To do so, PUT_ON executes the shell envelope shown in Fig. 8. This envelope creates a new agent which will execute CLEAR_SPACE[X] and CLEAR_SPACE[Y], returning "0" on success, and "1" on failure. This return code will direct MARVEL to assert the appropriate effect as defined in the PUT_ON rule (i.e., on success, the **move** operation is asserted). This process is recursive as the agent executing CLEAR_SPACE[X] might create a new agent to complete its task.

The final information MARVEL needs is the coordination model, which is defined in terms of CORD rules. Specifically, the MSL rules in Fig. 7 will produce a conflicting database access. Consider issuing the PUT_ON[**D,A**] rule on the example in Fig. 6. This, we have seen, will cause an agent to be created to invoke CLEAR_SPACE[**D**] and CLEAR_SPACE[**A**]. The original PUT_ON rule, however, must access the objects **D** and **A** in exclusive access mode, since it must prevent other agents from interfering with its operation. The objectbase would become inconsistent if another agent mistakenly placed another block on **D** after the CLEAR_SPACE[**D**] invocation has completed, but before CLEAR_SPACE[**A**] has started. However, CLEAR_SPACE[**D**] (invoked by the cooperating agent) needs to access **D** in an exclusive mode also, since it removes **G** from on top of **D**. We need some mechanism for allowing the cooperating agents to access information jointly, while preventing conflicting access by independent agents.

In our multiple agent block world example, there are four particular situations, labeled 1 through 4, which are resolved by the control rules in Fig. 10. These situations correspond exactly to those locking conflicts in Fig. 9. In each case, the CORD action simply ignores the conflict, allowing the lock request to succeed, and thus the entire process succeeds.

We now explain the process trace in Fig. 9, omitting all intention locks (these are normally acquired because of the composition of the objectbase; see [1]). When PUT_ON[**D,A**] is requested, the first PUT_ON rule is fired, and the three locks are acquired (**X1**[**D**] is the first exclusive lock requested for block **D**). This rule executes the `clear_space` envelope which invokes an agent to CLEAR_SPACE[**D**]. To execute this rule, two locks need to be acquired; however a conflict occurs as the second **X**[**D**] lock is requested, since the two locks are incompatible. This lock conflict is repaired by the second condition pair in the OBJECT_conflict CORD rule. Note that both **X** locks are set on **D**. The CLEAR_SPACE rule executes the `put_on` envelope which invokes another agent to PUT_ON[**G, Table**]. As these locks are acquired, three separate conflicts occur, and each is handled by the appropriate CORD condition pair. We omit the right side of the process tree (CLEAR_SPACE[**A**]) as its execution is identical.

```
# When ?src comes from on top of another object
put_on [?src:OBJECT, ?dst:OBJECT_CLASS]:
  (exists OBJECT ?under suchthat (member [?under.on_top_of ?src])):

  { CLEARER clear_space ?src.Name ?dst.Name }

  (and           (move [?src ?dst on_top_of ?under])
       no_chain (?under.clear = true));
  no_assertion;

# When ?src comes from the TABLE
put_on [?src:OBJECT, ?dst:OBJECT_CLASS]:
  (exists TABLE ?tbl suchthat (member [?tbl.on_top_of ?src])):

  { CLEARER clear_space ?src.Name ?dst.Name }

  (move [?src ?dst on_top_of ?tbl]);
  no_assertion;


hide auto_move[?o:OBJECT]:
  # This rule doesn't apply to the Table, since the Table is always clear
  (exists OBJECT_CLASS ?under suchthat (and (member [?under.on_top_of ?o])
                                  (?under.Movable = true))):
  { }
  (?under.clear = false);

clear_space [?tbl:TABLE]:
 :
 { }
 ;


clear_space [?object:OBJECT]:
 :
  no_chain (?object.clear = true)
 { }
 ;


clear_space [?under:OBJECT]:
  (exists OBJECT ?obj suchthat no_chain (member [?under.on_top_of ?obj])):
  no_chain (?under.clear = false)

  { PLACER put_on ?obj.Name "Table" }

  (?under.clear = true);
  no_assertion;
```

Fig. 7. MARVEL multiple agent solution

```
ENVELOPE clear_space;
INPUT
  string : SRC;
  string : DST;
OUTPUT none;
BEGIN
  ## Clear both objects by invoking an agent to
  ## execute: clear_space(SRC)  clear_space(DST)
  SCRIPT_FILE=/tmp/clear_space
  echo "#!marvel script"       > $SCRIPT_FILE
  echo "clear_space $SRC"     >> $SCRIPT_FILE
  echo "clear_space $DST"     >> $SCRIPT_FILE

  ## Invoke the agent ##
  OUTPUT_FILE=/tmp/OUTPUT
  marvel -b $SCRIPT_FILE > $OUTPUT_FILE

  ## Check status and clear up ##
  RC=1
  ERROR=`grep "Failed while interpreting ${SCRIPT_FILE}" ${OUTPUT_FILE}`
  if [ "x$ERROR" = "x" ]
  then
    RC=0      # Succeeded
  fi
  rm $OUTPUT_FILE
RETURN "$RC";
END
```

Fig. 8. SEL envelope for PUT_ON

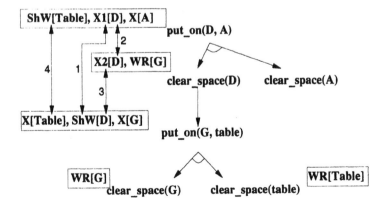

Fig. 9. Locking conflicts for PUT_ON[**D**, **A**]

```
OBJECT_conflict [ OBJECT ]
bindings:
   ?t1 = holds_lock ()
   ?t2 = requested_lock ()
body:
   if (and (?t1.rule = clear_space)      # An agent is using put_on[obj, table]
           (?t2.rule = put_on))          # to clear_space for user command
      then {                             # put_on[A, B], where object "obj" is sitting on
          notify(?t2, "Conflict-1")      # object A.
          ignore()
      }
   if (and (?t1.rule = put_on)           # An agent is using clear_space[obj] to
           (?t2.rule = clear_space))     # clear space for user command
      then {                             # put_on[obj, A] or put_on[A, obj].
          notify(?t2, "Conflict-2")
          ignore()
      }
   if (and (?t1.rule = put_on)           # An agent is using put_on(X, Y) and a
           (?t2.rule = put_on))          # subagent has been invoked to use
      then {                             # put_on(Y,table) to clear_space for Y.
          notify(?t2, "Conflict-3")
          ignore()
      }
end_body;

TABLE_conflict [ TABLE ]

bindings:
   ?t1 = holds_lock ()
   ?t2 = requested_lock ()
body:
   if (and (?t1.rule = put_on)           # Two agents are trying to place
           (?t2.rule = put_on))          # blocks on the same table
      then
        {
          notify(?t2, "Conflict-4")
          ignore()
        }
end_body;
```

Fig. 10. CORD coordination rules

4 Software Process Application

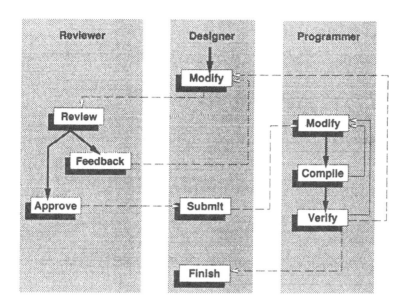

Fig. 11. Partial fragment from ISPW-7

Fig. 11 is a partial fragment from the ISPW-7 sample problem [4]. We apply the concepts shown in this paper to this fragment, and show how multiple agents can cooperate. There are three agents, the Reviewer, the Designer, and the Programmer. They each have a set of tasks (in white boxes) that they must perform. The solid arrows define the sequence of tasks for an individual agent and the dashed arrows show how the agents communicate with each other. The long grey vertical boxes represent the transactions encapsulating each agents's actions. The work starts when the Designer submits a modified design for review. The Reviewer either approves the design or produces feedback and replies to the Designer who either continues to modify the design, or submits it to the Programmer. Once the Programmer has made the necessary modifications, the code is compiled and verified, and the Designer is notified of either success or failure, in which case the design is finished, or further modified, respectively.

The data model and process model which specify this process are shown in Fig. 13 and Fig. 14. This somewhat complex-looking set of MSL rules is abstractly pictured in Fig. 12, where each rule is represented by a box whose logical condition is above the box and whose effects are below. A horizontal line of o's represents a rule invoking an agent. In order for these agents to cooperate, two conflicting situations need to be handled: when the Reviewer and the Programmer read the design which the Designer is modifying. We use the same lock compatibility table and mapping table from Fig. 4. The MODIFY_DESIGN rule invokes a separate agent to review the design and the locking conflict is resolved by the CORD rules in Fig. 15.

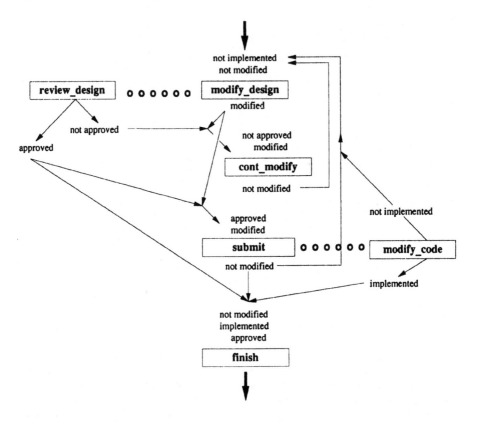

Fig. 12. Cooperative solution to ISPW-7 fragment

5 Conclusions

The CORD approach is similar to most investigations concerning cooperation mechanisms for database systems in that ACID transactions [2] are used as the underlying concept [6, 9]. CORD differs in that it can tailor the transctions to produce non-serializable behavior. Mneme [8] provides an interface between object-oriented languages and object-oriented databases so that the access policies to objects in the database can be specifically declared; the coding of the accesses are written directly by the programmer. The difference between Mneme and CORD is that CORD is involved only when non-serializable accesses occur. Hübel, et al., [5] propose a different cooperation control mechanism which defines the processing integrity of a set of activities with respect to their shared

```
OBJECT :: superclass ENTITY;
  design : DESIGN;
  code   : CODE;
end

DESIGN :: superclass ENTITY;
  contents    : text;
  modified    : (Yes, No, Initial) = Initial;
  approved    : (Yes, No, Initial) = Initial;
  implemented : (Yes, No, Initial) = Initial;
end

CODE :: superclass ENTITY;
  contents : text;
end
```

Fig. 13. Data model for fragment ISPW-7 solution

goal. Conflicts, in their model, occur when activities' goals are incompatible and negotiation between agents resolves the conflicts. CORD rules provide, then, a set of fixed negotiation tactics for particular situations which resolve conflicts without involving the user. To be sure, some conflicts are best resolved through human intervention, and we are considering adding such an action to the CORD language.

This research is similar in flavor to deliberative planning systems where one planner constructs a plan to be carried out later by several agents. Zlotkin and Rosenschein [10] present a strategy for autonomous agents to resolve conflicts through negotiation. Again, these conflicts occur on a more abstract level – goals – therefore, the resolution involves negotiations to restructure the goals of the agents. In addition, their context of noncooperative domains is different from our notion of a software process with cooperating agents. Macmillan [7] present an approach of emergent cooperation which is "discovered" by reasoning on the part of the planner. This contrasts with "scripted" cooperation which specifies all cooperation in advance. A software process is more likely to involve "scripted" cooperation since the modeling of the process reveals those steps which require cooperation among the agents.

The approach outlined in this paper has its shortcomings. In this prototype example of cooperating agents a new agent is created each time one is needed. In addition to wasting resources this will sometimes incorrectly model certain situations. The MARVEL system needs to be modified slightly to allow inter-agent communication between existing agents and this is one focus of future work. In addition, the CORD rule approach needs more extensions to be able to fully differentiate between interferences of cooperating agents and independent agents. We are in the process of enhancing CORD to address this issue. Finally, the approach of tailoring lock modes for rules, as described in Fig. 4, can be

```
modify_design[?o:OBJECT]:
  (exists DESIGN ?d suchthat (member [?o.design ?d])):
  (and (or no_backward (?d.modified = No)
           no_chain (?d.modified = Initial))
       (or no_backward (?d.implemented = No)
           no_chain (?d.implemented = Initial)))

  { MODIFY_TOOL modify_design ?o.Name }    # invokes separate agent to review design
  (and (?d.modified = Yes)
       (?d.implemented = No));
  no_assertion;

review_design[?o:OBJECT]:
  (exists DESIGN ?d suchthat (member [?o.design ?d])):
  { MODIFY_TOOL review_design }
  no_chain (?d.approved = No);
  no_chain (?d.approved = Yes);

hide continue_modify_design[?o:OBJECT]:
  (exists DESIGN ?d suchthat (member [?o.design ?d])):
  (and no_backward (?d.modified = Yes)
       no_backward (?d.approved = No))
  { }
  (and no_chain (?d.approved = Initial)
               (?d.modified = No));

hide submit[?o:OBJECT]:
  (exists DESIGN ?d suchthat (member [?o.design ?d])):
  (and no_backward (?d.modified = Yes)
       no_backward (?d.approved = Yes))
  { MODIFY_TOOL submit ?o.Name }    # invokes separate agent
  (?d.modified = No);

modify_code[?o:OBJECT]:
  (exists CODE   ?c suchthat (member [?o.code   ?c])):
  { MODIFY_TOOL verify_code ?o.Name }
  no_chain (?d.implemented = Yes);
  no_chain (?d.implemented = No);

hide finish[?o:OBJECT]:
  (and (exists DESIGN ?d suchthat (member [?o.design ?d]))
       (exists CODE   ?c suchthat (member [?o.code   ?c]))):
  (and no_backward (?d.modified    = No)
       no_backward (?d.implemented = Yes)
       no_backward (?d.approved    = Yes))
  { }
  (and no_chain (?d.modified    = Initial)
       no_chain (?d.implemented = Initial)
       no_chain (?d.approved    = Initial));
```

Fig. 14. MSL rules for fragment ISPW-7 solution

```
DESIGN_conflict [ DESIGN ]

bindings:
  ?t1 = holds_lock ()
  ?t2 = requested_lock ()
body:
  if (and (?t2.rule = review_design)   # A sub-agent requests to review a design
          (?t1.rule = modify_design))  # which has just been modified.
  then {
      notify(?t2, "DESIGN_conflict-1")
      ignore()
  }
  if (and (?t2.rule = modify_code)     # A sub-agent requests to review a design
          (?t1.rule = submit))         # which has just been modified
  then {
      notify(?t2, "DESIGN_conflict-2")
      ignore()
  }
end_body;
```

Fig. 15. CORD rules for ISPW fragment

too general to be of much use. Making all locks compatible avoids conflicts but introduces chaos since there would be no control over the operations. There currently exists in MARVEL a way to specifically determine lock modes for the activity section of a rule, but this needs to be extended to all symbols (and the objects bound to them) within the rule.

Even with its limitations this paper does address, and propose solutions to, certain issues regarding cooperating agents. The primary result of this work is to show how non-serializable behavior can be controlled by a set of coordination rules to allow cooperating agents to function properly, while still preventing independent agents from interfering with each other. The coordination rule approach can be applicable to any process modeling system, since the CORD rule language is orthogonal to the underlying PML which represents the process. We are currently implementing a transaction manager component, called PERN, which uses CORD to allow an application to tailor the concurrency control of a database to suit its needs.

References

1. Israel Z. Ben-Shaul, Gail E. Kaiser, and George T. Heineman. An architecture for multi-user software development environments. In Herbert Weber, editor, *5th ACM SIGSOFT Symposium on Software Development Environments*, pages 149–158, Tyson's Corner VA, December 1992. Special issue of *Software Engineering Notes*, 17(5), December 1992.

2. K. P. Eswaran, J. N. Gray, R. A. Lorie, and I. L. Traiger. The notions of consistency and predicate locks in a database system. *Communications of the ACM*, 19(11):624–632, November 1976.

3. Mark A. Gisi and Gail E. Kaiser. Extending a tool integration language. In Mark Dowson, editor, *1st International Conference on the Software Process: Manufacturing Complex Systems*, pages 218–227, Redondo Beach CA, October 1991. IEEE Computer Society Press.

4. Dennis Heimbigner and Marc Kellner. Software process example for ISPW-7, August 1991. /pub/cs/techreports/ISPW7/ispw7.ex.ps.Z available by anonymous ftp from ftp.cs.colorado.edu.

5. Christoph Hübel, Wolfgang Käfer, and Bernd Sutter. Controlling cooperation through design-object specification - a database-oriented approach. proceedings the european conference on design automation. In *Proceedings of the European Conference on Design Automation*, pages 30–35, Brussels, March 1992. IEEE Computer Society Press.

6. Henry F. Korth, Won Kim, and Francois Bancilhon. On long-duration CAD transactions. In Stanley B. Zdonik and David Maier, editors, *Readings in Object-Oriented Database Systems*, chapter 6.3, pages 408–431. Morgan Kaufman, San Mateo CA, 1990.

7. T. Richard Macmillan. Emergent cooperation in multi-agent deliberative planning. In *Proceedings of the IEEE 1991 National Aerospace and Electronics Conference NAECON*, pages 997–1003, Dayton, OH, May 1991. IEEE Computer Society Press.

8. J. Eliot B. Moss and Steven Sinofsky. Managing persistent data with mneme: Designing a reliable, shared object interface. In *Advances in Object-Oriented Database Systems*, volume 334 of *Lecture Notes in Computer Science*, pages 298–316. Springer-Verlag, September 1988.

9. Dan McNabb Won Kim, Raymond Lorie and Wil Plouffe. A transaction mechanism for engineering design databases. In *10th International Conference on Very Large Databases*, pages 355–362, Singapore, August 1984.

10. Gilad Zlotkin and Jeffrey S. Rosenschein. Cooperation and conflict resolution via negotiation among autonomous agents in noncooperative domains. *IEEE International Conference on Systems, Man, and Cybernetics*, 21(6):1317–1324, November 1991.

Towards Requirements for Enactment Mechanisms

Mark Dowson

Marlstone Software Technology Inc
525K East Market Street #303, Leesburg, Virginia 22075, USA
dowson@marlstone.com

Christer Fernström

Cap Gemini Innovation
Chemin du Vieux Chêne, ZIRST, 38240 Meylan, France
christer@capsogeti.fr

1   Introduction

Process centered (or process based or process sensitive) software development environments support teams of users in performing software projects in accord with some defined software process. Because different processes are appropriate for different projects, and because processes are likely to be improved and evolved over time, these environments should not be hard–wired to support a single process, but should include a mechanism for enacting (i.e., interpreting or executing) explicit software process definitions. This enactment mechanism will then interact with the environment users, and the other tools and components in the environment, to provide support consistent with the content of the definition.

In this paper we discuss what is involved in enacting process definitions to support software development, as a step toward deriving general requirements for enactment mechanisms. We recognize that there are several experimental and some commercial process centered environments available today, but consider that a deeper understanding of the requirements for their enactment mechanisms, especially with respect to flexibility, adaptability and dynamic process modification, could make a significant contribution to their evolution and to the design of future environments. We address two main issues which between them determine many of the requirements for enactment mechanisms: how a process centered environment should support process performance; and how generic process definitions that are applicable to a class of actual processes can be constructed, specialized and enacted. In discussing support, we recognize that it may not be possible or desirable to make process performance strictly conform to a process definition. This leads us to establish a conceptual separation of process definitions, process performance and process definition enactment that has significant implications for the definition formalisms and the environment mechanisms that are needed. Our discussion of generic definitions introduces the notion of process variables, that can have various kinds of values bound to them during process definition enactment. This leads to a discussion of strategies and mechanisms for dynamic process definition change.

Our conclusions are independent of any particular definition formalism or environment architecture, but do depend on some assumptions about the nature of process definitions and process support which are detailed below. In this work we have found it necessary to examine and clarify some of the basic concepts underlying process support, because a precise understanding of what a process centered environment is intended to do is essential for defining the requirements for mechanisms to do it.

2   Process Definitions, Process Performance, and Process Definition Enactment

We need to distinguish (static) process definitions from their dynamic enactment, and to recognize that process performance, even if supported by a process centered environment, may not conform to what is specified in a process definition. This leads us to identify three categorically different domains: a domain of process definitions; a domain of process performance; and a domain of process definition enactment (see Figure 1).

The *domain of process definitions* contains characterizations of processes or fragments of processes, expressed in some notation, in terms of how they could or should be performed. In this paper we are concerned with definitions that are enactable, i.e., that can be interpreted or executed by an enactment mechanism, to provide support and guidance for process performance. Enactable process definitions include information used to guide process performance, such as descriptions of how process steps should be performed, definitions of constraints on various aspects of process performance, or on the products produced by the process, statements of goals that process performance should achieve, etc.

The *domain of process performance* encompasses the actual activities or actions conducted by human agents (project staff including developers, managers, etc.) and non–human agents (generally computer programs) in the course of a software project. All project activities are part of process performance. Some will be conducted using software tools or other environment facilities; others will consist of thinking, writing, and formal or informal interactions between members of the project team not mediated by a computer based system. All software systems are produced by the performance of *some* process (that is, by some set of activities conducted in some order); but often the process is incoherent and lacks any explicit representation, leading to lack of project predictability, lack of process repeatability, and lack of a basis for process improvement. The main rationale for process centered environments is that by requiring explicit process definitions to be constructed, and by providing support for performing processes in conformance with them, predictability, repeatability and improvement will be facilitated.

The *domain of process definition enactment* is concerned with what takes place in a process centered environment to support process definition–governed process performance. It includes run–time occurrences of process definitions or process definition fragments that we call (process definition) *enactments*. An enactment is created by loading a copy of an enactable process definition or process definition fragment into an enactment mechanism. The enactment mechanism uses the definition to determine its interaction with the agents performing the process, and with other components of the environment, so as to support, guide, or enforce performance of the process in a way that is consistent with the process definition. Multiple simultaneous enactments of the same definition (supporting the performance of different projects) with independent enactment contexts should be possible. In this sense, process definitions are like the re–entrant code of a program.

By analogy with operating system processes, run time occurrences of process definitions have often been called "process instances" and the creation of an occurrence called "instantiation"; we prefer to avoid this terminology because of its somewhat confusing connotations. For example, operating system processes typically include parameters that must have values bound to them at instantiation time, and not changed thereafter. In contrast, process definition enactments may be created without binding any variables, and have values bound to their "parameters" incrementally throughout the progress of enactment.

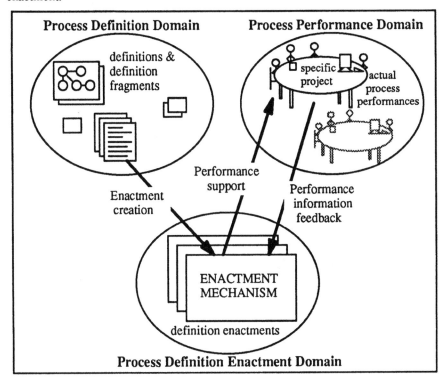

Figure 1. Process Domains

3   The Relationship between Enactment and Performance

The recognition that process definition enactment is different and separate from process performance has important consequences. A simulated enactment of a process definition, independent of the performance of any actual process, could provide analytical information on the definition enabling its improvement, or prediction of aspects of the performance of a process that conformed to the definition. For process definition enactment to provide support for the contemporaneous performance of a process, however, some degree of coupling between enactment and performance is needed.

There are two aspects to this coupling, which needs to be mediated by the enactment mechanism. Firstly, enactment needs to influence the way in which the process is performed. Actual performance of the process will then correspond, to some degree, to the definition's specification of how it should be performed. Secondly, the course of definition enactment may need to be contingent on events arising from actual process performance.

3.1 The Influence of Enactment on Performance

Process definition enactment is intended to influence the way in which a process is performed. Human environment users can be supported so that their activities tend to conform to the process definition. This support can take a variety of forms. At one extreme, a process definition enactment mechanism might constrain the actions of users to ensure that the process is performed in strict conformity with the process definition being enacted (in the same way that interpretation or execution of a program forces a computer to perform the computations specified in the program). On the other hand, an enactment mechanism might only support users by providing advice, derived from enactment of the definition, on how to perform the process; under some circumstances the users might, for good reason, ignore the advice, and perform part of the process in ways inconsistent with the definition. Any view of process enactment and process performance must accommodate both possible support paradigms (and others which lie on the spectrum between the two extremes of strict enforcement and complete liberality). We can characterize this spectrum by dividing it into four different general support categories or paradigms: passive guidance, active guidance, process enforcement, and process automation.

Passive guidance provides users, on request, with information that helps them to decide what actions they should perform if they are to conform to a process definition. Providing the text of a process definition for users to read, e.g., in the form of a "development policy and procedures" manual, would be an extremely limited form of passive guidance. With feedback from process performance influencing the enactment of a definition, the passive guidance available to process centered environment users can be made "context sensitive", i.e, dependent on the state of process performance, perhaps via a "what should I do next?" button. Providing useful passive guidance of this kind depends on obtaining feedback from process performance so that guidance appropriate to its current state can be provided. Essentially, this requires that the enactment must maintain an internal model of the state of process performance, and ensure a consistent relationship between it and the actual performance state. Other forms of passive guidance could include providing users with a view of the current process state (derived from an internal model created and maintained by the enactment), or a capability for exploring the effects of hypothetical actions on performance state.

Like passive guidance, *active guidance* depends on obtaining data from process performance so that the enactment mechanism can provide advice or information relevant to the current performance state. In this case, information is not provided passively, i.e., solicited by the user, but actively by the enactment mechanism under circumstances specified in the process definition. Such active guidance could take the form of adding tasks to users' "do lists", notifying users of significant events, supplying warnings, etc.

Process enforcement consists of forcing users to perform a process or part of a process in a specific way (in conformance with the process definition). The only way to achieve this is by controlling the user's access to data and tools, either indirectly by restricting access to a subset of the tools or data in the environment, or directly, by invoking, on the user's behalf, some interactive tool on the appropriate data object or objects. Such enforcement is essentially "negative", that is, it can prevent a user from performing any actions except those allowed by the enacting definition. This limitation on the way in which conformance to a process definition can be enforced does not imply a particular definition formalism, or determine the ways in which information about what must be done is presented. For example, a definition formalism might allow prescriptive statements (what should be done at some point in the process) or proscriptive statements (what should not be done at some point in the process), or a mixture of the two. In either case, the enactment mechanism needs to interpret the statements and constrain user access to tools and data appropriately. Similarly, presentation to the user might be inclusive (showing which actions are permitted), exclusive (showing which actions are forbidden), or consist of notifying the user if a forbidden action is attempted or a required action not performed.

Process automation consists of automatically performing some part of the process under the control of the process definition enactment. The Unix Make utility is a simple example of process automation, where a definition of the build process (a Make script) is used to control the performance of the steps needed to build a system. Process automation is appropriate for parts of the process that consist of complex, stereotyped sequences of system development actions that can be performed by non–human agents (e.g., software tools) with little or no user intervention or decision making. Existing environments that emphasize process automation include Marvel [7], where actions are triggered by the fulfillment of rule pre–conditions, and Adele [1], where actions are triggered by changes in an active database.

The boundaries between passive guidance, active guidance, enforcement, and process automation are not sharply defined. For example, invoking an interactive tool on a user's behalf might be considered active guidance (if the user can dismiss the tool without using it), enforcement, or process automation (if little or no interaction with the tool is needed). Neither is a single support paradigm likely to be appropriate for all aspects of the same process, or even for the same aspects of a process at different times. For example, if a process definition prescribes filling in a timesheet on a weekly basis, support might move from passive guidance, through active guidance to enforcement in the course of a single (Friday) afternoon.

Most existing process centered environments are restricted to a single support paradigm. Consequently, little attention has been paid to the problem of specifying support paradigm aspects of process as part of process definitions. Certainly, *some* aspects of process need to be enforced, e.g., configuration management discipline, even if others are supported merely by providing advice on what should be done. The ability to specify types of support as part of a process definition is likely to be an important feature of future process centered environments. Providing this feature, however, does raise some significant problems for designers of definition formalisms and enactment mechanisms. Over–detailed specification of support style, e.g., precise definition of the form of user interaction, would be inappropriate, hiding the commonality of definitions that differed only in fine details of what should be presented to users, and reducing the portability of definitions between environments with even slightly differing enactment mechanisms. On the other hand, the precise form of interaction has to be specified somewhere (unless some default interaction style is always acceptable), and needs to be related to the content of the process definition.

3.2 Feedback from Performance

Enacting a process definition "open loop" without feedback from actual process performance would be of little value (except, as noted above, for simulation purposes).

Most activities that are part of software development have uncertain outcomes, and the progress of enactment needs to be contingent on actual process performance if it is to provide useful support. Essentially the problem is one of maintaining a consistent relationship between the state of the enactment and the state of the performance of the process it is supporting.

As a useful analogy, consider the execution of a real time control system (such as a power station control system where both the power station and its operators constitute the environment of the control system). Like a real time control system, an enactment interacts with an external "real world", only a subset of whose state is accessible. To do this successfully, both a real time control system and a process definition enactment must include some representation of the state of the external world. There is, however, a fundamental difference in that control systems are usually designed to filter and highly constrain the interaction between their operators and the controlled system; commands to the system are given via the control system, which attempts to ensure that the controlled system is always in some predictable (and safe) state. In contrast, significant aspects of software process performance, which includes activities such as thinking and informal interaction between project team members, are outside the control of the process definition enactment mechanism; environment users can and do operate directly on the "controlled system" changing its state in potentially unpredicted ways.

Feedback from process performance needed to maintain the consistency between enactment state and performance state can be obtained from a variety of sources. For example, for appropriate enactment of the definition fragment "when task T1 (creating a new version of module M1) is finished, task T2 should be performed", feedback is needed to determine when T1 is finished. Possible sources of this process performance information include:

- explicit user actions, e.g., pressing a "done" button.
- results of requests for information from a user, e.g., "have more than 80% of the tests on Module M1 been completed?"
- tool–generated events, e.g., a "compilation of M1 complete" event generated by a compiler.
- interrogation of a passive product database, e.g., "does version V2 of module M1 exist?"
- events generated by an active product database, e.g., "version V2 of module M1 has been checked in."

While, as indicated above, there are some cases where feedback about significant process performance events can be generated automatically, this is the exception rather than the rule. In most cases, some kind of user decision and input is needed to provide information about significant events, signaling, for example, when a task is finished, or whether some document being reviewed is satisfactory. These events are not necessarily synchronized with events that the environment can detect automatically, such as creation of an artifact, tool invocation, or tool termination, so there can be a high degree of dependence on users for appropriate feedback about the state of process performance. Human users can, of course, forget to provide the needed input, or make mistakes in what they provide, or take creative short–cuts that bypass the points at which expected feedback would have occurred. This leads to the possibility of inconsistency (i.e., loss of correlation) between the state of process performance and the state of the process definition enactment intended to influence it, drastically reducing the ability of the enactment to provide useful support to performance.

Inconsistency of this kind is closely analogous to the inconsistency, familiar to project managers, that can arise between a project plan and the progress of a project. If progress is not correctly reported, or planned tasks cannot be completed, or project team members find effective ways to achieve project goals that do not correspond to the plan, the plan can become progressively less useful as a guide to action, and restorative actions need to be taken by the manager. These might consist of either correcting the record of project progress, or of altering the plan (re–planning) to be appropriate to the new situation.

Similar considerations apply to process definition enactments. Inconsistencies need to be detected (preferably before they cause catastrophic failure of the enactment) and corrective actions undertaken, either by manipulating the enactment's definition of process performance state to correspond to reality, or by making (small or large) changes to the enactment.

Some existing PSEs, e.g., Marvel [7] and Process WEAVER [2], avoid the possibility of inconsistency between enactment state and performance state by blocking the relevant thread of enactment until some expected feedback is received. This forces environment users to either strictly conform to the definition being enacted, or to fake conformance to the definition (e.g., pressing a "task complete" button even though the task has not been performed), if the enactment is to proceed and provide further support. For example, if a process definition fragment specifies "perform task T1, then perform task T2", a user who recognizes that task T1 is redundant (perhaps because project circumstances have changed) must still perform it (or fake its performance) before the enactment can proceed to suggesting or enforcing the performance of T2. In PSEs that do not adopt such limiting and potentially undesirable avoidance strategies, inconsistencies will need to be detected and corrected before they drastically reduce the effectiveness of the support that the environment is providing. Correction may involve manipulating the enactment's implicit or explicit model of process performance state to correspond to reality, or making (small or large) changes to other aspects of the enactment. While detecting inconsistency may be partially automatable, it seems unlikely that much can be done, except in trivial cases, to automatically restore consistency without human intervention. We therefore envisage the need for a human "process manager" or "process administrator" whose job it is to monitor process definition enactment and process performance, and to take corrective action when inconsistencies arise. Some of this corrective action will require dynamic changes to ongoing process definition enactments. The problems that this involves are discussed in section 5 below.

4 Process Variables as a Fundamental Mechanism for Process Change

One of the main potential benefits of process definitions is that they can capture generic information about how a class of processes should be performed. This allows the effort of developing effective definitions to be amortized over a large number of specific projects, provides a single locus for improvement–related feedback from multiple process performances, and ensures that definition improvements can be applied to a large number of future projects. Definitions, therefore, ought to be generic, but capable of particularization or specialization to meet the needs of a specific project. Some of this specialization may be conducted in the process definition domain, before an enactment of the definition is created. Much of it, however, will need to take place during the course of definition enactment, in response to the information produced as a result of process performance. One way to fulfill these requirements is to incorporate variables in process definitions to which project–specific values can be bound. Such *process variables* can represent the generic aspects of process definitions and provide a locus for static and dynamic process definition change. Process variables are not intended as a concrete feature of a specific process definition language or formalism. Rather, their description below characterizes a set of features needed by *any* effective process definition formalism, that can be realized in different ways (and by different constructs) in different formalisms. In this sense, process variables constitute a requirement specification or reference model for some important aspects of process definition formalisms, defining required features of new formalisms and allowing comparison of existing formalisms.

Process variables have many similarities with conventional programming language variables. They are introduced in the "text" of a process definition, and can be associated there with type specifications and default values. Like programming language variables they can have values bound to them at run time (process definition enactment time). They differ, however, both in the way they are used, and also in how and to what kinds of values they may be bound.

Process variables need to represent a wide variety of different aspects of a process. For example, they can be used to represent products that will be produced by a performance of the process, roles that need to be occupied by some agent, constraints on values of other process variables or on other aspects of process performance, tools to be used in performing the process, project specific goals or subgoals, or variant process definition fragments (e.g., from a library of such fragments).

Process variable binding, by which process variables acquire values during the enactment of the process definition that contains them, needs to be incremental and multi–faceted. For example, a process variable might be first bound to a type specification, constraining the actual values to which it can be bound, and have actual values conforming to that specification bound later during enactment. The precise rules governing process variable binding, determining, for example, whether a type once bound to a variable can be arbitrarily changed or only refined, or even be "unbound" from the variable, are properties of the enactment mechanism (which can be regarded as determining the operational semantics of the process definition formalism).

In many ways, process variables resemble slots in AI–style frame representations more than they resemble programming language variables. A frame represents a real–world entity by a set of slots that contain the attributes and relationships of the frame. Slots are furthermore structured into dynamically modifiable "facets" that describe different aspects of the slot. One facet is the "value" facet, which is intended to hold the value assigned to the slot. Another facet contains a "type" reference (which may be represented by an "is–a" relationship to another frame). Additional facets could contain other kinds of constraints on slot values (perhaps relative to values of other variables), default values, or functions that compute the slot value when needed (see Figure 2).

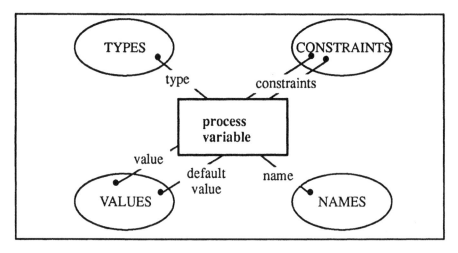

Figure 2. Process Variable Bindings

Different process definition notations or formalisms will represent process variables in different ways, and allow the variables to stand for more or less different kinds of values. The critical point is that any useful process definition notation must have some way of representing as–yet undefined aspects of the processes it is used to define.

The text of a process definition can be specialized or particularized to apply to a smaller class of software projects (or a single project) by replacing some of its process variables with constant values, by providing default values that will be initially bound to the variables at enactment time, or by tightening the type or other constraints that restrict the range of values they may be assigned. Such changes are not bindings or re–bindings, but textual substitutions in the definition.

During enactment of a definition, the values of process variables will generally be determined as a result of performing part of the defined process. For example, consider a process variable representing the name of the human agent who should perform some process step. Apart from a value computed from information already present within a definition, there are two possible sources of information for the value that is bound to the variable during definition enactment:

- Human agents. For example, the enactment mechanism might interact with the project manager, who supplies the name of the agent who should be assigned to perform a step.

- Other environment services. For example, the enactment mechanism might interact with a scheduling and resource assignment tool which supplies the name of an available resource (a human agent) to perform a step.

Process variables whose values are process definition fragments are of particular interest. For example, the detailed process definition for performing a process step might be represented by a process variable to which alternative definition fragments could be bound, and the appropriate fragment selected depending on the experience level of the agent assigned to perform the step. Apart from their use for handling planned alternatives for parts of the process, process variables which represent process fragments provide a mechanism for disciplined management of some aspects of dynamic process change, as described in the next section.

During enactment of a process definition, its process variables will be referenced, i.e., their values will be read, perhaps to determine the course of the enactment. Referencing a process variable which has not been bound to a value is an enactment time error (analogous to a run time error in program execution) and the effect of such an error is a property of the enactment mechanism. Raising an exception to be handled as part of the process definition, or if not handled, then addressed to a human "process manager" would be one possibility.

5 Process Change

Process definitions need to undergo continual change. Some of this change will be a normal, pre–planned part of the enactment of a definition, as it is incrementally specialized during enactment. Other changes will be more radical, creating a *different process*. Some of these changes will be static, in the sense that they consist of changes to the text of a process definition that has no effect on any current enactments of the definition, but only on future enactments. Definitions will need to be specialized, generalized, adapted to different classes of projects, or improved and evolved in the light of experience, organizational changes, or a better understanding of how (future) processes should be performed. Other changes will be dynamic, altering definitions while they are being enacted, perhaps because faults are discovered in the definition, because changes to project circumstances or goals make a different process more appropriate, because feedback from the performance of the project (or of other projects) suggests process improvements, or simply because some aspects of how best to perform a project could not be determined in advance of its inception.

5.1 Design for Change

Some changes, whether static or dynamic, are easier to make than others. In particular, it is useful to distinguish between *anticipated* change and *unanticipated* change. For example, a definition designer might include a section defining a code inspection method, knowing that an improved inspection method is being developed elsewhere in the organization. Replacing the old inspection method process definition fragment with a fragment representing the improved inspection method would then be an anticipated change. Definitions can be structured to reduce the difficulty of making anticipated changes (whether static or dynamic), and a skillful process designer is likely to anticipate that many aspects of a definition might be changed at some future time, identify them, and structure the definition accordingly. This kind of structuring is analogous to the structuring needed to make computer programs easier to maintain and evolve, requiring support (in the language) and use (by the program designer) of modularity, information hiding, and scope rules that limit the global side effects of local program changes. With some notable exceptions, however, program change is confined to changes to static program text, rather than to running instances of programs. In contrast, dynamic changes to process definition enactments are likely to be relatively common, and the linguistic and run time mechanisms provided to support change must reflect this bias.

Process variables provide a common abstraction for making anticipated changes in a disciplined way both statically in the process definition domain, and dynamically, in the enactment domain. Using them to represent potentially changeable aspects of a definition, ranging from integer values through specifications of constraints on performance to complete process definition fragments can reduce (although by no means eliminate) the difficulty of ensuring that changes do not compromise the integrity of the definition as a whole. Using process variables in this way does not obviate the need for scope rules, modularity and information hiding, but does provide a focus for the application of these mechanisms and techniques in a way that allows dynamic change (by binding new values to variables) to be supported in a coherent way. Unanticipated changes, to aspects of definitions that have not previously been identified and represented as process variables, will still be needed. In these cases, analyzing the effects of change, and, in the case of dynamic change ensuring or restoring consistency will be more difficult.

5.2 Static Change

Static anticipated change, i.e., changes to process variables that create a new definition from an existing one without affecting any ongoing definition enactment, is the most manageable case. Such change might result in a specialization, a generalization or a variant of the original definition.

A specialization of an existing definition is achieved by process variable refinement, further constraining the range of values that can be bound to a process variable. This could consist of changing the variable type to a more restrictive type, providing additional constraint bindings, supplying a default value, or replacing a variable by a constant or a more elaborate value such as a definition fragment. A generalization of an existing definition is achieved correspondingly by relaxing constraints on process variable values (perhaps in accordance with documented modification rules). A variant, finally, is created by a generalization followed by a specialization (or vice versa).

Analysis of the effect of specialization is relatively straightforward. Provided that the range of values that can be bound to a process variable in the revised definition is a subset of the values permitted in the original definition, many properties of the definition (and of process performances that conform to it) will be unchanged. Generalization poses greater problems. For example, if constraints on a process variable representing a process fragment are relaxed, so that a wider range of fragments can be bound to it, it will be necessary to ensure (at least) that all the data referenced by the new fragments exists in the rest of the definition (and is of an appropriate type), and that all existing references to the process variable are still legal whichever fragment it is bound to.

Unanticipated changes to a definition, that is, changes that go beyond specialization and generalization of process variables, are likely to result in a definition that has no clear relationship to the original definition. We therefore consider this as a general case of process definition, where the process designer uses an existing definition informally as a basis for the new definition. We refer to this as process re–definition.

5.3 Dynamic Change

Dynamic changes to a definition that affect ongoing enactments may be needed for a variety of reasons. Sometimes the sources of change will be external to definition enactment. For example, project circumstances may change, making a revised definition more appropriate, or an improved method for performing some part of the process is developed and needs to be incorporated in the definition. More often, dynamic change will be needed in response to some condition arising from project performance or the interaction of project performance and definition enactment. In some cases, decisions as to details of the process definition may have to be deferred, and made in the light of project progress and events. In other cases, the original process definition may turn out to be inappropriate to the project in unexpected ways. Finally, a detected discrepancy between definition enactment state and project performance state may require consistency–restoring adjustments to the enactment.

Dynamic change presents considerable problems. Essentially, the enactment state of the revised definition must be consistent with the enactment state of the original definition. For example, if the original definition includes a representation of a process step that is currently being performed, that step also needs to be represented in the revised definition. Similarly, if the revised definition refers to some aspect of past process performance state, that aspect needs to have been captured by the enactment of the original definition (and preserved across the process change).

In principle, there are a variety of different ways to perform dynamic process definition change, all of which pose consistency problems. At one extreme, a process designer could be allowed to make arbitrary changes to an enacting process definition, and bear the responsibility for ensuring the consistency of these changes. At the other extreme, an enacting definition could be brought to a consistent, stable state (implying that process performance was halted), before being replaced by a revised definition (this would not eliminate the consistency problem, but would make consistency analysis and restoration more tractable).

Our view is that neither of these alternatives is desirable. Allowing arbitrary change is risky (it is rather like patching the running code of a real–time control system), and insisting on halting process performance before making any change is impractical on a large multi–person project. Whenever possible, process changes that involve changes to enactments should be anticipated changes, and restricted to pre–defined, confined fragments of process definitions represented by process variables. Process variables provide a *mechanism* for this kind of change, because they can be bound (during enactment) to more or less restrictive constraints, and to different values, including different variants of process fragments; but do not solve the problem of ensuring that the revised definition is consistent, which may still require extensive analysis. This approach is similar to that adopted for allowing dynamic evolution of user functionality in, e.g., telephone switching systems. In such systems new functionality must be provided without interrupting ongoing calls, and without compromising the consistency of the database (which, for example, may be holding dynamically created "call waiting" information). To achieve this, new functions are often provided as "procedure parameters" dynamically linked in to pre–defined procedures in the system.

When the necessary dynamic change to the enactment is unanticipated, i.e., not confined to changing values of process variables, but involving structural changes to the enacting definition, its outcome is hard to predict and such "enactment surgery" should only be performed in extreme cases and with the same precautions as when doing on–line "patching" of any complex software system. However, since there are cases where such changes are necessary, the enactment mechanism needs to provide assistance. Such assistance should include facilities to locate active threads of enactment, to block further actions in parts of the enactment, and to introduce changes atomically (i.e., several changes in a single transaction).

5.4 Performance Change

Dynamic process change cannot necessarily be restricted to an enactment, but will usually require corresponding compensatory changes to the process performance. Some backtracking may be needed, such as changes (e.g., deletions or undoing modifications) to a product database, removal of tasks from users' do lists or cancellation of ongoing tasks, or even undoing the results of some external effect of project performance (such as a communication with the client). Where the change to the process is substantial, more far reaching changes to the process performance are likely to be needed. As a minimum, users performing the process need to be made aware that it is changing and, depending on the complexity of the change, it may be preferable to introduce the changes in several stages. If this is the case, it is useful to define a *process change process*, (which could be defined by a process definition for process change). A change process would include steps for changing performance, and others for introducing changes in enactment. For example, user awareness and training with respect to a new tool would be a step in changing the performance, while binding the new tool to an enactment constitutes a step of changing the enactment.

5.5 Support for Change

The need to support dynamic change implies the need for a number of definition formalism and enactment mechanism features. These features, discussed in Section 6 below, provide constructs for structuring definitions to make them easier to change and mechanisms for implementing dynamic changes to enactments. In addition to these constructs and mechanisms, support (in the form of methods and tools) is needed to help ensure that definitions are appropriately structured, and that changes can be made without compromising the integrity of definition enactment and process performance.

As noted above, designing definitions for change involves many of the same considerations as designing programs for change. What is needed are design methods that encourage modularity, information hiding, and the encapsulation of parts of definitions in which change can be anticipated. While these design methods will be different from program design methods that have similar objectives, to the extent that process definition formalisms and process definitions are different from programming languages and programs, it is likely that we can build on our experience with program design to develop the needed methods.

Changing definitions, particularly dynamic change to enactments, will require support in the form of tools for inspection and analysis. At the very least, a process manager making a change to an enactment needs to be able to inspect its current state, and tools supporting the presentation of views of enactment state are needed.

Analysis tools will be needed to help determine the impact of change. Static analysis tools will find, for example, the location of all references to a given process variable, while dynamic analysis tools could help to identify aspects of performance that will need compensatory changes to maintain consistency when dynamic changes are made to an enactment.

6   Conclusions

The issues we have discussed above have a number of implications for the design of formalisms or languages for constructing enactable process definitions, and for the design of process definition enactment mechanisms that would form part of process centered environments. At this stage, it would be premature to regard these implications as requirements, even in an informal sense, but we believe that they can provide a starting point for developing a systematic set of requirements in the near future.

We have also attempted to avoid making premature design decisions. For example, our discussion of process variables is, as far as possible, independent of any particular process definition paradigm. Constructs that corresponded to our notion of process variables could be included in a wide variety of new formalisms, or introduced as extensions to various existing formalisms, such as the programming language–like formalism of APPLA/A [8], the extended Petri net notations used in Archipel [5] or Process WEAVER [2], the goal oriented formalisms proposed by Huff [6] and others, or the active database approach of Adele [1].

The design of a process definition formalism is, of course, intimately related to the design of an enactment mechanism for that formalism (which must implement the operational semantics of the formalism as well as providing run time services to users and other environment components). In what follows, these two issues are discussed separately, but it is important to recognize that design decisions about definition formalisms cannot be made independently of decisions about enactment mechanisms.

6.1 Implications for Process Definition Formalisms

Existing definition formalisms for enactable process definitions provide various kinds of facilities for control and data structuring, based on a variety of paradigms. These facilities are, of course, essential, but we believe that any effective definition formalism needs to include a number of additional facilities in two main areas: facilities that allow the definition of interactions between an ongoing enactment and the environment users and other components; and facilities that allow the definition and manipulation of process variables.

As discussed in Section 3, an enactment needs to influence the course of process performance, and itself needs to be influenced by feedback from performance. A definition formalism, therefore, must include constructs which allow definition of the way in which this mutual interaction will take place. An enactment can support performance in different ways ranging from passive support to enforcement and process automation, and a formalism needs the ability to define different support paradigms for different processes or for different parts of the same process, and even for the same process part under different circumstances. It is therefore important that the formalism allows support paradigms to be expressed separately from other aspects of processes, and that it allows the explicit manipulation of their relationships.

To support the construction of generic definitions, and as a mechanism for facilitating process change, a definition formalism needs to include a construct corresponding to the notion of process variable, together with operations for manipulating and accessing process variable values.

As indicated in Section 4, process variables differ considerably from programming language variables, both in the kinds of values that can be bound to them, and in the binding mechanisms that are needed. We have presented process variables as if they are a single, uniform concept, and as if they are the only form of variable needed in a process definition. An actual definition formalism does not have to adopt this uniform view, but could use different constructs for the various functions that process variables might perform in a definition. These include use as:

- local or global variables (in the programming language sense) for creating non–persistent data structures and (as part of expressions) for influencing the "flow of control" in a definition.

- parameters of definitions, whose values are set externally to determine some specific course of definition enactment, or reset to implement dynamic enactment change.

- representations of generic aspects of definitions, with values that are incrementally bound to specific values as a result of enactment.

- representations of variant process definition fragments.

6.2 Implications for Process Definition Enactment Mechanisms

An enactment mechanism provides run–time services to process definition enactments, and implements the operational semantics of the language used to construct enactable process definitions. The need to support dynamic process definition change in general, and in particular to detect and correct any inconsistencies that arise between the state of definition enactment and the state of process performance, implies the need for some specific enactment mechanism facilities. Some of the most significant of these are outlined in this section. They are largely independent of any particular definition paradigm or formalism; we assume only that enactments are *multi–threaded*, and that definitions can include *variables* to which various kinds of values can be bound during enactment.

To support dynamic change, the enactment mechanism needs to include a dynamic binding mechanism, which supports process variable bindings involving types, constraints, data and process fragments. This binding mechanism needs to be available to the enactment itself (implied by the need for incremental binding), to tools used by a process manager (implied by the need for dynamic change to the enactments), and to *other* enactments (implied by the need for enactment–supported change processes). The enactment state (i.e., the states of the various active threads of enactment) must be accessible and manipulable both by the enactment itself and by tools used by a process manager. Part of this state information may be encoded in definition variables, but access to the internal state of the enactment mechanism run–time system will also be needed. This property is known as *self referentiality*. In addition to the ability to monitor the enactment state, the enactment mechanism must provide a means to block certain threads of enactment to prepare for a binding operation. These two facilities (monitoring and blocking) must furthermore be provided in the form of a "test–and–set" primitive, since they will be subject to shared access (by enactments and process managers). Consistent process variable re–binding may require that the binding primitives are available as transactions (several bindings accomplished as an atomic operation). In addition, enactments need to be responsive to requests for storing their current state and to initializing their state from previously stored state information.

Because significant performance events may not occur synchronously with the progress of an enactment, enactable definitions need to include *event handlers* to asynchronously detect and respond to external events. Possible responses to performance events include recording them (as part of building an internal representation of performance state), and making changes to other aspects of the state of the enactment.

Some inconsistencies may be detectable because they cause enactment time errors (analogous to run time errors in program execution) such as references to unassigned definition variables. Rather than aborting the enactment, such errors should raise *enactment time exceptions*, and definitions should be able to include *exception handlers* to take appropriate action (such as bringing an exception to the attention of a process manager who can take corrective action).

Allowing for dynamic modifications and replacements of process fragments puts requirements both on the enactment mechanism and the language on the one hand, and on the process definitions on the other. The requirements on the enactment mechanism and language are mainly that they must support some form of dynamic binding of both data and process definition fragments, and that the binding mechanism can be controlled both by explicit commands in the process definitions and externally by tools supporting enactment adaptation. Dynamic binding of process definition fragments to process variables can be realized in the form of procedure parameters, message passing or "dynamic libraries" like those supported by some operating systems.

7 Acknowledgements

Preliminary versions of some of the ideas in this paper were developed as part of the Software Design & Analysis Inc. Process Management Project [4], and during extended discussions with Ian Thomas, some results of which appear in [3].

We also would like to thank Maryse Bourdon of Cap Gemini Innovation, and Lyn Uzzle, of Marlstone Software Technology, for numerous helpful comments on earlier drafts.

8 References

[1] N. Belkhatir, J. Estublier, and W. Melo, *Adele 2: A Support to Large Software Development Processes*, Proc. 1st International Conference on the Software Process, IEEE Computer Society Press, October 1991.

[2] C. Fernström, *Process WEAVER: Adding Process Support to UNIX*, Proc. 2nd International Conference on the Software Process, IEEE Computer Society Press, March 1993.

[3] M. Dowson, *Process and Project Management*, Proceedings of the 7th International Software Process Workshop, IEEE Computer Society Press, 1993.

[4] M. Dowson, B. Nejmeh & L. Uzzle, *Concepts for a Prototype Process Based Environment*, Software Design & Analysis Inc. Technical Report Ref. No. 7–50–4, Software Design & Analysis, Boulder CO., September 1991.

[5] C. Fernström and L. Ohlsson, *Integration Needs in Process Enacted Environments*, Proc. 1st International Conference on the Software Process, IEEE Computer Society Press, October 1991.

[6] K. E. Huff and V. R. Lesser, *A Plan–based Intelligent Assistant that Supports the Software Development Process*, Proc. ACM SIGSOFT/SIGPLAN Software

Engineering Symposium on Practical Software Development Environments, ACM Press, Nov. 1988.

[7]   G. Kaiser, P. Feiler, and S. Popovich, *Intelligent Assistance for Software Development and Maintenance*, IEEE Software, May 1988.

[8]   S. M. Sutton Jr., D. Heimbigner, and L. J. Osterweil, *Language constructs for managing change in process centered environments,* Proc. 4th ACM SIGSOFT/SIGPLAN Software Engineering Symposium on Practical Software Development Environments, ACM Press, 1990.

Enactment Control in Interact/Intermediate

AT&T Bell Laboratories, 600 Mountain Avenue, Murray Hill, NJ 07974 USA

Abstract. Interact/Intermediate supports goal-directed process modeling in such a way as to maximize the concurrency of activities and to minimize the direct control of humans in the process. In this context, there are three different and interacting loci of control which we illustrate and discuss with an example: an implicit, internal locus of control; an external, arbitrary locus of control; and an explicit, internal locus of control.

1   Introduction

The philosophy of Interact/Intermediate [1-3] is to support goal-directed process modeling in such a way as to maximize the concurrency of activities and to minimize the direct control of the human element in the process. Interact is the process description language by which the necessary artifacts, project structures, organizational structures, and process activities are defined; Intermediate is the support environment which, via the process models, provides the context for the process being enacted by both humans and tools.

Interact's emphasis is on specifying the assumptions and goals of the various process activities while, in general, leaving the details of the activities implementation to the enactor. Providing guidance in implementing the structure of an activity is one of the primary purposes of Intermediate.

However, there are times when the modeler will want to define in some detail the enactment structure of an activity. For example, the detailed description may be the result of a desire for a particular approach to avoid some particular problem, a desire for some standard steps in certain activities across a particular project, or a desire to automate a particular routine activity.

Two further considerations are important in the design of the enactment control mechanisms of Interact: dynamism and reflectivity. The process by which we build and evolve large software systems is of necessity an extremely dynamic one. The activities required at any particular point in time are dependent on the state of the artifacts being produced, the state of the project and organization, and the state of the process itself. Only by being able to reify both the state of a process and the process itself can the process be sufficiently adaptive and dynamic. Not only will the human enactor dynamically create processes out of the activity fragments, but the process itself will dynamically create the necessary enactment control structures for the particular state of the product, project and process.

Given these various requirements on the design of the description language and the support environment, it is worth noting that there are three different loci of control that will interact with each other in controlling the enactment of any given process: an implicit, internal locus of control, an arbitrary, external locus of control, and an explicit, internal locus of control.

In the subsequent sections, we discuss these three loci and indicate how they interact with each other.

2 Implicit, Internal Locus of Control

Activity descriptions are the basic process fragments from which an enacted process is constructed. An activity description consists of an activity name, a set of typed parameters, a set of policies (policies are first order predicates over finite sets) that represent the assumptions that must be satisfied before enactment of the activity can begin (that is, preconditions), the internal structure of the activity (which may be **primitive** — meaning that the implementation is left to the enactor — or some explicit control structure), and a sequence of results (one or more of which may be designated by the enactor as the results of the enacted activity) each of which consists of a set of policies that represent assertions about the resulting state of the activity (that is, postconditions), and a set of of policies that must be eventually satisfied by enactors of the process (that is, obligations). Consider the example activity description.

Because of the preconditions, postconditions and obligations, there are dependencies among the defined activities in a process model that yield a partial-ordering of those activities. Preconditions and obligations must be satisfied by some set of state and postconditions provide that state. Thus there is an implicit ordering, an implicit control, that is exerted on the activities that are enacted within a particular model. An activity instantiation (such as Determine-Dependencies) can only be enacted when its assumptions are satisfied. Until that happens, the activity cannot proceed no matter what explicit control structure it may be embedded in.

This partial order is the fundamental global form of enactment control.

3 Arbitrary, External Locus of Control

There are three different kinds of user-directed (and apparently, arbitrary) enactment control: activity elaboration, state restoration and enactment scheduling. The first is considered to be normal enactment control; the second is considered to be abnormal enactment control (that is, it is the handling of exceptional circumstances by moving the process state to some — possibly previous — consistent state) by the human enactor; the third is an external constraint on either the beginning or the completion of an enactment.

In the example, we have a detailed activity structure specified for the integration activity. Given that our approach is to underspecify rather than overspecify activity structures, activity structures will range from the primitive structure (which must be elaborated at enactment time) through a variety of incompletely

```
activity Integrate ( )
  preconditions { Release-Approved(Tool-Release-Board) }
  {
    for each  tool t  in  {tool t | submitted(t) }
    until  Current-Time == Deadline:
      <
        Determine-Dependencies(t, dependencies) ,
        let  testset' = testset + t ,
        Build(testset', result) ,
        ( result == false, tool-rejected(t)  )  ,
        ( result == true,
          <
            < for each  person P
                in {person p | owner[t1] == p & t1 in  dependencies }:
                  bind  Evaluate(t, t1) to  P
            > ,
            Await-Acceptance/Rejection(t)
          >
        )
      >
  }
  results
    <
      ( postconditions {
              approvedset = { tool t | tool-approved(t) },
              exportset = exportset + approvedset,
              tools-released(exportset) }  ,
        obligations  { }
      ) ,
      ( postconditions {  rejectset = { tool t | tool-rejected(t) }  }  ,
        obligations { for each  tool t in  reject-set: modify-tool(t)  }
      )
    >
```

specified structures to completely specified structures. Since the general intent is for an incomplete structure rather than a complete one, the human enactor will interact heavily with the support environment to elaborate the incomplete activity structures by means of the various Intermediate environment commands and the various language control statements.

The interaction between the enactor and the internal and implicit partial-ordering of activities is a direct one. The primary purpose of the enactor is to achieve one or more results within a given activity. One way to achieve those results is to backchain through the activity dependency graph to find activities that will produce the desired results. This backchaining results in a non-classical transformation of an incomplete activity structure into a complete one.

For those activities that are independent and also for those activities that have been enabled, the enactor is free first to choose which activities to enact and in which order. Their freedom is constrained only by the implicit priority defined by the specific schedule applied to those activities. For those activities that are in the process of enactment, the enactor is free to multiplex between them arbitrarily by means of activity suspension and resumption. It should be noted, however, that mere caprice is not likely to result in an effective or efficient process.

It may well be the case that because of the incompatible dependencies or conflicting enactments, a particular activity may get permanently stalled (or, if you will, starved or deadlocked). Often the way to recover from this situation is to change the current state of the process by enacting various environmental commands or recovery activities.

Again, the interaction between this form of control and the implicit partial-order control is a direct one. The recoverer must understand those dependencies and, via recovery activities, adjust the process state to some state in which progress can be made.

4 Explicit, Internal Locus of Control

Explicit enactment control is provided in Interact via basic enactment commands, enactment control, and control generation. Basic enactment commands are the units of work within an activity and are performed either by the human, a tool or the Intermediate support environment. Enactment control indicates how these individual enactment commands will be executed in relation to each other. The control generation mechanisms enable one to generate families of structures with a basic structure that is individuated either statically with distinct arguments or dynamically with different values. We see illustrations of each of these in the example.

4.1 Enactment Commands

There are three kinds of enactment commands: local equations, activity instantiations, and Intermediate commands. Local equations enable the modeler to bind values to names. On the one hand, this enables one to construct or deconstruct values for local names used only within the context of the local equation — that is, import values. On the other hand, this enables one to construct or deconstruct values for global names — that is export values. The constructive aspects of local equations enable one to construct larger structures out of component parts; the deconstructive aspects enable one to extract desired pieces from complex structures.

The local variable, testset', is defined and and assigned its value of the current test set with the addition of the particular tool t.

Activity instantiations are analogous to function or procedure calls: the activity is named and given a set of arguments. However, as we mentioned in the section on implicit control, the activity cannot be enacted until the assumed policies have been satisfied. Once the assumptions have been satisfied, the activity can be enacted. If the activity is bound to a tool, then that tool will be executed by the support environment; if the activity is bound to a human, then it is the responsibility of the that human to enact that activity.

Determine-Dependencies and Build are two examples where the instantiated activities are bound to tools. Evaluate, however, is bound to the appropriate owners of tools that are dependent on the tool to be evaluated.

An Intermediate command is one of the basic underlying process enactment and inspection primitives (such as binding commands, event commands, eval, etc.). These commands are the primitives for process definition, administration and enactment. We leave the discussion of them to a later paper.

4.2 Enactment Control

There are three enactment control structures: guarded enactment, sequential enactment and arbitrary enactment. Guarded enactment is represented by a tuple in which the first element in the tuple is the guard and the second is the enactment statement (which is either an enactment command, enactment control or control generation statement).

We test the results of the the build activity with two guarded enactment statements: the first specifies what to do if the build fails, the second specifies what to to if the build succeeds.

Sequential enactment is denoted by the structure $< \ldots >$ — literally, this is a sequence of enactment statements which are to be executed in sequence. Note, however, that the semantics of the individual enactment statements must be observed. In particular, if the assumptions of an activity have not been satisfied, the execution sequence will not proceed further until that does occur. Thus some other activity or set of activities will eventually have to be enacted to satisfy the assumptions of the stalled activity.

We have three sequential enactments in the example. The first is the sequence of steps that applies to each submitted tool. The second is the sequence of steps that applies when the build succeeds. The third, we defer to the discussion of control generation.

Arbitrary enactment is denoted by the structure $\{ \ldots \}$. Where in sets of data, we have no particular ordering of that data, so in sets of enactment statements, we have no particular ordering of those statements. The enactor (whether it is a human, a tool, or the support environment in the case of local equations and primitive commands) is free to select the order arbitrarily doing as much concurrently as is desired. Remember, however, that activities can only proceed when their assumptions have been satisfied. The defined activities' partial ordering takes precedence over the arbitrary ordering.

We have a single arbitrary enactment statement in the example. It is coupled with a set generation statement which we will discuss in the next section. In this case, the enactments generated are to be done in arbitrary order. It is likely that each of the enactments generated is independent of the others and can be done in truly arbitrary order — concurrently, randomly, etc.

Note that we have combined sequential and arbitrary enactments: we have an arbitrary enactment of sequences as the basic structure of the activity. We could just as easily have had a sequence of arbitrary enactments. Note that a arbitrary enactment of arbitrary enactments just reduces to a single arbitrary enactment. That is,

{ {A, B} {C, D} } is effectively { A, B, C, D }.

4.3 Control Generation

Given the set orientation of Interact, a useful thing to be able to do is to apply some enactment to each member of the set. We do that with the set generation command. This command generates an enactment for each member of the specified set. The order in which the enactments are done depends on the encompassing enactment control.

We have two such instances in the example. The first applies the sequence enactment to each submitted tool. Note that this set generation command is contained within the arbitrary enactment command: the evaluation sequences for each tool may be done arbitrarily (though, of course, the sequences themselves must be done in sequence). Note also that we have a termination expression that allows the set generation to continue until the deadline has been reached. As additional tools are submitted (that is, as the set of tools satisfying the policy tool-submitted gets new members), the evaluation sequence is applied to those newly submitted tools.

In the second instance, we have an illustration of the set generation command within a sequence enactment. This produces an enactment sequence that is analogous to iteration (though strictly speaking, it is iteration unrolled). An instantiation of the evaluation activity is bound to each person who owns a tool dependent on the particular submitted tool. Note that it is the binding of the activity not the enactment of the activity itself that is done in sequence. [1] The actual enactment of each of those instantiated activities takes place outside the scope of this activity and is subject to the standard partial ordering rules.

5 Summary

We have illustrated three loci of enactment control: internal and implicit, external and arbitrary, and internal and explicit. The partial order inherent in the precondition and obligation dependencies is paramount. It is fundamental in the

---

[1] Note that we could just have easily done the binding in arbitrary order — that is, enclosed this part of the activity implementation in { } instead of < >. We enclosed it in a sequence here for pedagogical reasons.

sense of global control of activity enactment. Within this global control, the human has a great degree of latitude to choose which of the prescribed activities to enact as long as it is consistent with the modeled enactment ordering.

References

1. Perry, Dewayne E.: Policy and Product-Directed Process Instantiation. Proceedings of the 6th International Software Process Workshop, 28-31 October 1990, Hakodate, Japan.
2. Perry, Dewayne E.: Policy-Directed Coordination and Cooperation, Proceedings of the 7th International Software Process Workshop, October 1991, Yountville CA.
3. Perry, Dewayne E.: Humans in the Process: Architectural Implications, Proceedings of the 8th International Software Process Workshop, March 1993, Schloss Dagstuhl, Germany.

Supporting informality in the software process

Ian Sommerville and Simon Monk

Department of Computing,
Lancaster University,
Lancaster LA1 4YR,
United Kingdom.
telephone: +44 524 593795
e-mail: is@comp.lancs.ac.uk

1   Introduction

Since the emergence of software engineering as a discipline in the late 1960's, the conventional wisdom has been, in essence, that many of the problems underlying the software 'crisis' were due to the fact that the methods used to develop software products were informal and, indeed, that the software process itself was an informal process. The proposed solutions were therefore that we should formalise, as far as possible, the methods used for development. Initial efforts at formalisation focused on the programming process but the emergence of structured methods and, later, formal specifications, reinforced this assumption that a more formal approach was likely to be more productive at least in terms of quality if not in cost.

In the 1980's comparable assumptions were made about the software process (and other business processes) itself. Early attempts at process modelling dived into formality and were, in my view, misguided [1, 2] Later work has recognised that human activities are really very hard to formalise and have introduced more flexibility. Nevertheless, formalisation, in some form, is still seen as the key to process improvement. Indeed, this is reflected in one of the goals of this workshop namely the discussion of novel formalisms for SPT. In this paper, we wish to question the notion that a continuing concentration on formalisms is the right way to improve the software process.

It is clearly the case that the software 'crisis' remains with us. We believe that both software quality and productivity have improved significantly over the past 20 years and that most of this improvement is due to the increased level of formality which has been adopted. However, there have not been orders of magnitude improvement in either quality or productivity and it is not at all clear that continuing the trend towards formality will ever produce such orders of magnitude improvements. Indeed, we may have arrived at a situation of diminishing returns where further investment in formality is not a particularly cost-effective way of improving quality and productivity.

A consequence of moving towards a formal approach to software development is to impose control on that process. Structured programming controls the programming process by limiting the programmer's ability to use the constructs of the programming language in an unfettered way. Design methods, whether they be structured or formal methods, impose control by limiting the expressiveness of notations and by proposing a 'standard' approach to the development of a design. Process models impose control by limiting the range of activities and tool applications which can be incorporated into a process. It can be argued, in fact, that this imposition of control is the reason why design methods have resulted in improved quality - the method itself is irrelevant - it is the control that is important.

At this stage it is important to emphasise that we are completely supportive of the need to impose some control on the software process and that the formalisation of that process which has occurred over the last 20 years has been worthwhile. It is clearly impossible for software teams to work effectively without some control. However, we argue that by focusing on improved process control and by developing tools which assist with the imposition of this control, we have lost sight of the need to support all process activities.

It is manifestly the case that there are many critical activities involved in the software development process which cannot, in practice, be formalised because we don't know how to formalise them. A few examples of such activities are:

1. Calling in an expert to assist with a very specific problem which is domain-based.
2. Negotiating system changes due to budget reductions. Again, there can be no procedural way of doing this.
3. Re-planning to cope with an unexpected change in resources.
4. Understanding a program.

All of these activities (and there are many more of the same type) are characterised by the fact that they are unpredictable (although not necessarily unanticipated) and that the response of the software development manager and software engineers is not only determined by the problem but by wider organisational factors.

Other activities are very hard to formalise because they are collaborative in nature and take place in the context of meetings. Except for very specific types of meetings (e.g. program inspections), the dynamics of meetings are determined by the participants and the current state of the organisation. We do not believe that these can sensibly be formalised.

We have undertaken studies of processes in two different organisations [3] who are both concerned with the development of large, embedded software systems. These studies indicated that for many engineers, particularly senior engineers and management, participation in these informal activities took up the vast majority of their time.

2 Supporting informal activities

We argue that it may be more cost-effective to provide support for these informal activities rather than on attempting to extend the range of activities in which formal notations can be used. In particular, we do not believe that formalising what are currently informal collaborative activities is an effective strategy.

We propose two complementary approaches for providing support for informal activities:

1. Provide generalised tools for supporting cooperation. Many if not most informal process activities are explicitly collaborative activities so it may be possible

to use general CSCW (Computer Support for Cooperative Work) systems and integrate these with other tools for process support. Examples of this class of systems include structured messaging systems, computer conferencing systems, meeting room systems, etc. [4].

2. Provide tools for informal information capture, processing and retrieval. In the vast majority of cases, the information generated during informal process activities is lost because it does not fit neatly with the structured information generated from more formal notations. This informal information is usually unstructured, may be inconsistent and incomplete and may be extremely difficult to categorise. Nevertheless, it can be extremely useful particularly during system evolution as it captures the rationale for decisions which affect the structure and implementation of the system.

Tools for informal information capture must meet a number of requirements if they are to provide cost-effective support:

1. It must be possible to collect informal information in several stages and to add to that information as further details become available. An inherent characteristic of informal information is incompleteness so we must always allow more information to be provided.

2. The tools must, as far as possible, be unobtrusive as far as existing working practice is concerned. This means that their use should not significantly change the nature of an activity and that they should be easy and convenient to use. In this respect, they are quite different from tools to support formalisms as the introduction of formalisms normally constitutes a change of practice.

3. It must be possible to learn how to use these tools effectively with a few minutes of practice. As discussed above, those involved in generating informal information are often the most senior staff working on a project. They do not have the time to learn how to use a complex system.

4. It must be possible to access both informal information and formal project documents through the same interface and to link formal and informal information. Few specification, design or programming support tools allow informal information to be collected directly (except as comments). We need to be able to annotate the outputs from these tools with informal information.

5. It must be possible to impose structure on the informal information either as it is being generated or after it has been generated. Informal information is not necessarily unstructured but we may not know its structure in advance. We should be able to structure that information when it has been collected. This requirement is one reason why collecting informal information as textual comments is ineffective.

6. The tools must support the definition of new types of entity and relationship. Whatever the formal or structured notation used, any complex project will include entities and relationships which cannot be denoted by the 'standard' notation. Either these are transformed into known entity or relation types or are discarded. We believe that neither of these approaches is sensible so an extensible mechanism for defining entities and relations is necessary.

7. The tool must provide retrieval capabilities so that the relevant informal information can be discovered. In a large project, a vast amount of informal information

may be collected so we need powerful information browsers and query languages to find the information required.

These requirements mean that it is generally impractical to include support for informal information capture and retrieval in tools designed to manage formal or structured notations. Rather, the approach that we are adopting is to develop an information system which acts as a catalogue to the formal project documents and provides annotation and grouping facilities which allow new informal information to be associated with these documents.

Our recent work, undertaken as part of the ESPRIT project Proteus, has been concerned with providing this latter form of support. We are developing a Process and Product Information System (PPIS) which can be integrated with existing design tools to provide a basis for the capture of design rationale [5, 6]. The PPIS is a hypertext system with facilities to reference external documents and to run tools to view and edit these documents. We meet the above requirements in the following way:

1. The interaction metaphor is through electronic notes like 'Post-it' notes. These are familiar and easy to use. We allow notes to be structured or unstructured and provide a simple information retrieval system to find specific notes.
2. The note facility allows information to be captured incrementally. The different note types allow information from different sources to be identified.
3. We provide a facility to create and link entities and relationships and to add type information to these entities and relationships. Different views may be defined and the same entity may have a different type in different views. Entities may be grouped and ungrouped, organised into a hierarchy, easily moved from place to place in the hierarchy etc. The entities may be 'external entities' representing documents created using some other tool. However, these external entities may be annotated in exactly the same way as other entities.

The first planned application of this system is to retrofit design rationale to existing designs which have been created in the HOOD notation. Most current work on Design Rationale is based on the notion that rationale is collected during the design process. This may sometimes happen but we believe that a more pressing need arises during the process of system evolution where those responsible for making system changes must try to understand why design decisions are made. This understanding, typically. emerges slowly and its derivation may be a collaborative effort involving different engineers who making changes to the system over a period of time.

In summary, we believe that it is time to accept that formality will never be able to solve all or even most of the problems of software development and that we must also consider the informal, human aspects of software engineering if we are to provide effective process support. One way to do this is to recognise the inherent informality in human communications and to provide tool support for this.

3   Acknowledgements

The work described here was partially funded by the European Commission's ESPRIT programme (Project 6068, Proteus). Thanks are due to our collaborators in that project and, in particular, to Matra Marconi Espace, Toulouse, who are acting as an evaluation site for the PPIS.

References

1. Ellis, C.A., 'Information Control Nets: A mathematical model of office information systems', Proc. 1979 ACM Conf. on Simulation, Measurement and Modelling of Computer Systems, ACM Press, 225-239, 1979.
2. Osterweil, L., 'Software Processes are software too', Proc. 9th Int. Conf. on Software Engineering, IEEE Press, 1987.
3. Rodden, T.A., King, V., Hughes, J. and Sommerville, I., 'Process modelling and development practice', Proc. 2nd European Workshop on Software Process Technology, Springer, 1994.
4. Rodden, T.A., 'A survey of CSCW systems', Interacting with Computers, 3 (3), 319-353, 1991.
5. Twidale, M., Rodden, T., Sommerville, I., 'The Designer's Notepad: Supporting and understanding cooperative design', Proc. ECSCW'93, 93-108, 1993.
6. Haddley, N. and Sommerville, I., 'Integrated Support for Systems Design', BCS/IEE Software Engineering J., 5 (6), 331-338, 1990.

Navigation in Process Models

Gerhard Chroust

Systems Engineering and Automation
Kepler University Linz, Austria
CHROUST @ SEA.UNI-LINZ.AC.AT

1.0 Process Models

The problems of today's software engineering discipline are deeply rooted in the nature of software. Quality products can only be the result of a quality production process [Crosby_80] [Humphrey_89]. which has to be defined in advance by a *process model* [Chroust_92a]. A process model cannot specify in advance the exact sequence of activities to be taken. Thus it is necessary to provide to the individual user guidance as to the specific sequencing of activities: we speak about *navigation*.

Based on the cascade model [Chroust_92a] we see a process model in its simplest form as the tupel:

$$PM = < A, R, i, o, ... >$$

A: set of activity classes. An instance is represented by a_i.

R: set of result classes. an instances is represented by r_i

i: $i(r_i, a_j)$ defines the inputs r_i of activity a_j.

o: $o(r_i, a_j)$ defines the outputs r_i of activity a_j.

We can distinguish 4 different scenarios. They require different navigation strategies which are supported with different adequacy by the various representations.

straight-forward development: This is the standard development process implied by most methods, e.g. the waterfall model [Royce_70].

iterative forward development: Development is in a forward direction with the proviso (like the spiral model [Boehm_88]) that activities are iterates to provide further refinement.

work-ahead: Despite the absence of the final version of inputs activities are started for reasons of balancing manpower or tight schedules. Before finishing the activity one has to check, however, whether the results is in line with the final version of the inputs [Phillips_88].

rework: For various reasons (change of requirements, actual mistakes etc.) it is often necessary to go back and change some already finished intermediate results.

2.0 Process Models and Navigation

We discuss several common representations of process models, cf. [Chroust_92a], and their ability to describe navigation. For this purpose we define a predicate *is-made-ready*(a_i, a_j) which states that if a_i becomes finished, a_j becomes ready. We ignore the fact that a_j might already be ready or finished. This question would justify an investigation of its own.

2.1 Activity Network: The process is seen as a network of activities, irrespective of the used results, e.g. as in Boehm's waterfall model [Boehm_84].

$is\text{-}made\text{-}ready(a_i, a_j) = is\text{-}successor\ (a_j, a_i)\ \&\ finished(a_i)$

- An activity becomes ready as soon as its predecessor becomes finished.
- Complications arise if the successor relationship is not 1:1, i.e. if an activity can have several predecessors and/or successors.

2.2 Activity-Result Network: For each activity its successor(s) is/are defined together with the data to be passed on, e.g. the German V-Model [Brohl_93]. This representation has many properties of data flow diagrams.

$is\text{-}made\text{-}ready(a_i, a_j) = is\text{-}successor\ (a_j, a_i)\ \&\ finished(a_i)\ \&$
$(forall\ r_k\ /\ i(r_k, a_j)\ finished\ (r_k)).$

- The process interpreter has more flexibility since additionally the passed results have to be in a finished state.
- Multiple successors can be handled by assigning different states to results.

2.3 Result-correlated Activities: Activity classes are described with their inputs and outputs. Identically named result classes correspond to one another, cf. ADPS [Chroust_89d]. Sequencing not described.

$is\text{-}made\text{-}ready(\ null, a_j\ ) = (forall\ r_k\ /\ i(r_k, a_i)\ finished\ (r_k)).$

- Readiness is not dependent on a specific predecessor.
- A tacid assumption is that only finished results are acceptable as inputs.
- No special assumption about the connection between the individual activities is made, the set of activities does not necessarily form a network, giving considerable freedom for choosing different enactment sequences.
- Obviously ambiguity arises as soon as the same result class is output from and input to at least two activity classes.

2.4 Pre-conditioned Activity Classes: The previous representation proved difficult to impose some meaningful control over the development process, especially if results were output of different activities and the network of activites was large. In order to be able to restrict the set of activities to be considered one can add preconditions, e.g. LARS [Hagemann_87].

$is\text{-}made\text{-}ready(\ a_i, a_j\ ) = is\text{-}entry\text{-}predicate\ (\ a_j, ...)$

- The expressive power depends on the type of variables permissible in the preconditions. Allowing external states (e.g. management decisions, time) can provide complete control of the development process.
- It is directly compatible with result-correlated networks but almost incompatible with activity networks and activity-result networks (predicates can halt execution but do not offer any alternatives).

2.5 Pre- and Post-Condition (ETVX-paradigm):   [Phillips_88]   chooses   a representation which uses both entry and exit criteria. The basic building block of the representation provides also integrated verification/validation (but this will not be further considered here). In the sequel we assume that the exit criterion is a condition for leaving the activity (there exist also other interpretations).

is-made-ready(a_i, a_j) = is-successor (a_j, a_i) & is-entry-predicate (a_j), ...) & is-exit.predicate (a_i), ...).

- Quality assurance can be handled very well.
- Work-ahead is easily handled since the post-condition can check the fulfillment of all pre-conditions.

2.6 Trigger: Certain process models, cf. [Chroust_90b], use explicit triggers for making a successor activity 'ready'.

is-made-ready(a_i, a_j) = is-triggered (a_0, a_j) for some a_0.

- This does not introduce a new concept since it is largely equivalent to an an activity network, probably restricting the successor-function to a 1:1 or n:1-relationship.
- Explicit triggering makes parallel paths difficult to handle.

2.7 Petri-Nets: Various process models have been implemented using concepts of Petri-nets, e.g. the LION environment [Gruhn_93].

- This paradigm can be largely reduced to the ones before.
- Names of the result types have to be associated with places in the Petri-net.
- Problems arise with assigning states to results and activities.

3.0 Summary

Process model descriptions can be evaluated with respect to their ability to express navigational strategies and constraints in relation to the four important development scenarios (cf. table below).

Being still far from an optimal representation, we need more experiments and at the same time we need to understand better the requirements of the different development scenarios in order to to represent the navigation within them.

	forward	*iterat.*	*w ahead*	*rework*
Activity Network	+	-	-	--
Activity-Result Netw.	++	0	+	-
Result-correlated Act.	0	+	0	+
Pre-conditioned Act.	++	+	0	++
pre- and post-cond.	++	+	++	+
Trigger	++	--	-	--
Petri-nets	++	-	--	--

[Boehm_84] Boehm B.W.: Software Life Cycle Factors.- in Vick C.R., Ramamoorthy C.C. (eds.): Handbook of Software Engineering, Van Nostrand New York 1984 pp. 494-518

[Boehm_88] Boehm B.: Applying Process Programming to the Spiral Model.- Dowson M. (ed.): Representing and Enacting the Software Process.- Proc. 4th Int'l Software Process Workshop, IEEE 1988, pp.1-11

[Broehl_93] Bröhl A.P., Dröschel W. (eds.): Das V-Modell - Der Standard für die Softwareentwicklung mit Praxisleitfaden.- Oldenbourg 1993

[Chroust_89d] Chroust G.: Application Development Project Support (ADPS) - An Environment for Industrial Application Development.- ACM Software Engineering Notes, vol. 14 (1989) no. 5, pp. 83-104

[Chroust_90b] Chroust G., Goldmann H., Gschwandtner O.: The Role of Work Management in application development.- IBM System Journal, vol. 29 (1990) no. 2, pp. 189-208

[Chroust_92a] Chroust G.: Modelle der Software-Entwicklung - Aufbau und Interpretation von Vorgehensmodellen.- Oldenbourg Verlag, 1992

[Crosby_80] Crosby P.B.: Quality is Free.- Mentor Books / New American Library 1980

[Humphrey_89] Humphrey W.S.: Managing the Software Process.- Addison-Wesley Reading Mass. 1989

[Merbeth_92] Merbeth G.: MAESTRO-II - das Integrierte CASE-System von Softlab.- Balzert H. (ed.): CASE - Systeme und Werkzeuge.- 4. Auflage, B-I Wissenschaftsverlag 1992, pp.215-232

[Phillips_88] Phillips R.W.: State Change Architecture: A Protocol for Executable Process Models.- Tully C. (ed.): Representating and Enacting the Software Process.- Proc. 4th Int. Software Process Workshop, May 1988 ACM Software Engineering Notes vol. 14 (1989), no. 4., pp. 129-132

[Royce_70] Royce W.W.: Managing the Development of Large Software Systems.- Proc. IEEE WESCON, Aug. 1970, pp.1-9

Multi-View Modeling of Software Processes

Martin Verlage

Fachbereich Informatik, Universität Kaiserslautern, 67653 Kaiserslautern, Germany

1 Introduction

The objective of software process technology is to support the derivation and analysis of software process models, and their use in projects. Software process models should represent as much as possible of a project, and thereby support as many project members as possible. But a very rare few people ever understand a large project as a whole. The first problem is that every process element is viewed differently depending on the contexts of the project members. The second problem is that different roles exist within a software project. I believe that a useful software process model can only be derived by describing the process from different perspectives. Concentration on a subset of information (e.g., product flow) during modeling is helpful [1]. The part of a software process model which corresponds to a role (i.e., supports the role's tasks) is called a *view*. Views may overlap and have to be integrated to produce a comprehensive software process model. I believe that development and use of comprehensive software process models should be performed by the application of the following three steps:

1. **Modeling.** Every participating role develops its own view. This results in a role-specific description which is more likely to represent the real world than a description made by other people.
2. **Integration.** The separately developed views have to be integrated into a comprehensive software process model. Because all roles have described the same project, there has to be a match. If views cannot be connected, the project itself is misunderstood; cooperative work is based on no common basis.
3. **Use.** Every role uses its own view during project guidance. The comprehensive software process model is not presented as a whole, and unnecessary information is filtered. The process is presented using the role's own terms defined in the corresponding view.

It is my belief that the views developed in step 1 are the elements to be reused, and not the comprehensive software process model. Each view represents a set of processes aiming at a goal (e.g., verification); a project represents a collection of goals. This collection is unique in every project, but the single goals represented by a view remain stable over project lifetime.

2 Requirements for Multi–View Approaches

Models to be integrated may represent complex processes and may overlap. Therefore, multi–view modeling requires powerful approaches. In our opinion, at least the following requirements for supporting approaches must be fulfilled by a supporting approach:

R1. **Different perspectives on the same process element must be offered.** Different roles need different information about a product, process or resource.

R2. **Tailorable (user-defined) perspectives.** We can not assume a static set of predefined perspectives will be sufficient since it is impossible to define a static set of roles.

R3. **Structuring of views.** Process elements should be explicitly grouped to form a view.

R4. **Independent modeling of views.** The description of views may not be influenced by other views. Correspondence between views should be established after their description.

R5. **Detecting similarities between views.** Separately defined views may describe the same process elements. Similarities have to be detected to connect views.

R6. **Detecting inconsistencies between views.** Views developed independently may contain inconsistent information. Semantic information about software processes has to be provided in order to detect such situations.

R7. **Dynamic change of perspectives.** Not all roles participate during the whole project. Actors are assigned and released asynchronously; even the same process element may be viewed differently by the same role in different situations. Mechanisms are needed to support a change of perspectives.

R8. **Concurrent views.** Many people are involved in a project. Different views should be presented concurrently to the different people.

R1–R4 belong to modeling (step 1); R5 and R6 support integration (step 2); and R7 and R8 allow independent use of views (step 3).

3 Does Existing Technology Meet the Requirements?

Various approaches exist in the area of system development which support simultaneously displaying information. We describe a few approaches briefly.

The idea of defining system functionality by different approaches is rooted in the context of multiparadigm languages [2]. Different vies (files) may be described by using languages employing different programming paradigms. Merging different views is established by procedure calls.

Software Engineering Environments may offer multiple views simultaneously to the user (e.g., Pecan [3]). Separate views are derived from an internal representation based on abstract syntax trees.

These two approaches offer support for solo programming. An approach explicitly supporting parallel development is ViewPoint specification [4]. Evolutions of software specifications are performed by using associated ViewPoints, which are built out of five slots: a style, a domain (in our case fixed: software process), the specification, a work plan and a work record, which contain operations on the specification and the history of applied operations. ViewPoints are related by identical entities, which are propagated top–down.

An approach developed for the specification of systems but also used to model software processes is STATEMATE [1]. It has been used to describe software processes from three predefined perspectives, namely the organizational, the behavioral, and the functional view.

Independent evolution of multiple specification lines and later integration is described in [6]. The main problems occur when detecting correspondences and inconsistencies [7].

ORM is used as an object–oriented basis for integration of classes with roles (i.e., sets of features) [8]. The approach developed within the ITHACA ESPRIT project employs general but simple techniques in order to detect correspondence between classes.

ES-TAME [5] is a modeling tool for specifying high–level software process models. Templates for measurement plans, which express development goals in an operational and measurable manner, may also be defined. Users modify process elements by using viewpoints, which are defined in the elements itself. Every model defines its own appearance to the real world.

The following table expresses which requirements are fulfilled by the presented approaches. A '×' denotes that a requirement is fulfilled, '(×)' means that the approach covers only a subset of the corresponding problem. An empty box means that this requirement is not fulfilled by the approach.

Approach	R1	R2	R3	R4	R5	R6	R7	R8
Multi-Paradigm Languages		×	×	×				
SEEs	×	×						
ViewPoints	×	×	×	×		(×)		(×)
STATEMATE	×					(×)	×	×
Multi-Line Specification	×		×	×	(×)	(×)		
ITHACA (ORM)	×		×	×	(×)	(×)	(×)	(×)
ES-TAME	×	×		×			×	

Table 1: Requirements Satisfaction of Multi-View Techniques

4   What is Needed for Multi–View Modeling

The requirements introduced in Section 2 are not fulfilled completely by any of the seven approaches shown in Table 1. The two main reasons are that they do not support all three steps presented in Section 1, and are not tailored to the specific needs of multi-view modeling of software processes (except ES-TAME). The second reason means that the approaches lack the knowledge about software processes which is primarily needed during integration of views (R5 and R6). Therefore, I identify the following points as important for future research efforts:

Do any standard views exist? Experience has shown a distinction between managerial and technical perspectives on a software development or maintenance project. Refinement of these views is needed in order to describe the relevant aspects on which a role should concentrate, i.e. to support learning and integration of new project members. Company–wide standard views ease reuse of process knowledge.

How are identical objects identified in different views? Matching identical information in separate views is needed to connect views. This becomes more evident when aspects of different views have only small intersections, e.g. one view shows product flow, whereas a second presents process attributes.

Where to begin when merging different views? Does there exist an order, determined by the roles, which eases the merging of models? For instance, selecting a high–level role like project manager as a starting point for merging activities could serve as a framework for integration.

How is consistency achieved when merging different views? Specifying a project from different viewpoints can lead to inconsistent descriptions. Sometimes this inconsistency may be required, for example when the roles misunderstand the processes. Finding these inconsistencies requires additional semantic knowledge about software processes.

Finding solutions to these problems will allow describing software process models from different perspectives. This requires a tailoring of existing approaches to the specific needs of multi–view modeling of software processes. Additional semantic information about software processes has to be considered in the design of future tools and methods to support development and use of software process models.

References

1. Humphrey, Watts S. and Kellner, Marc I. "Software Process Modeling: Principles of Entity Process Models", Proceedings of the 11th International Conference on Software Engineering, May 1989, pp. 331–342.
2. Brent Hailpern, "Guest Editor's Introduction: Multiparadigm Languages", IEEE Software, January 1986, pp. 6-9
3. Steven P. Reiss, "PECAN: Program Development Systems That Support Multiple Views", Proceedings 7th International Conference on Software Engineering, 1984, pp. 324-333
4. A. Finkelstein, D. Gabbay, A. Hunter, J. Kramer, B. Nuseibeh, "Inconsistency Handling in Multi-Perspective Specifications", Proceedings European Software Engineering Conference, Garmisch-Partenkirchen, Germany, 1993
5. Markku Oivo, Victor R. Basili, "Representing Software Engineering Models: The TAME Goal Oriented Approach", IEEE Transactions on Software Engineering, October 1992
6. W.N. Robinson, "Integrating Multiple Specifications Using Domain Goals", 5th Int. WS on Software Specification and Design, Pittsburgh, USA, May 1989
7. M.S. Feather, "Detecting Interference when Merging Specification Evolutions", 5th Int. WS on Software Specification and Design, Pittsburgh, USA, May 1989
8. C. Francalanci, B. Pernici, "Object-Oriented View Integration to Support Reuse of Requirement Specifications", Proc. 2nd International Computer Science Conference, Hong Kong, December 1992

PML Concepts and Paradigms Session

Alfonso Fuggetta

Politecnico di Milano and CEFRIEL

Several Process Modelling Languages (PMLs) have been developed in recent years, based on different paradigms and linguistic approaches. Existing PMLs range from Petri-nets-based approaches such as SLANG, Melmac, and Process Weaver, to logic-based languages such as Peace and Alf, rule-based systems such as Merlin and Marvel, and other languages developed in the area of concurrent, dynamically reconfigurable systems (e.g., derived from Milner's π-calculus). An overview of existing approaches can be found in [1, 2].

The papers in this session highlight several critical issues that are currently being addressed in the research community. Existing PMLs suffer from a series of limitations and drawbacks that must be solved in order to make it possible an industrial exploitation of this technology. In particular, it seems that the most critical issues that still hamper the adoption of process technology can be summarized as follows:

- How can a process model evolve even during its enactment in order to reflect changes occurring in the modeled process? How is it possible to model and control the way such evolution is accomplished? How can we reason about changes before they are applied and incorporated in the process model being enacted?
- How can we build process models (and the corresponding enactment environments) that really support process agents (e.g., software engineers) without forcing or prescribing specific behaviour or sequences of actions? How can we really provide process guidance? How can we specify agents' goals without forcing a specific ordering of steps or actions?
- How can we describe the behaviour of a group of people cooperating to achieve a common goal? How can we specify dependencies and relationships among different process agents? How can we manage coordinated access to the process artifacts developed and managed in the software process?

These problems are quite critical and there are no definitive results yet. The papers in this session provide valid contributions and suggestions towards their solution.

References

1. Pasquale Armenise, Sergio Bandinelli, Carlo Ghezzi, and Angelo Morzenti. A Survey and assessment of Software Process Representation Formalisms. To appear on the International Journal of Software Engineering & Knowledge Engineering.
2. Chunnian Liu and Reidar Conradi. Process Modeling Paradigms: An Evaluation. In Alfonso Fuggetta, Reidar Conradi, and Vincenzo Ambriola, editors, *Proceedings of the First European Workshop on Software Process Modeling*, pages 39–52, Milano (Italy), May 1991. AICA–Italian National Association for Computer Science.

Specification of Coordinated Behaviour by SOCCA

Gregor Engels and Luuk Groenewegen *

University of Leiden, Department of Computer Science
P.O. Box 9512, NL-2300 RA Leiden, The Netherlands
email: engels,luuk@wi.leidenuniv.nl

Abstract. The software process situations to be modelled usually exhibit a great diversity and complexity, as data, local behaviour as well as coordination of behaviour of human and non-human agents have to be modelled on a fine-grained level. Unfortunately no existing specification formalism seems to be sufficiently suitable. To this aim the paper proposes a specification formalism, which combines the best fitting (parts of) different formalisms, in order to attain a satisfactory specification. The combination discussed in this paper is SOCCA (Specifications Of Coordinated and Cooperative Activities), composed of Extended Entity-Relationship (EER) based object-oriented modelling for the data perspective, state transition diagrams for the local behaviour perspective, and PARADIGM for the coordination of behaviour perspective.

Keywords: Process Modeling, Object-Oriented Concepts, State Transition Diagrams, Coordinated Behaviour

1 Introduction

Software process modelling is a relatively new branch at the software engineering tree. Through software process modelling a computer model is to be implemented for the lifecycle of an arbitrary software engineering project. Such a computer model should be such that all in the software process involved human and non-human agents get appropriate support and all kinds of relevant information from it. For instance, from a project management perspective, this relevant information ranges from relatively simple topics like the current project status, what tasks have been assigned to whom, what documents do exist and what versions, to more difficult questions and topics as for instance, is the project or whatever part of it on schedule, what is the prediction of the (near) future of the project, what happens to the project if a different approach is taken or the current model is changed into a new one.

A variety of multi-paradigm approaches has been proposed to model software processes. All of them are centered around one main paradigm like rules (e.g. Marvel [16], Merlin [21], Oikos [1]), imperative programs (e.g. APPL/A [15],

---

* Work supported by PROMOTER, ESPRIT BRWG 7082

IPSE 2.5 [24]) or Petri Nets (e.g. Slang [2]). Two main characteristics of these approaches are that first with an exception for the Petri Net based approaches, all of them use textual representations. Second, most of them are already on the abstraction level of programming languages. They thus hamper a direct modeling of a problem situation, while forcing the designer to take into account a lot of technical features of the modeling formalism.

Furthermore, all of these approaches do not support a separate modeling of the different perspectives of the software process. In case of rule-based as well as imperative languages, the modeling of the static and dynamic perspective is mixed within the same description. While this can be separated by using (coloured) Petri Nets, the modeling of local dynamics in Petri Nets is completely intertwined with the modeling of the global dynamics.

Due to the complexity and due to the requirements of software process modeling it seems to be much more appropriate that each low-level modeling or even implementation of a software process is proceeded by a high-level specification step, where all perspectives can be modelled separately on the one hand and as integrated component of a complete specification on the other hand. Such a modular specification decreases the complexity of the modelling activity and increases the changeabiltiy and evolvability of software process models.

So far the proposal contains nothing unexpected from a software engineering point of view. In this case however, the problem is that the system to be implemented should not only contain code which models the technical parts of the software process. Examples of these technical parts are the documents and deliverables to be produced, how are they developped, where and when are they released. The tools used in the software process are another example, where, when and how are they used. But the system to be implemented should also contain code modelling the human parts or rather members of the software process. In addition, the system should reflect all kinds of interaction between the various parts, the non-human as well as the human parts. Incorporating human parts and interaction where human parts are participating in, into an automated system, is highly unusual in software engineering. Human parts usually belong to the environment of the system. Therefore they are far less explicitly modelled. The consequence of this is, that the specification does not reflect the human parts and the interaction they are involved in, at least not as detailed as the non-human parts.

In the situation of software process modelling, it is essential to incorporate into the specification the human parts and the interaction they participate in. This incorporation should be have the same characteristics as the non-human parts. So data aspects, behavioural aspects and algorithmic aspects must be clearly recognizable in the specification of the human parts. In this paper a specification formalism for software process modelling is proposed, called SOCCA (Specification of Coordinated and Cooperative Acitivities), which explicitly incorporates the human parts together with the interaction they are involved in. This approach does fully justice to the aspects mentioned.

The paper has been organized as follows. After the introductory section 1, section 2 gives a problem description serving as the explanatory example of SOCCA. In section 3 it is argued why our approach of combining the best from different formalisms, is necessary, and from what formalisms SOCCA is composed. These formalisms are object-oriented modeling based on Extended Entity-Relationship (EER) modeling, and state transition diagrams in combination with PARADIGM. Object-oriented modeling applied to the explanatory example is the topic of section 4. Section 5 gives the state transition diagrams for this example. These state transition diagrams are essential for the PARADIGM description presented in section 6. Conclusions and a brief discussion of future work finish the paper in section 7.

2 Problem description

In the world of software process modelling the ISWP-6 and ISWP-7 examples consist of a problem description which has the same function as the so-called CRIS-case has in information system modelling. Its role is to provide a standard problem, to which all modelling approaches can be applied, and through which they can be evaluated and compared. This is the reason we also take the ISWP-6 example as the problem to model. As the complete specification would result in too many pages for this paper, only a subproblem will be discussed here.

The complete description of the example can be found in [17]. A brief overview of it will be given here. After that the restriction to the subproblem relevant to this paper will be indicated.

A software project has the following structure. The project is handled by a project team, and different kinds of project documents are to be produced. To this aim the project team consists of engineers, one of which is the project manager. The other members are the design engineers and the quality assurance engineers. The project documents consist of design parts and code parts. All versions of these design and code parts are kept. Moreover, based on each version of any design part, a test plan and a test package also belong to the project documents. By the direction of the project manager, a design engineer has to modify a design part, or to review a design part, or to modify a code part in conformity with the correponding design part, or to test the code part along the guidelines of the corresponding test package. Modification may also mean creation, i.e. modifying nothing into a first version. If a design engineer has done the modification, she or he is not allowed to do the reviewing or the testing. By the direction of the same project manager, a quality assurance engineer has to make a test plan, or to make a test package, or to test the code part according to the guidelines of the corresponding test package. After having scheduled and assigned these tasks, the project manager monitors their progress. Summarized the following tasks exist for the team as a whole:

– schedule and assign tasks
– modify design
– review design

- modify code
- make test plan
- make test package
- test code
- monitor progress

As already remarked above, this example would be too large for this paper. Therefore, the problem is restricted to the subproblem of doing the modification and review of designs. So the model of this subproblem is restricted to design engineers and versions of design parts. A very global data flow diagram of this subproblem is given in Figure 1.

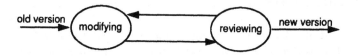

Fig. 1. Global data flow

It will be the topic of section 4 to 6 to work out the details of this rough model by means of different and detailed formalisms. In the next section the discussion is about the reasons for mixing different specification formalisms.

3   Rationale

In the field of software engineering as well as in the field of information systems much experience exists in formally describing large, complex systems. It is well known, see e.g. [22], that such a system can be viewed and described from different so-called perspectives. These perspectives are the data perspective, the process perspective and the behaviour perspective. The data perspective concentrates on the static structure of the system, on what the system is concerned with, on what is influenced by the system and on what is influencing the system.

The other two perspectives address the dynamic behaviour of the system, the things that are taking place within the system, or even outside the system but more or less connected to it. The central theme of the process perspective is the question what transformations are performed on the data and how do the data flow from transformation to transformation. So the process perspective addresses the functionality of the system. The behaviour perspective concentrates on the algorithms, especially their step sequences, establishing the transformations on the data.

Exisiting formalisms for describing the system to be developped, are specialized in the description according to only one of these perspectives. For instance, the extended Entity-Relationship model (EER) is appropriate for the data perspective. Data flow diagrams (DFD) are appropriate for the process perspective.

And state transition diagrams (STD) are appropriate for the behaviour perspective. The problem with these different formalisms is that it is still unclear how to integrate them into one large formalism covering all perspectives. Some integration has been successful, see e.g. [22, 20, 23] but the integration reached so far is certainly not completely satisfying.

For the situation discussed here, object-oriented class diagrams, based on Extended Entity-Relationship concepts, will be chosen to model the data perspective. The behaviour perspective and, in particulur, the coordination of behaviour will be described by STDs and by PARADIGM on top of STDs. PARADIGM is a specification formalism, which was originally being developed and restricted to the specification of parallel processes [12]. At last, object flow diagrams (OFD) will be chosen for modelling the process perspective. OFDs are an extended version of data flow diagrams with operations derived from the class diagram specifications. In our opinion a better integration, although at this moment not yet complete, is reached by carefully choosing some ingredients from the description according to one formalism in order to continue the development of the description according to the next formalism. In view of selecting these ingredients the formalisms are not only differentiated according to perspective, but also according to scale. This results into the matrix-like overview of Figure 2, with the perspectives on the horizontal axis, and the scale on the vertical axis.

	data	behaviour	process
local	class attributes operations	external behaviour states transitions	process components inputs/outputs
nearby	relationships part-of is-a	internal behaviour states transitions	(de)composition
global	relationships general uses	coordinated behaviour manager processes subprocesses traps	flow objects from/to
SOCCA concepts	EER	STD + PARADIGM	OFD

Fig. 2. Specification perspectives of different scale

SOCCA, the modelling approach proposed here, picks its way through the indicated formalisms in the following manner. Starting from some problem description, possibly formulated in terms of a very global data flow process, one first concentrates on a suitable class diagram. These class descriptions not only allow for attributes, but also for operations, the so-called export operations of the class. Based on these export operations one is able to switch to state transition (STD) diagrams and PARADIGM. The external behaviour of each class is modelled as an STD exhibiting all possible sequences of answering the calls for its export operations. Then, from studying where the export operations are imported, the various internal behaviours of the operations of a class are modelled as STDs exhibiting all possible sequences of calling imported operations.

So far, all external and internal behaviours are modelled as sequential processes without any respect to coordination with other processes. This is done in the next step by reusing the STDs which model the external behaviour as so-called (PARADIGM) managerprocesses. They coordinate the communication between various internal behaviours, now called (PARADIGM) employee processes. By this, it can explicitly modelled what kind of asynchronous resp. synchronous communication takes place between two internal behaviours.

Only after the communication between the various behaviours is made explicit through the PARADIGM notions, inserts, updates and deletes of objects and relationships can be described as caused by other objects. This leads to descriptions of the transformations of the objects and how the objects flow from one transformation to another by object flow diagrams. As these object flow diagrams are not in the focus of this paper, we do not explain them in more detail here [8, 14].

Due to complexity and size of software process models, the resulting SOCCA specifications are complex and large, too. But, the explicit separate modeling of each perspective enhances modularity and thus evolvability, changeability, and adaptability of the model. The price for these advantages is a large, but well-defined set of consistency constraints for a SOCCA specification. But this results not in a serious objection against SOCCA, as all these constraints can automatically checked by appropriate editing and analyzing tools in a software process modeling support environment. For instance, it can automatically be checked whether all exported operations of a certain class occur at least once in the corresponding STD describing the allowed external behaviour of this class.

This finishes the rationale for using and integrating different formalisms within SOCCA. The next sections give more details about SOCCA and show how the problem situation defined in section 2 is modelled by SOCCA.

4 Class diagrams

In this section a class diagram for the problem from section 2 is to be formulated and discussed. As class diagram modelling based on EER concepts is fairly common, the discussion will be brief ([7]). To structure this discussion, the class diagram will be introduced in a step-wise manner.

First, complex structured objects are described by class hierarchies consisting of class definitions as well as of part-of and is-a relationships. This covers the 'local' as well as the 'nearby' scale of the data perspective of Figure 2.

Second, the missing general relationships are added.

Third, as an extra feature to the usual EER models, it will be indicated which of the objects indeed use the operations exported by other objects. So it is explicitly indicated by a further relationship type, called *uses* relationship, where the various export operations are imported. This is expressed in a separate diagram referred to as interaction diagram.

The first step gives the result as shown in Figure 3. It describes a part of the ISPW6 case, more than is actually needed here to model the subproblem defined in section 2. The reason is that this gives a better impression of the usefulness of all offered Extended Entity-Relationship concepts within SOCCA. Object classes are denoted by rectangles. For the sake of readability, attributes and operations of the classes relevant for the subproblem are given separately in Figure 4. Moreover only those attributes and operations are indicated that will return later in other parts of the total SOCCA specification. In Figure 3, the small triangles indicate is-a relationships, and the small diamonds indicate part-of relationships. A triangle being black means that the is-a relationship is not disjoint. For instance, an **Engineer** may act as **ProjectManager** as well as **DesignEngineer**. A black dot indicates that the number of instances participating in a relationship may between zero and n, while no dot indicates that exactly one instance participates. For instance, a project team consists of exactly one **ProjectManager** and between zero and n **DesignEngineers**.

The second step restricts the diagram to the classes **DesignEngineer**, **ProjectDocs** and **Design** and gives the (general) relationships **modifies** and **reviews** within this subdiagram (cf. Figure 5). A hollow dot indicates that an entity participates zero or one time in this relationship. For instance, a **DesignDocument** may be (currently) modified by no or one **DesignEngineer**. On the other hand, each **DesignEngineer** modifies between zero and n **DesignDocuments**.

The third step actually extends the entity descriptions occurring in the class diagram from the first step with information usually not given in an EER model. By means of a new binary relationship type called **uses** it is indicated where the various export operations are imported. The result of this step is drawn in the interaction diagram in Figure 6.

Each **uses** relationship has an attribute **import_list** for keeping the list of names of actually imported operations. The list of imported operations may differ between different instances of the same type depending on the role of this instance. For instance, a **DesignEngineer** needs and imports different operations from a **Design** when he acts as a designer in comparison with acting as a reviewer. We come back to this point in the next section where we discuss the definition of the internal behaviour of a class.

This finishes the discussion of the class diagram, covering the data perspective within SOCCA.

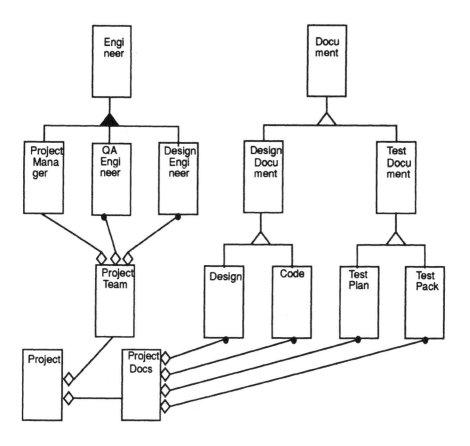

Fig. 3. Class diagram: object types and is-a and part-of relationships

Design Engineer	Project Docs	Document	DesignDocument
name		documentname	versionnumber content
design review	create_version	open_for_modif. modify close_modif.	prepare create_first create_next open_for_review review close_for_review_ok close_for_review_not_ok copy

Fig. 4. Class diagram: attributes and operations

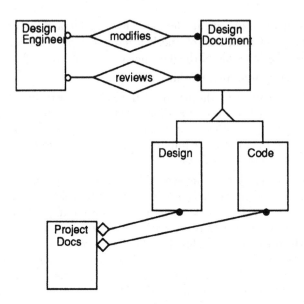

Fig. 5. Class diagram: classes and general relationships

5 State transition diagrams

The previous section discusses a class diagram for our example system. All classes are defined by fixing their attributes and by the (syntactical) signature of their operations. Up to now, no dynamics or behaviour of these operations have been defined. This will be the topic of this and the following section. In this section, we restrict our attention to the behaviour of a class on its own, its local behaviour. This local behaviour consists of two different types of behaviour, the external behaviour and the internal behaviour. The external behaviour is the behaviour visible from outside, specifying the allowed sequences for calling the exported operations. The internal behaviour consists of the actions the class performs on its own, and of the actions the class performs on behalf of the calling of imported operations. This internal behaviour specifies the allowed sequences of private operations and of calls of operations imported from elsewhere.

In view of this, the section has the following structure. First the external behaviour is specified for each class. Second it is indicated for each class which (export) operations it imports from elsewhere. And third the internal behaviour of each class is specified. In this example the internal behaviours mainly consist of the calling sequences with respect to the imported operations.

Before giving the various behaviours, a short remark is made about the execution model of these behaviours. For the time being it is assumed that each behaviour has its own processor to execute on. In the next section it will be discussed how the various behaviours are coordinated. It will be indicated how the PARADIGM notions of subprocess and trap are used from within a behaviour to influence the execution of other behaviours. At the end of that same section

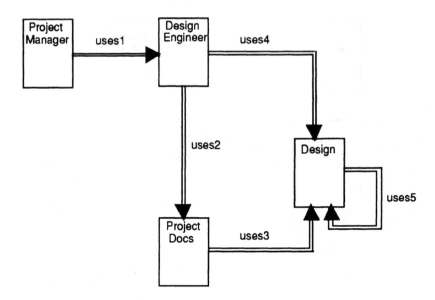

Fig. 6. Interaction diagram

some attention is given to a number of behaviours sharing the same processor.

As a vehicle for the behaviour specifications we use state transition diagrams (STDs). So we leave out all the details concerning data, but instead we now add details about the order of the operations. To make this more concrete, we start specifying the external behaviour of **DesignEngineer**, followed by the external behaviour of **ProjectDocs** and of **Design**.

In order to see exactly what has to be ordered, the export operations of **DesignEngineer** are listed once more. Remember that we restrict ourselves to those relevant for producing a new version of a document. The export operations of **DesignEngineer** are:

```
design (doc-name)
review (doc-name)
```

By parametrizing these two operations, the number of export operations effectively equals twice the number of document names.

As any design engineer may be simultaneously involved in several designs as well as reviews of different documents, there is no definite order for calling these operations. So we propose the state transition diagram of Figure 7 for the external behaviour of a **DesignEngineer**, allowing for any order of starting any number of design and review activities

In this STD all states are labeled by a short, informal comment, indicating the interpretation of a state. All transitions are labeled by (the call of) an exported operations or are unlabeled.

The state labeled **neutral** is the state the design engineer returns to after whatever design or review activity has been started by her or him.

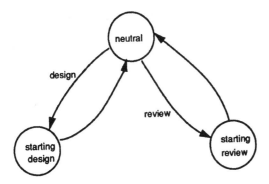

Fig. 7. DesignEngineer: STD of the external behaviour

The state **starting design** can be viewed as marking the beginning of the design activity. Note that the transition from this state back to state **neutral** has not been labeled. So there is no export operation corresponding to this transition. This transition is actually made without any calling initiative from elsewhere. To be slightly more accurate however, this transition is made only after the (internal) design activity has really started.

The state **starting review** can be viewed as marking the beginning of the review activity. The transition from this state back to **neutral** is also made without any call from outside as well as after the (internal) design activity has really started.

Further down within this section the internal behaviours of **DesignEngineer** will be discussed. Only in the next section about PARADIGM we will see how the dependencies between external and internal behaviour of the same class are formally specified.

We now proceed with the second class, **ProjectDocs**. Its export operations are:

create-version (doc-name)

As versions of other documents may be created after one creation has started but before it has been finished, the external behaviour just specifies the start of the creation, followed by returning as soon as possible to a neutral state. This leads to the diagram of Figure 8 for **ProjectDocs**.

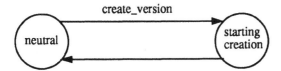

Fig. 8. ProjectDocs: STD of its external behaviour

The third and final class whose external behaviour we want to model, is **Design**. This has far more export operations than the other two. Most of these are actually inherited from some superclass. As in this paper we are not going to discuss inheritance of behaviour, we simply incorporate the operations into our behaviour description. The complete list is as follows.

```
prepare
create-first
create-next
open_for_modif.
modify
close_modif.
open_for_review
review
close_and_review_OK
close_and_review_not_OK
copy
```

In view of possible orders of these operations it is important to keep in mind that each instance of **Design** represents exactly one version of a design document. And for one version on its own highly sequencialized behaviour seems to be most appropriate. So we propose the diagram given in Figure 9 for **Design**.

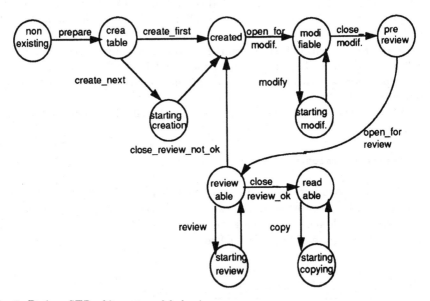

Fig. 9. Design: STD of its external behaviour

Note that for the sake of brevity we have left out all the details concerning the reading of the document version.

After the specification of the external behaviours, we proceed by specifying the internal behaviours. These would have to correspond to the various export operations when being called from elsewhere. This calling from elsewhere is typically done inside some internal behaviour as it takes place at the very same elsewhere. This elsewhere is the class where the export operation is imported. In order to prepare the specification of the internal behaviours, we present for each **uses** relationship of the interaction diagram in Figure 6 a list of possibly imported operations. This list actually states more precisely the value domain of the attribute **import_list** of a **uses** relationship.

```
uses1
  design (doc-name)
  review (doc-name)

uses2
  create_version (doc-name)

uses3
  create_first
  create_next

uses4
  open_for_modification      % used as designer
  modify
  close_modification
  open_for_review            % used as reviewer
  review
  close_and_review_OK
  close_and_review_not_OK

uses5
  copy
  prepare
```

These list of operation names indicate all possibly imported operations. Depending on the role of a certain object, only a subset of these operations are actually imported. For instance, a **DesignEngineer** needs as designer the first three operations of the **uses4** relationship, whereas he needs as reviewer the last four operations of the **uses4** relationship.

For the sake of completeness only we have indicated that the **ProjectManager** is allowed to call **DesignEngineer**'s export operations **design** and **review**. In the sequel we don't pay any attention to the **ProjectManager**, as she or he falls outside the scope of our example restrictions.

We now arrive at the internal behaviour specification. As we shall see, only three of these are really interesting within the context of this paper. These three internal behaviours are: **int-design, int-review** and **int-create_version**.

In the name giving to these internal behaviours we use the convention of adding 'int-' as a prefix to the possibly abbreviated name of the corresponding external behaviour.

Within the internal behaviour specification of any exported operation two different types of operations can occur. First of all, the imported operations can be used. When we do this, we follow the convention of using the name of the elsewhere exported operation, preceeded by the word 'call'. We could have omitted 'call', but we prefer to have it explicitly present as a reminder that the transition (execution) of the correponding external operation as well as the internal behaviour of that external operation are not necessarily synchronized, i.e. taking place at the time of the call. In this respect our approach greatly differs from approaches like state charts [13] or CCS [19].

The internal behaviour specifications are given in Figures 10 up to 12.

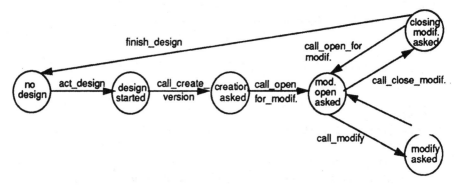

Fig. 10. int-design: STD of its internal behaviour

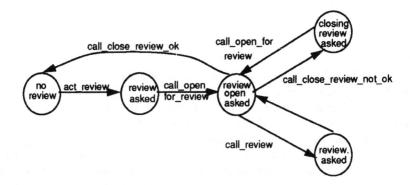

Fig. 11. int-review: STD of its internal behaviour

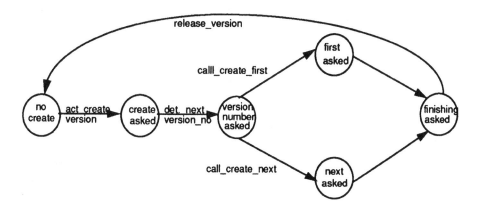

Fig. 12. int-create_version: STD of its internal behaviour

Note that both internal behaviours of **DesignEngineer** together, i.e., **int-design** and **int-review**, contain all operations imported in **DesignEngineer**. This can be immediately verified from the import list given above. A similar property holds for the one internal behaviour of **ProjectDocs** - **int-create_version**.

Another common feature of these internal behaviours we want to comment on, is their first internal operation. These are called **act-design, act-review**, and **act-create_version** respectively. The prefix **act** is an abbreviation for **activate**. It denotes the preliminary activation of the internal behaviour as a whole, without its having got actually going. This can be compared to a computer program already submitted to the operating system of a computer without having started its execution: it has only been scheduled.

From the foregoing discussion it is clear that the number of STDs becomes quite large. To be more precise, we can say the following about this number. For each class there is one STD describing the external behaviour of objects of this class. In addition, for each exported operation there is another STD describing the internal behaviour of this operation. In the above discussion we have only incorporated the interesting ones.

So far we have not discussed the coordination between the various external and internal behaviours. This is the topic of the next section. This moreover means that within SOCCA the state transition diagrams cover the behaviour perspective only as if each diagram represents a sequential behaviour executing on its own processor, completely independent from the other behaviours.

6 PARADIGM

In section 5 we discussed several external and internal behaviours. All these behaviours are strictly sequential. Moreover, as already has been remarked informally, the execution of any export operation occurring somewhere in an external behaviour, starts the execution of the corresponding internal behaviour. And the other way round, calling an export operation from inside an internal behaviour starts the execution of that export operation. As this starting of the execution of some sequential behaviour is caused by the execution from within some other sequential behaviour, this is characteristic for communication, and in particular it is characteristic for communication between these two sequential behaviours.

In view of observing two different ways of starting the execution of some sequential behaviour from within some other sequential behaviour, we could group this communication into two categories. The first category is the communication taking place between any internal behaviour and some external behaviour of another entity. This communication is the immediate result of the internal behaviour's calling an operation as exported by the other entity through its external behaviour. The second category is the communication taking place between any external behaviour and the internal behaviours belonging to the same object. This communication is the immediate result of the actual start of the execution of the external operation.

As it turns out, these two categories of communication can be combined into one category of communication, denoted as *type-1*, where the external behaviour is the intermediate between the internal behaviours from other objects and those from its own object.

In addition to this communication of type-1, another category of communication exists. This category consists of the communication taking place in order to determine and to control order, priority and similar other dependencies of all behaviours of the same object, the internals as well as the external. This category will be denoted as communication of *type-2*. Until the discussion of the type-2 communication the assumption about the execution model of the behaviours remains unchanged: each behaviour is being executed on its private processor. It is through the PARADIGM notions of subprocess, trap and manager process, that restrictions on the behaviours, i.e. on the execution of the behaviours, are enforced.

PARADIGM was originally being developed for the specification of coordinated parallel processes [12, 23, 20]. The basic underlying idea of modeling can be described by the following four steps:

1. The sequential behaviour of each process is described by a STD.
2. Within each STD significant subdiagrams, called subprocesses, with respect to coordination with other processes (also described by STDs) are identified.
3. Within each subprocess (sets of) states, so-called traps, are identified, which describe situations where an object is ready to switch from one subprocess to another.
4. The possible transitions between subprocesses of all objects, the behaviours of which have to be coordinated, are once more described by a STD, a so-called manager process.

In the following we first discuss how PARADIGM can be applied to the running example to define the communication of type-1. After that we only generally discuss the communication of type-2.

It has been already observed above that the external behaviour is an intermediate to the internal behaviours from other objects on the one hand, and the internal behaviours of its own object on the other hand. This makes each external behaviour a useful candidate for serving as a manager process in the PARADIGM model. The employees of this manager then are the internal behaviours executing the calling of an imported operation on the one hand, and on the other hand the internal behaviours of its own object executing the internal operations of the called export operation.

According to the PARADIGM formalism this means the following. Each state of an external behaviour, being a state of a manager, corresponds to a behaviour restriction. a so-called subprocess, of each of its employees. The correspondence means that when the manager is in a state, it actually prescribes its employees to restrict their behaviour to this subprocess. This behaviour restriction is thus called the current behaviour restriction, depending on the current state of the manager. In addition, each transition of an external behaviour, being a transition of a manager, corresponds to a certain final part, a so-called trap, of the current behaviour restriction(s) that is (are) to change on behalf of the change of the current state of the manager by making this transition. In this case the correspondence means that the manager is allowed to make a transition only when the relevant employees have entered these traps. So by entering a trap of the current behaviour restriction, an employee actually prescribes the manager a new behaviour in which the transition corresponding to this trap is allowed, which was not the case before the trap was entered.

As the introduction and discussion of a complete PARADIGM description is quite complicated, this discussion will be structured according to the following rules. First, an overview is given of the manager and the employees. Second, of each of the employees the subprocesses and traps are given with respect to this manager. Third, the correspondence is indicated between the manager's states and transitions on the one hand and the subprocesses and traps of its employees on the other hand. The graphical representation of subprocesses and traps is as follows. A subprocess, being a restriction of the complete behaviour as represented by the orginal state transition diagram, is itself represented as a state transition diagram, being a restriction of the original one. A trap of a subprocess is represented as a shaded polygon around the states being part of the trap.

The first example of a PARADIGM description of type-1 communication takes the external behaviour of DesignEngineer as manager. The employees here are the two internal behaviours of DesignEngineer, int-design and int-review. Properly speaking the internal behaviours of ProjectManager calling design or review are employees too, but in this paper we leave out all details concerning ProjectManager. This makes the first example relatively simple.

The subprocesses and traps of int-design and of int-review are given in Figure 13 and 14.

The correpondence between manager's states and subprocesses, and between manager's transitions and traps are visualized in Figure 15. The subprocesses occur as state labels, and the traps occur as transition labels.

Note that trap t-2 and t-4 are chosen as large as possible, in order to enable

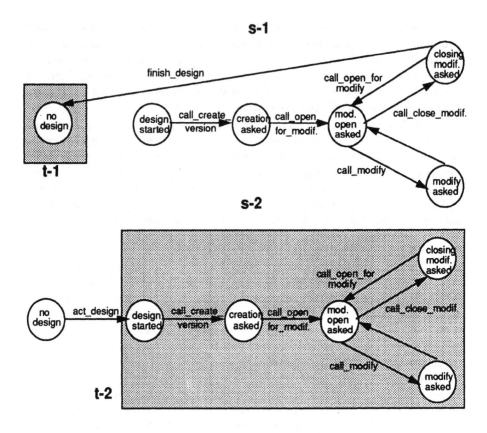

Fig. 13. int-design's subprocesses and traps w.r.t. DesignEngineer

the manager to return as soon as possible to its neutral state, after having started one of its internal behaviours by prescribing s-2 or s-4 to one of them. This is characteristic for all communication between a manager and its internal behaviours.

The second example of type-1 communication has **ProjectDocs** as manager. The employees are **int-create_version** being the internal behaviour of the same object the manager belongs to, and also **int-design**, being the only internal behaviour from another object calling **create**, the only export operation of this manager. The subprocesses and traps of these employees are given in Figure 16 and 17.

How the manager prescribes subprocesses and reacts to traps entered is described in Figure 18.

The new feature of this example is how the manager reacts to the call of **create**. By prescribing subprocess s-5 it allows for the call and it even waits for the call. Only after the call has been executed - **int-design** then has entered its trap t-5 - the manager starts its internal behaviour for the real creation, thereby

s-3

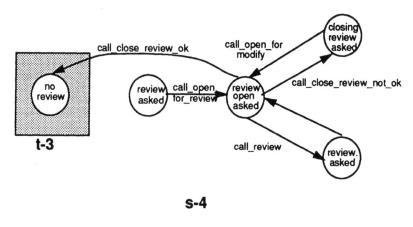

s-4

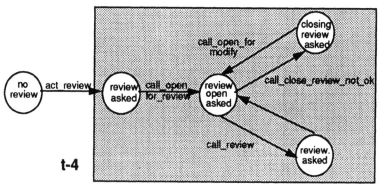

Fig. 14. int-review's subprocesses and traps w.r.t. DesignEngineer

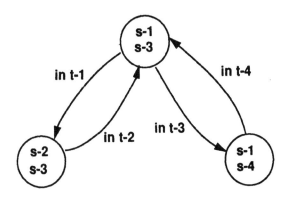

Fig. 15. DesignEngineer, manager of int-design and int-review

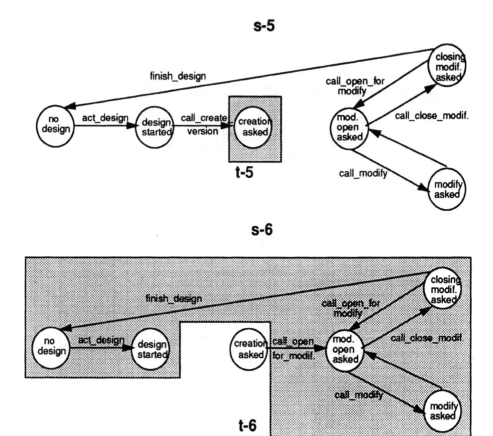

Fig. 16. int-design's subprocess and traps w.r.t. ProjectDocs

releasing **int-design** from its trap by prescribing subprocess s-6 to it. As soon as both employees have left their former traps - a direct consequence of entering their new traps t-6 and t-8 respectively - the manager returns to its neutral state.

As this finishes the discussion of the type-1 communication, the type-2 communication is the next topic. It has already been remarked, that type-2 communication consist of controlling order, priority and similar other dependencies between all behaviours belonging to one object. For an arbitrary object of type **DesignEngineer** this means the following. The instance, or the person, has three roles, corresponding to its three behaviours. In order to perform these roles in an adequate manner, it is necessary to switch from one role to another. The type-2 communication is exactly taking care of this switching, completely analogous to an operating system being reponsible for all jobs - to be considered as roles here - submitted to it. So each instance is supposed to have its private operating system for performing the type-2 communication.

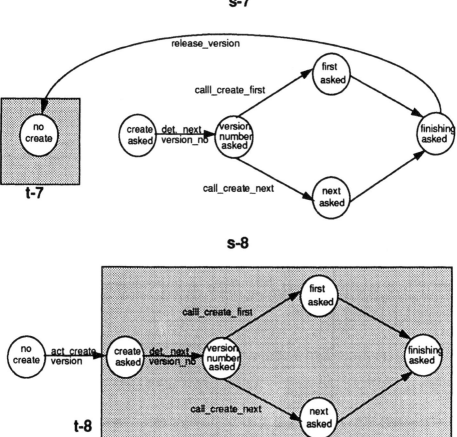

Fig. 17. int-create_version's subprocesses and traps w.r.t. ProjectDocs

This assumption can be weakened in the following sense. The behaviours of the non-human entity instances are supposed to be executed on some processor. If the behaviours of more than one object are running on the same processor, the type-2 communication of all these entity instances is performed by the operating system of this processor. On the other hand, if each behaviour, external or internal, has its private processor to be executed on, then there is no type-2 communication, so there is no need for operating systems on these dedicated processors.

It is interesting to note a similar property for the instances which behaviour is executed by a human being. If the behaviours of more than one instance are executed by one human being, then the type-2 communication between all these behaviours is in one hand, the highly sophisticated but nevertheless operating system like control of this human being. And if on the other hand each instance has its behaviours performed by a small organization on its own, one separate

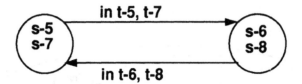

Fig. 18. ProjectDocs, manager of int-design and int-create_version

person for each separate behaviour, then there is no type-2 communication.

The description of this type-2 communication will be omitted, as on the specification level it is of no concern. The occurrence and the structure of the type-2 communication completely depends on the mapping of the model into the architecture of the machines as well as of the human organization. This causes the type-2 communication to belong to the domain of implementing and enacting the process model, and not to the domain of high-level process modelling. On the other hand, PARADIGM can be very useful in describing this type-2 communication control, as PARADIGM has been successfully applied to the domain of operating systems, see [23]. This finishes the discussion about PARADIGM. As state transition diagrams are part of PARADIGM, PARADIGM covers the complete behaviour perspective within SOCCA.

7 Conclusions and Future Work

The above discussion shows how class diagrams and PARADIGM models can be used and combined to specify the data and behaviour perspectives of a software process on a high level of abstraction. Extending this by the formalism of object flow diagrams, SOCCA indeed provides a design formalism unifying the data, behaviour and process perspectives. Based on experiences with the separate formalisms SOCCA consists of, it is to be expected that any concrete SOCCA specification will facilitate implementing the code for the software process model under consideration. Future research will certainly address this topic, probably combining SOCCA with existing, lower level languages for software process modeling.

Other topics of future research are the investigation of possible relations between the various key notions discussed in [18] and features of SOCCA. Furthermore, inheritance of behaviour and of roles seems an interesting topic. Finally, editing, analyzing and animation tools supporting SOCCA are subject of future research.

References

1. Ambriola V., Jaccheri M.L., *Definition and Enactment of Oikos Software Process Entities*, First European Workshop on Software Process Modelling, Milano, May 1991.

2. Bandinelli S., Fuggetta A., Ghezzi C., *Software Processes as Real Time Systems: A case study using High-Level Petri nets*, First European Workshop on Software Process Modelling, Milano, Italy, May 1991.
3. Belkhatir N., Estublier J. and Melo W., *Adele 2: An Approach to Software Development Coordination*, First European Workshop on Software Process Modelling, Milano, May 1991.
4. Benali K., Boudjlida N., Charoy F., Derniame J.C., Godart C., Griffiths P., Gruhn V., Jamart P., Legait A., Oldfield D., Oquendo F., *Presentation of the ALF Project*, First Int. Conf. on System Development Environments and Factories, Berlin, May 1989.
5. Conradi R., Osjord E., Westby P., Liu C., *Initial Software Process Management in EPOS*, Software Engineering Journal, Special Issue on Software Environments and Factories, September 1991.
6. Deiters W., Gruhn V., *Managing Software Processes in MELMAC*, Fourth ACM SIGSOFT Symposium on Software Developments Environments, Irvine, December 1990.
7. G. Engels, M. Gogolla, U. Hohenstein, K. Hülsmann, P. Löhr-Richter, G. Saake, H.D. Ehrich: *Conceptual Modelling of Database Applications Using an Extended ER Model*. Data & Knowledge Engineering, North-Holland, Vol. 9, 157-204, 1992
8. G. Engels, L.P.J. Groenewegen: *Specification of Coordinated Behaviour in the Software Development Process* (Position Paper). In J.C. Derniame (ed.): Proc. 2nd European Workshop on Software Process Technology (EWSPT 92), Trondheim (Norway), Springer-Verlag, Berlin, LNCS 635, 58-60, 1992
9. Emmerich W., Junkermann G., Schäfer W., *MERLIN: Knowledge-Based Process Modelling*, First European Workshop on Software Process Modelling, Milano, May 1991.
10. Fernström C., *PROCESS WEAVER: adding process support to UNIX*, In Proceedings of the 2nd International Conference on the Software Process Berlin, Germany, February 1993, pp.12 - 26.
11. Peter H. Feiler and Watts S. Humphrey, *Software Process Development and Enactment: Concepts and Definitions*, In Proceedings of the 2nd International Conference on the Software Process, pages 28–40, Berlin, Germany, February 1993.
12. Groenewegen, L.P.J., *Parallel phenomena 1 - 14*. University of Leiden, Dep. of Computer Sc., Techn. Rep. 86-20, 87-01, 87-05, 87-06, 87-11, 87-18, 87-21, 87-29, 87-32, 88-15, 88-17, 88-18, 90-18, 91-19. 1986 - 1991.
13. Harel, D.: *Statecharts: A Visual Formalism for Complex Systems*, in Science of Computer Programming, Vol. 8, No. 3, pp. 231-274, June 1987
14. Hennemann, Chr., Schacht, J.: *Design and Implementation of a Language for the Visual Specification of Actions on Extended Entity-Relationship Databases*. Diploma Thesis (german), Technical University of Braunschweig, 1991
15. Heimbigner, D., Sutton, St.M., Osterweil, L.: *Managing Change in Process-Centered Environments*. In Proc. of the 4th ACM/SIGSOFT Symposium on Software Development Environments, Dec. 1990
16. Kaiser, G.E., Feiler, P.H., Popovich, St.S.: *Intelligent Assistance for Software Development and Maintenance*. IEEE Software, 40-49, May 1988
17. Kellner, M., P. Feiler, A. Finkelstein, T. Katayama, L. Osterweil, M. Penedo, H. Rombach, ISWP-6 Software process example. In: Proc. of the 6th Int. Software Process Workshop: support for the software process. Japan, October 1991.

18. Jacques Lonchamp, *A Structured Conceptual and Terminological Framework for Software Process Engineering*, In Proceedings of the 2nd International Conference on the Software Process, pages 41–53, Berlin, Germany, February 1993.
19. Milner, R.: *Communication and Concurrency.* Prentice-Hall, Englewood Cliffs, 1989
20. Morssink, P.J.A., Behaviour modelling in information systems design: application of the PARADIGM formalism. Ph.D. Thesis, University of Leiden, Dep. of Computer Science, 1993
21. Peuschel, B., Schäfer, W., Wolf, St.: *A Knowledge-Based Software Development Environment Supporting Cooperative Work.* To appear in International Journal on Software Engineering and Knowledge Engineering
22. Rumbaugh, J., Blaha, M., Premerlani, W., Eddy, F., Lorensen, W.: *Object-Oriented Modeling and Design.* Englewood Cliffs, Prentice-Hall 1991
23. Steen, M.R. van, Modelling dynamic systems by paralle decision processes. Ph.D. Thesis, University of Leiden, Dep. of Computer Sc., 1988.
24. Warboys B., *The IPSE 2.5 Project: Process Modelling as the basis for a support Environment*, First Int. Conf. on System Development Environments and Factories, Berlin, 1989.

Distribution and Change: Investigating Two Challenges for Process Enactment Systems

Neil Berrington, David De Roure
R. Mark Greenwood and Peter Henderson

University of Southampton
Department of Electronics and Computer Science
Southampton, UK. SO9 5NH *

Abstract. Process enactment systems are inherently distributed; a single central server cannot be assumed, and the configuration and behaviour of nodes is dynamic. Hence we require distributed enactment models majoring on process mobility, with a framework for reasoning about and controlling change. We have built tools to investigate such dynamic process enactment systems, using the *Document Flow Model* (DFM) as a vehicle and adopting ideas from Milner's π-calculus.

1 Introduction

In this paper we describe our ongoing work investigating distribution and change in the context of process enactment systems. We have developed the *Document Flow Model* (DFM) as a paradigm for providing process support through a network of distributed sub-processes. These sub-processes are not only distributed, but also mobile in the sense that they can change their configuration, and may even change the physical processor on which they are running. The objectives which guided the development of DFM are presented in section 2, DFM is outlined in section 3, and our initial experiences are described in section 4. Milner's π-calculus has been a source of ideas on DFM's ability to describe a changing configuration of sub-processes; this, and other related work, are described in section 5. Finally, we discuss some preliminary conclusions based on our work to date in section 6.

2 Objectives

We believe that a process enactment system whose architecture corresponds closely to that of the process being modelled offers significant benefits. It affords a degree of simplicity by supporting a model close to the application domain (though it may pose particular challenges), it provides a natural support for evolution of the process, and it provides a degree of resilience to failure of nodes. An architecture with client processes accessing a central server does not capture the inherently distributed nature of most problems.

We have identified three primary objectives:

---

* email: {nb88r,dder,rmg91r,ph}@ecs.soton.ac.uk

- Process mobility,
- Framework for change,
- Simplicity.

In considering a process as a distributed system, one natural view is to think of the process as a network (connected graph) of sub-processes. These sub-processes are elements of distribution, and each is a separate "thread" in the process execution. The links between the sub-processes represent their ability to communicate.[2]

From this viewpoint we can broadly define two types of change: changes in the links of the network, and changes in the internal behaviour of a sub-process. If we extend our model to consider how the sub-processes are mapped onto processors, which could be machines or people, then there is a third type of change: the migration of sub-processes between processors. We want to be able to reason about these change issues and Milner's π-calculus [16, 17] offers a powerful formalism. This is not surprising, as the ability to describe process mobility, that is changing configuration, was the goal which shaped the π-calculus. In addition, we have experience, at the implementation level, of established techniques for process migration in distributed systems [19], and of incremental change in a process enactment system [11].

One important approach to mobility and change issues is to make use of reflection. This enables the system to take hold of structures to do with the executing process and to handle them as first class citizens within the model; for example, the state of a process could be captured as data for migration. Reflective techniques are adopted in meta-object protocols to give the user control over the behaviour of the system—Kiczales proposes that this interface to the behaviour of process should be part of the interface to a process [13].

We make two important decisions to support the objectives above, and their effect is pervasive:

- Independent processes;
- Asynchronous communication.

By *independent processes* we mean that all processes are *first class citizens* within the model: there is no master process (except as designated in the execution of a particular enactment), and new processes can join the evolving network. Asynchronous communication captures the asynchronous nature of process execution—there is no global clock, and our concern is only with maintaining the event ordering required by rules of causality. It also affords interoperability with foreign processes across standard interfaces, and promotes resilience by employing a store-and-forward model. These latter aspects are exemplified in electronic mail systems.

As a concrete example consider the problem of providing support for a customer fault reporting process, where the customer is one of the people supported. This is inherently distributed with part of the process at the customer's site and part, which itself might be distributed, at the supplier's site. In addition, the people involved would have different requirements for process evolution. The customer would want

---

[2] So far we have taken the simple view that these sub-processes are atomic in the sense that they are not themselves formed of a network of sub-sub-processes and so on. This is analogous to looking at a human network performing a process and taking each individual as a natural unit.

a common interface for reporting all faults. First line customer support would want to categorize faults, perhaps according to their contractual commitments to the customer and whether the fault had been previously reported. Finally, technical fault investigators would want a very flexible process which could evolve as more was learnt about the problem and hence who should investigate it. In addition, customers might want to be able to specialize their part of the process, for example to access their own fault reports database. A network of processes, with asynchronous communication between them, seems a simple and natural way to support such a process. The required flexibility can be provided by the evolution of this network[3].

3 DFM–A preliminary model

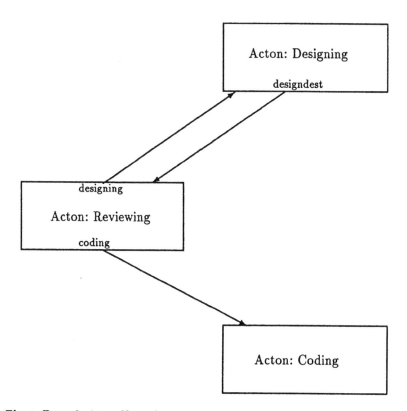

Fig. 1. Example Acton Network

---

[3] Another distributed process which you might ponder how to support is the composition of a collaborative research proposal, by *l* researchers in *m* institutions, spread over *n* countries.

Document Flow Model (DFM) is a process enactment paradigm which we are developing, guided by the objectives outlined above. In DFM there are two principal object classes: *documents* and *actons*. A process is a network of actons, so named because each "acts on" the documents which it holds. Each acton has three parts:

a collection of documents — sometimes referred to as the acton's in-tray;

a set of rules — which are the operations the acton can perform on its documents;

a binding table — which associates the addresses of other actons in the network with local names which are used in the rules. (The binding table thus describes the network links.)

Figure 1 shows how the binding tables represent the links in the acton network. The Reviewing acton knows the address of the other two actons, referring to them as designing and coding respectively. As we shall see below, the evolution of this network of links is an important part of the process.

Documents represent the data which is manipulated by the process. They arrive in an acton's document collection, asynchronously, and can be sent there by any acton whose binding table contains the appropriate link. The arrows in figure 1 thus represent paths along which documents travel.

Each rule has a name, a guard and an action. The guard is a predicate over a fixed number of documents. If it is possible to select documents from the collection such that the guard is true, then the rule is ready to fire. When a rule which is ready is selected, then the code in the action part is executed. This will extract the selected documents from the collection, possibly create some new documents, possibly set document fields to new values, and send them to their destination actons. (We have also started to investigate action parts which add or delete rules from their acton.)

```
(defrule reviewRework ((comnts Report)(des Design))"Send Design...Rework"
 guard: (eq (Report-pass comnts) 'Rework)
 action: (send designing (make-ChangeReq 'text (Report-text comnts)))
         (send designing des)
         (setbinding designing designdest (lookup-binding 'coding)))
```

Fig. 2. Example DFM rule

Figure 2 shows an example rule called reviewRework. This is taken from a reviewing acton in a simplified design, review, implement model. This rule works on two documents, one of type Report which it calls comments, and one of type Design. The rule's guard will be true if its acton's in-tray contains two documents of the appropriate type and the pass field of comments is Rework. The rules action part dispatches three documents. The acton which this acton knows by the label designing is sent a document of type ChangeReq and the design. In addition, designing is also sent a document which tells it to overwrite the acton address which it refers to as designdest, to the address which the reviewing acton refers to as coding. All actons have built-in rules for handling these "setbinding" documents, so enabling the process network to evolve. (In the reviewing acton there are two other rules: one simply sends an approved design to coding, the other sends a design which did not pass review to the designing acton but does not change its `designdest` link. The rule above represents the middle ground where there are corrections to be made but another review is unnecessary.)

In DFM our focus is on investigating distribution and change, rather than developing a state of the art process enactment system. There are therefore no specific proposals about a human computer interface, or facilities for integrating external tools.

4 Experiences with DFM

In order to investigate the Document Flow Model a sequential evaluator has been implemented. This is written in EuLisp [18], a modern object-oriented dialect of Lisp.

Actons, rules and documents are all modelled as objects, with their classes installed in the EuLisp object system. A document type is modelled as a class, with slots in that class representing document parts.

An acton engine maintains all actons in the system. Primitives are provided to the programmer to define new document types (which automatically generates new primitives to create instances of the document, and read and update it slots), create actons and send documents to actons.

Rules and bindings are special cases of sending a document to an acton. Adding a rule to an acton is the equivalent of sending it a document of type `add-rule` containing the rule to be added. Upon receipt of such a document, the acton engine automatically processes it by firing a pre-installed rule which installs and initializes the new rule. Bindings are added or updated when an acton receives a `set-binding` document.

Upon receipt of a standard document the acton engine places the document in the actons collection of documents (a slot in the acton object) and tests the document with permutations of existing documents against the guards of all the rules installed in the acton.

Once a network of actons has been defined, the system is run by starting a stepper. This requests a list of rules whose guards hold from each acton in the system. The stepper then presents all the ready rules in a menu, allowing the user to select a rule to fire. A new menu is then presented, and thus the user can direct the progress of all the actons in the system (figure 4).

A number of examples, covering a broad range of problems, have been written to test the model. These include the mobile phones example from Milner's π-calculus tutorial [16], a distributed solution to the dining philosophers problem taken from [15], and a distributed deadlock detection algorithm taken from [12].

A fully distributed implementation is under design using a Scheme compiler with a message passing library. It is envisaged that there will be multiple acton evaluators running on a network of heterogeneous machines, with 'listeners' providing interfaces to a number of users.

5 Related Work

5.1 The π-calculus

action terms A ::= $\bar{x}y.P$ send y along x

            $x(y).P$ receive any y along x

    terms P ::= $A\_1 + \ldots + A\_n$ alternative action

             $P\_1 \mid P\_2$ composition

             $\nu y P$ restriction (new y in P)

             $!P$ replication ($!P = P \mid !P$)

basic rule of computation :
$$x(y).P\_1[y] \mid \bar{x}z.P\_2 \rightarrow P\_1[z] \mid P\_2$$

Fig. 3. π-calculus constructs

"The π-calculus is a way of describing and analysing systems consisting of agents which interact among each other, and whose configuration or neighbourhood is continually changing" [16]. In the case of DFM the agents are actons and the changes in configuration are changes to their binding tables. In reasoning about DFM we have used π-calculus in its simplest form, the monadic π-calculus. For the sake of completeness we give a brief description here; for a fuller treatment please see [16, 17].

In the monadic π-calculus there are two entities. The most primitive is the name (or link, or channel). Processes are the only other entity in the system, with names used to specify links between processes. If two processes have access to a name (using normal lexical scoping rules) then those two processes can communicate using that name.

Communication between processes is synchronous. Values may be transmitted one way during a communication. In the case of the monadic π-calculus, only names may be transmitted during a communication. This implies that names are dynamic, allowing networks of processes to reconfigure themselves during execution.

Constructs for the specification and creation of processes allow systems to be defined. The dynamic nature of the π-calculus extends to processes, with constructs provided to create new processes during execution, again dynamically changing the structure of the network.

The constructs of the monadic π-calculus are shown in figure 3 (which is taken from [17]). Using π-calculus as a formalism for reasoning about DFM is based on the similarity between the basic rule of computation given in figure 3, and a system containing actons P1 and P2 where a rule in P2 performs

```
(setbinding mya1ref y (lookup-binding 'z))
```

where mya1ref in P2's binding table is the address of P1. This will result in P1's binding table having y bound to what P2 has bound to z.

In DFM we have talked about an acton's binding table containing the address of other actons, while π-calculus makes a policy of naming channels and not naming processes. In addition, π-calculus is based on synchronous communication while DFM is asynchronous. Despite these differences we have found π-calculus a powerful formalism for reasoning about DFM models. One approach to resolving the differences is to consider the address of an acton as just the ability to put a document in its in-tray. An acton is always ready to accept documents into its in-tray. The address can thus be thought of as the name of a channel which the acton will always receive input on. As far as the sending process can tell the communication is synchronous.

In the context of the example given above, the problem, which we have not yet solved, is how to formalize in the π-calculus the placing of the new value for y in P1's binding table.

In [16] the property that a name is uniquely handled, that is at any time only one process uses that name for input, is described. It is suggested that this is a property which you might want to ensure holds for a given process network, and a set of syntactic rules over a system described in π-calculus, which are sufficient to ensure this property is given. Thinking about this property in the context of DFM we can see that all names are uniquely handled because it is only the ability to use a name for output which is ever communicated over the network.

In order to address the communication of processes over channels as well as channels over channels, we are working informally with an extended CSP notation, which itself draws ideas from π-calculus. We would like to formalize this into a system which will help us both present and reason about the evolution of our systems.

In summary, we do not yet have a formal translation from DFM to the π-calculus, but it has proved very valuable in thinking about the evolving configuration of a DFM model, and we expect to do further work in this area.

5.2 Distributed Systems

Our current work on DFM does not address the issues of mapping distributed subprocesses to processors. There are benefits in supporting process migration, both in terms of effective machine utilisation, and providing support on a machine which a person is currently using. In the future we hope to make use of the techniques of ICSLA [19], a concurrent and distributed lisp which supports process migration. In contrast to DFM, ICSLA adopts a distributed shared memory concept so reasoning about a process's configuration involves reasoning about the variables which are in scope.

Our view of a process enactment systems as a set of independent processes linked by asynchronous communication is broadly the same as a number of other systems, notably Actors [1] and the ANSA architecture for distributed systems [2, 3, 4]. ANSA contrast their "open" distributed approach with systems "designed to work within 'closed' localized contexts, either within limited physical areas, or within limited logical boundaries" [3]. They propose that the open approach offers increased flexibility, scaleability and resilience. DFM provides an example of the "open" approach as a contrast to the current tendency for process enactment systems to be "closed". In ANSA the network evolution is achieved through trading: a process by which the services offered by servers and those requested by clients are matched. This is done by specific trader processes. The work on evolution within ANSA has mainly focussed on providing resilience to node failure, rather than evolution to support change.

The need to support change is addressed in configurable distributed systems [14, 15], and in particular in the approach of configuration programming. This "advocates the use of a separate language for describing program structure (configuration model) than that used for component programming (computation model)" [14]. In DFM we do not have such separate languages, however, there is a distinction between changes to the structure of the process network (changing actons' binding tables) and changes to the distributed sub-processes (adding and deleting rules). It is interesting to note that at least one configuration language has looked at π-calculus as an appropriate formalism [9].

5.3 Process Enactment Systems supporting Evolution

The IPSE 2.5 (now ProcessWise Integrator[4]) system [6, 7] has influenced DFM. It executes processes which are networks of PML roles linked by interactions. The evolution of the network is achieved by communicating interactions over interactions, while the evolution of roles is supported by incremental compilation using reflective features of the underlying implementation [11]. Unfortunately, the semantics of evolution in PML are complex. We believe that the simplicity of DFM offers a better framework for investigating process change. In addition, there are a few features of the system which rely on a "closed" world. An example is the ability of any role to make a synchronous, incremental change to any other role to which it has a reference. (A reference to a role is a pointer, and quite distinct from interactions which provide many-to-one asynchronous, buffered communication between roles.)

The SLANG system also uses reflective capabilities to support process evolution [5]. The system is based on hierarchical Petri-nets and sub-nets are represented as tokens which can be modified, prior to instantiation. The sub-net instantiation rules and synchronisation requirements mean that the transitions will be managed by a central server. This contrasts with DFM where there is a single level of actons which only require asynchronous communication between them.

In some process enactment systems, for example Process WEAVER [10] and EPOS [8], evolution is supported through the binding of process variables in an explicit instantiation phase before a process model fragment is executed. We believe that this could be subsumed, as it is in IPSE 2.5, by the sort of process change facilities we have described. However, the fact that this blurs the distinction between the process and the meta-process may be considered a disadvantage.

6 Discussion

We have adopted a viewpoint that many processes are inherently distributed, and therefore it is natural to develop distributed process enactment systems. In particu-

---

[4] The Alvey IPSE 2.5 project developed a process modelling language PML and a process control engine which executed PML models. This system was further developed first as PSS, and more recently as ICL's ProcessWise Integrator

lar, there are benefits in ensuring a close match between the structure of the process and the structure of an enactment system supporting the process. These systems can be viewed as a network where the nodes are distributed sub-processes, and the links are communication channels. In such a system we can categorize changes into three types:

mobility – a sub-process changing its neighbourhood, that is, changing the network configuration.

internal change – a sub-process changing its internal behaviour.

migration – changes of the mapping between the sub-processes and processors

This categorisation suggests an interplay between distribution and change which has influenced our decision to investigate them together. In our investigations we have used ideas from the related areas of π-calculus, which provides a formalism for reasoning about mobility, and distributed systems, where reflective capabilities and configuration languages have been used to address change issues.

The Document Flow Model (DFM) has been developed as a vehicle which we can use to test out our ideas. Initial experiences suggest that mobility is a common form of process change, and improved support for mobility encourages its use. The π-calculus is a fundamental calculus and we are working on how to use it to analyse DFM models. We expect that it will assist in both the rigourous definition of change in a DFM model, and in comparing the change capabilities of DFM with other process enactment systems.

References

1. G. A. Agha. *Actors: A Model of Concurrent Computation in Distributed Systems* MIT Press, Cambridge, Massachusetts, 1986.
2. ANSA: An engineer's introduction to the architecture. available from Architecture Projects Management Limited, November 1989. Release TR.03.02.
3. ANSA: A system designer's introduction to the architecture. available from Architecture Projects Management Limited, April 1991. Release RC.253.00.
4. ANSA: An application programmer's introduction to the architecture. available from Architecture Projects Management Limited, November 1991. Release TR.017.00.
5. S. Bandinelli and A. Fuggetta. Computational reflection in software process modelling: the SLANG approach. In *Proceeding of 15th International Conference on Software Engineering*, Baltimore, Maryland, May 17-23 1993.
6. R.F. Bruynooghe, R.M. Greenwood, I. Robertson, J. Sa, R.A. Snowdon, and B.C. Warboys. Towards a total process modelling system: A case study using ISPW-6. book chapter - in preparation.
7. R.F. Bruynooghe, J.M. Parker, and J.S. Rowles. PSS: A system for process enactment. In *Proceedings of the First International Conference on the Software Process*, pages 142–158, Redondo Beach, California USA, October 1991.
8. R. Conradi and M.L. Jaccheri Techniques for process model evolution in EPOS *IEEE Transactions in Software Engineering*, 19(9), September 1993. to appear.
9. S. Eisenbach and R. Paterson. π-calculus semantics for concurrent configuration language Darwin. to appear in Hawaii International Conference on System Sciences, Koloa, Hawaii, 1993.

10. C. Fernström. PROCESS WEAVER: Adding process support to UNIX. In *Proceedings of the Second International Conference on the Software Process*, pages 12–26, Berlin, Germany, February 1993.

11. R.M. Greenwood, M.R. Guy, and D.J.K. Robinson. The use of a persistent language in the implementation of a process support system. *ICL Technical Journal*, 8(1):108–130, May 1992.

12. S. Hilditch and T. Thomson. Distributed detection of deadlock. *ICL Technical Journal*, May 1993.

13. G. Kiczales, J. des Rivieres, and D. Bobrow. *The Art of the Metaobject Protocol.* MIT Press, Cambridge, Massachusetts, 1991.

14. J. Kramer. Configurable distributed systems - editorial. *Software Engineering Journal*, March 1993.

15. J. Kramer and J. Magee. The evolving philosophers problem: Dynamic change management. *IEEE Transactions on Software Engineering*, 16(11), November 1990.

16. R. Milner. The polyadic π-calculus: a tutorial. In *The Proceedings of the International Summer School on Logic and Algebra of Specification*, Marktobberdorf, 1991. modified version of Report ECS-LFCS-91-180 from LFCS Edinburgh.

17. R. Milner. Elements of interaction. *Communications of the ACM*, 36(1):78–89, January 1993.

18. J.A. Padget et al. Special edition of *Lisp and Symbolic Computation*, 6(1–2), September 1993.

19. C. Queinnec and D. De Roure. Design of a concurrent and distributed language. In *Parallel Symbolic Computing: Languages, Systems, and Applic ations*, Cambridge, Massachusetts, October 14-17 1992.

A   DFM Stepper Example

Figure 4 shows a primitive stepping interface to our example (see figure 1). At each step, the contents of all the actons' in-trays are show, followed by the rules which are currently ready to fire. One rule is selected and the system steps on. Note that after the ''Send Design for Rework'' rules (see figure 2), the next ''Do Design'' results in the design and report being sent straight to the acton Coding.

```
In Trays:
Designing: (#<Design: 22d410> #<ChangeReq: 22c738>)
Coding: ()
Reviewing: ()
Options:
1. Designing: Do Design
Stepper> 1

In Trays:
Designing: ()
Coding: ()
Reviewing: (#<Report: 2327d0> #<Design: 230648>)
Options:
1. Reviewing: Review decides Design ok
2. Reviewing: Review decides Design fails
3. Reviewing: Review decides Design needs rework
Stepper> 3

In Trays:
Designing: ()
Coding: ()
Reviewing: (#<Report: 2327d0> #<Design: 230648>)
Options:
1. Reviewing: Send Design for Rework
2. Reviewing: Review decision revoked
Stepper> 1

In Trays:
Designing: (#<Design: 230648> #<ChangeReq: 23e490>)
Coding: ()
Reviewing: ()
Options:
1. Designing: Do Design
Stepper> 1

In Trays:
Designing: ()
Coding: (#<Report: 2407e0> #<Design: 2401f8>)
Reviewing: ()
Options:
1. Coding: Do Coding
Stepper>
```

Fig. 4. DFM Stepper

Why is Process Modelling so Difficult?

Gernot Starke

Lehrstuhl Informatik III, Technical University of Aachen,
Ahornstr. 55, D-52074 Aachen, Germany
☎: (+49) (0)241-8021 311
Fax: (+49) (0)241-8021 329

E-Mail: gernot@rwthi3.informatik.rwth-aachen.de

Abstract. This paper outlines some major problems in software process modelling. The first is the *terminology* and *language* problem: there is still no accepted consensus among the process modelling community about a common terminology or appropriate modelling languages. Next we present the *type-instance* problem: process models are usually given on a *type* level, whereas activities are carried out on an *instance* level. Then we point out *reflexivity* as an inherent problem, followed by a brief discussion of process model *dynamics*. Finally there is a strong lack of appropriate process *standards*.

Introduction

There are several reasons why software process modelling is very different from other modelling disciplines:

- models of software development processes contains many *creative* activities, especially in requirements and design, which cannot be formally described.
- Process models contains many activities which are carried out by *humans rather than machines*. Human behaviour is error-prone and subject to a variety of modifications [Starke 93].
- Process structures are highly *dynamic* and are likely to *change during development*.

In the following paragraphs we detail some principal problems occurring in process modelling, namely the *terminology* and *language/paradigm* problem, the *type-instance* problem, furthermore *reflexivity*, *dynamics* and *standards*.

Problem 1: Terminology

Although Process Modelling has established its position within the software engineering community, still no agreed-upon common terminology exists. The approaches of [Dowson+91], [Feiler+93] and [Lonchamp 93] are excellent and complete introductions, but still some problems remain with these proposals:

- There should be a precise definition what the requirements of a process model are: Who are users of process models ?, Who expects what benefit? Those answers will be used to distinguish it from simple *work flow models*.
- It is distinguished between task (= managed process step) and activity (= unmanaged process step), but leave this decision completely to the process model designer. In our experience this distinction is too artificial and leads to a great deal of confusion among users.
- Real processes are based upon human interactions like decisions, argumentations, discussions etc. A terminology should support those concepts.

- It is not distinguished between *goal* and the *actions* which satisfy that goal. Often the actions are not specified, but left over to the actor.
- *Resources* can evolve from artifacts. For example a result (=artifact) of an early activity within the process model could be the construction of a test-tool, which is definitely a resource in later phases. Such typical type-changes of process entities have to be supported.

Problem 2: Languages and Paradigms

A variety of about 50 different languages and paradigms exist to model software processes. Still no approach exists to systematically evaluate these languages or paradigms. The effort of the International Software Process Workshops (e.g. [Kellner+90]) in that direction has not been continued systematically. It requires a common terminology (see problem 1 above).

Problem 3: Types and Instances

Every system can be structured from several perspectives. The most important from the *construction* point of view are the product (PS) and activity structures (AS). An example is given in figure 1.

Each of the perspectives PS and AS can have a hierarchical substructure of arbitrary depth. At the leafs of the resulting structure trees the basic building blocks respectively the basic process activities are listed. These are called product respectively activity *instances*.

The problem is that the complete structures are not known in advance. A process model is therefore a more or less rough anticipation of what those structures will look like. They are determined in detail during the actual system development.

There is no principle difference between the dynamic behaviour of activity and product structure. Both evolve during system development time, both are completely known by the end of the project.

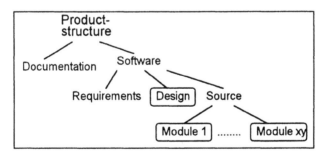

Figure 1: *Sample product structure*

A closer inspection of the term *activity* shows, that there exist two interpretations:
1. activity *type*, denoting that (during actual development) several *instances* of that activity have to be created. Example: the implementation activity, where a distinct instance of that activity *type* has to be created for every module that will be implemented.

2. activity *instance*, denoting a distinct piece of work carried out during actual development. An example is the activity *implement user interface module.* Activity instances work on product instances, in this case on the user interface module and the design document (in contrast: Activity *types* refer to both product *types* and product *instances*.)

In the example the number of *instances* of the implementation activity (= the number of modules to be implemented, see figure 2) is determined by the contents of the system design document. This serves as a typical example of the tight relationship between activity and product structure. In general an arbitrary number of instances might be created from every activity *type* during development. The scenario is clarified in figure 2.

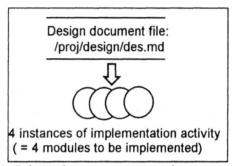

Figure 2: *Relation between structure and contents (example)*

A result from this observation is that parts of the activity structure are determined by contents of elements of the product structure. In virtually every development process several activities are determined by contents of certain sub-products. Main consequence is the inherent *reflexivity* of process models: a detailed process model can only be constructed during development by taking into account contents of the process model itself, namely results of prior activities. Contents of documents have to be interpreted during run-time of the process.

Most existing approaches to software process modelling fail to recognise the reflexivity as an important property of processes and therefore process models.

Problem 4: Dynamic Changes
Within any development process a variety of dynamic changes is likely to occur, which can alter process structure. Examples include schedule and budget modifications, changes to user requirements, change of implementation paradigm etc.

In most cases these changes induce changes to the underlying process model. Then the question arises, which of the already produced results are still valid or needed within the new model. Obviously it is impractical to start the complete process over from scratch in case of a model modification.

Problem 5: Standards
From the field of software quality, several standards are known: ISO 9000-9004, DoD 2167, AQUAP 13 etc. They provide both customers and developers with a

mutual understanding of the quality assurance activities and required documents. Furthermore compliance to standards is often used as an acquisition instrument.

Industrial practice would need process standards, as the existing standardisation approaches like the official German V-model or the ISO (draft) process standard do not tackle the problems mentioned so far.

Conclusion

We are currently systematically evaluating process modelling languages by mapping the appropriate language constructs to the elements of an abstract *basic terminology*: how does this language represent the basic process elements? By comparing these mappings it is possible to judge the suitability for specific purposes.

Furthermore we are working on formalising the *instantiation* process from *type* to *instance* level within process models.

Bibliography

[Dowson+91]   M. Dowson, B. Nejmeh & W. Riddle. Fundamental Software Process Concepts. Proceedings of the First European Workshop on Software Process Modelling, CEFRIEL, Mailand, Italien, Mai 1991, pp 15-38, AICA (Italian Computer Association)

[Feiler+93]   P. Feiler & W. Humphrey. Software Process Development and Enactment: Concepts and Definitions. Proceedings of the Second International Conference on the Software Process, Februar 1993, Berlin, pp. 28-40. IEEE Computer Society Press, 1993.

[Kellner+90]   M.I. Kellner & H.D. Rombach. Comparisons of Software Process Descriptions. In: T. Katayama, editor. Proceedings of the 6th International Software Process Workshop, Hakodate, Japan, Oktober 1990, pp. 7-18. IEEE Computer Society Press.

[Lonchamp 93]   J. Lonchamp. A Structured Conceptual and Terminological Framework for Software Process Engineering. Proceedings of the Second International Conference on the Software Process, Februar 1993, Berlin, pp. 41-53. IEEE Computer Society Press, 1993

[Starke 93]   Gernot Starke. People and Process Models. In: Proceeding of the International Conference on Information Technology and People, Moscow, Russia, May 1993, pp. II/112-II-120. Published by the Institute for Scientific and Technical Information, Kuusinena str. 21-b, Moscow, Russia.

Acknowledgements

The author would like to thank Uli, Stefan Hardt and Professor Gerhard Chroust for interesting comments and fruitful discussions, not only on the Software Process.

Modelling Processes with Constraints

R. Mark Greenwood

University of Southampton
Department of Electronics and Computer Science
Southampton SO9 5NH *

Introduction

Process change was a major theme of EWSPT'92, and has received a good deal of attention within the software process community [1, 4, 8, 10]. However, most of this attention has been on the process change mechanisms which enable a process support environment to cope with evolving processes. This position paper outlines a constraint-oriented process modelling language (coPML) which aims to assist in the design of process changes. The description uses a small example based on two of Dowson's global process constraints [5]. In this way, coPML begins to address another EWSPT'92 challenge, "that emerging process modelling languages do not appear to lend themselves to writing global process constraints" [4].

Process Design Focus

In developing coPML, the target users are process designers. They need the ability to produce a number of process descriptions which can be discussed, examined, refined and so on. Processes are about what happens over a period of time, but it is not easy to infer this dynamic behaviour from a textual or graphical description, especially when changes are being considered. In coPML this investigation of process behaviour is supported by enabling designers to "play" coPML models, as executable specifications.

Constraint Focus

We believe that many processes can be efficiently specified by a number of constraints. In addition, the adding, removing, relaxing or strengthening of these constraints is a natural way for these processes to evolve. By capturing constraints directly, such changes can be reflected by small changes in the model. This increases the designers' capability to do rapid prototyping and investigate alternative designs. (In contrast, our experience with PSS' PML[2] [2] suggests that in many process modelling formalisms a conceptually small change in the process can result in large

---

* email: rmg91r@ecs.soton.ac.uk

[2] PML was developed in the Alvey IPSE 2.5 project, which developed a process support system programmed in PML. This system was further developed as PSS, and renamed as ICL's ProcessWise Integrator

changes in the model.) The use of constraints complements the executable specification focus. The process is captured in a declarative manner, but the execution capability enables designers to understand the implied dynamic behaviour pattern.

coPML example

The basic concepts of coPML are entities, invariants and events. These will be described in the context of a simple example development process. This process involves a team of people who have to code and test a number of modules. Initially, there are only two constraints (based on those given in [5]):

1. No person should be allocated more than three jobs simultaneously. (Coding one module is a single job.)
2. All modules should be independently tested

The basic approach of coPML is to express these constraints as invariants which apply to **entities**. This is an object-based approach: the model is composed of instances of entity classes, and the aim is to have a simple mapping between the "real world" and the model. In the example there are two entity classes: Person and Module. Each entity has:

- a *State*,
- *Operations* which may modify its state,
- *Invariants* which are predicates over the state.

An entity is considered to be in a valid state if its state satisfies all its **invariants**. At any time the operations which an entity can engage in are precisely those which leave it in a valid state.

In the example, a Person entity might simply have a state giving the list of jobs allocated to that person, and an invariant:

$$0 \leq length(PersonState) \leq 3$$

which states that the length of this list is always between 0 and 3. It will also have operations which add a new job, and remove a job.

In coPML operations do not call operations of other entities; the synchronisation of operations is done by **events**. The events also manage any exchange of data between entities which is required. The event instances provide the alphabet for observing and interacting with the model as it executes. (There is a strong link here with process algebras such as CSP [7], CCS, π-calculus [9].) Each event instance refers to a number of entity instances, which will normally be passed to the event's constructor function. For example, assigning events:

$$AssignCode(p1, m1), AssignCode(p1, m2), AssignCode(p1, m3)$$
$$AssignTest(p1, m1), AssignTest(p1, m2), AssignTest(p1, m3) \ldots$$
$$where\ p1\ is\ a\ Person\ and\ m1, m2, m3\ are\ Modules.$$

An *AssignCode* event will involve an operation call on each of the person and module involved. If three assigns are done for person *p1*, then the constraint above will ensure future assigns for *p1* are impossible until one of the jobs has been done. In addition, once *AssignCode(p1,m1)* is done an invariant will ensure that *AssignTest(p1,m1)* is no longer a valid event. Each event has two parts: a guard and an action. The guard part is a predicate which returns true if the event is valid, that is, it would not result in any entity being in an invalid state. The action part corresponds to the event occurring and actually updates the entities.

The mode of interaction is that the user is presented with a list of valid next events, picks one which is performed, giving a new set of next events, and so on. In addition, it is also possible to investigate change by modifying the constraints (perhaps allowing one person to be allocated up to five jobs simultaneously) during an interaction. In this manner the changes which can be modelled are more than simply several instantiations of a generic model with different parameters.

The generic approach to developing a coPML model can be summarised:

1. define Entity classes,
2. define Event classes,
3. create Entity instances,
4. create Event instances,
5. interact with model to observe its behaviour,
6. if necessary revise and repeat,
   or alter entity instance invariants to reflect a change and continue interaction.

In the example, it is quickly revealed that the above two constraints are insufficient to precisely describe the process which we have in mind. A number of other constraints need to be added. Perhaps:

- all modules must be coded before they are tested,
- jobs must be allocated before they are done,
- a constraint covering the re-allocation of jobs, etc.

Discussion

The aim of coPML is to provide a process modelling formalism which enables designers to rapidly produce executable models and investigate alternative processes. Its ability to assist in process change design is dependent on most likely changes being reflected in simple changes to the model. Initial investigations on a range of exemplar processes are encouraging; constraints appear to be a good unit of changeability.

The development of coPML is ongoing. We are developing a suite of exemplar models to evaluate and refine the ideas. These, including the one described here, have been developed in Peter Henderson's object-oriented modelling language *enact* [6]. One future refinement is to extend events so that they include the dynamic creation of entity and event instances. In the area of modelling change, one planned experiment is to make entity invariants part of the entity's state. This would allow us to model processes which control their own evolution.

We have not achieved Mark Dowson's aim of representing global process constraints. This can be approached by attaching invariants to an entity class rather than an entity instance, ensuring that all instances of the class satisfy the invariant.

There is scope for expanding the types of constraint which coPML can handle; we hope to adopt techniques from other constraint languages such as Prolog-III [3].

Of course step-through simulation does not prove that a model is correct. Such proof requires the ability to formally reason about coPML models which is an area of future work. As the current evolution of coPML is based on a number of small exemplar processes, there is a need for further investigation on how well it scales up to cope with larger processes.

Acknowledgements

Thanks are due to the Southampton University Process Modelling Group: Peter Henderson, David De Roure, and Neil Berrington. They, along with colleagues from Manchester University and ICL's Process Support team, have been the source of many fruitful discussions. The author is supported by an SERC studentship.

References

1. S. Bandinelli and A. Fuggetta. Computational reflection in software process modelling: the SLANG approach. In *Proceedings of ICSE 15*, 1993.
2. R.F. Bruynooghe, R.M. Greenwood, I. Robertson, J. Sa, R.A. Snowdon, and B.C. Warboys. Towards a total process modelling system: A case study using ISPW-6. book chapter - in publication.
3. Alain Colmerauer. An introduction to Prolog-III. *Communications of the ACM*, 33(7):69-90, July 1990.
4. J.C. Derniame. EWSPT'92 report. In *Proc of the Second International Conference on the Software Process*, pages 160–164, Berlin, Germany, February 1993. IEEE Computer Society Press.
5. M. Dowson. Software process themes and issues. In *Proc of the Second International Conference on the Software Process*, pages 54–62, Berlin, Germany, February 1993. IEEE Computer Society Press.
6. Peter Henderson. *Object-Oriented Specification and Design with C++*. International Series in Software Engineering. McGraw-Hill, 1993.
7. C.A.R. Hoare. *Communicating Sequential Processes*. Prentice-Hall International Series in Computer Science. Prentice-Hall, 1985.
8. Karen E. Huff and Gail E. Kaiser. Change in the software process - session summary. In *Proc of the Seventh International Software Process Workshop*, pages 10–13, Yountville, California, October 1991. IEEE Computer Society Press.
9. Robin Milner. Elements of interaction. *Communications of the ACM*, 36(1):78–89, January 1993.
10. R.A. Snowdon. An example of process change. In J.C. Derniame, editor, *Software Process Technology: Second European Workshop, EWSPT'92*, pages 178–195, Trondheim, Norway, September 1992. Springer-Verlag. Lecture Notes in Computer Science 635.

Goal Oriented vs. Activity Oriented Process Modelling and Enactment: Issues and Perspectives

Selma Arbaoui and Flavio Oquendo

CRISS – Université Pierre Mendès France
B.P. 47 - 38040 Grenoble Cédex 9 - FRANCE
E-mails: {arbaoui, oquendo}@criss.fr

1 Introduction

The study of current software process models suggests a set of requirements that a software process modelling formalism must meet [Arbaoui & Oquendo 1991]. Among these, in order to support real industrial software processes, an important requirement is:

> *The formalism should support dynamic ordering of software process activities.*

The main rational of this requirement is that a Process Sensitive Environment (PSE) must provide assistance to software process performers rather than to prescribe them a rigid process model. If orderings of activities can be dynamically built and modified, i.e. during model enactment, the PSE enactment engine will be able to continue to support and assist process performance. Otherwise, process performance will diverge from process enactment, and thereby no process support will be possible [Dowson 1992], [Arbaoui & Oquendo 1993b].

When we examine how some existing software process modelling formalisms meet this requirement we remark that there are two approaches: the activity oriented and the goal oriented. We present in this paper, the definition of these approaches, their advantages and drawbacks and how they are used by some of the studied systems. We propose as perspective an approach based on both concepts, i.e. goal and activity, for modelling and enacting software processes.

2 The activity oriented approach

In the activity oriented approach, ordering of activities is a function of these activities, i.e. during process modelling we describe possible sequences of activities that should be performed (the *how*). Environments based on this approach are called *prescriptive* [Heimbigner 1990] to indicate that the process model and the enactment engine closely control the order in which activities have to be performed.

Advantages

Therefore, in the activity oriented approach, i.e. in a prescriptive environment, modelling a software process requires the description of all the process activities along with their scheduling, i.e. possible orderings of activities are pre-established, and the enactment of the resulting model constrains performers to carry out the process exactly as it was described[1]. Modelling, enacting and performing software processes in such environments have several advantages:

- Process models that are built following an activity oriented approach are in general precise, unambiguous and understandable. Indeed, all the activities that compose a process are detailed in the model along with their scheduling.
- The enactment of such process models is easy to realise and the model enactment control is facilitated by the fact that all process characteristics are defined in the model. Therefore supervising process model enactment requires only to check if the process state is consistent with what is described in the model.
- Prescriptive environments can provide an effective support to software process performance. This is the case when performers are for example novices that have to follow a particular software method. A prescriptive environment provide substantial feedback to the performer when s/he deviates from the specified process or ignores at a given time the way to pursue process performance.

Drawbacks

However, prescriptive environments often fail in supporting real industrial software processes. Their drawbacks related to modelling and performance support are:

- Modelling software processes in this approach requires a beforehand knowledge of the complete software process. The process engineer has to forecast all the exceptional situations that may occur during the process model enactment. This is the case for foreseen activities in an unforeseen order and the case of unforeseen activities. The ordering of activities is predetermined and any exception must be handled by changing the process model by hand, in advance.
- In the most general case, process performance support in prescriptive environments is too restrictive. Indeed, the control is taken away by the environment, and performers creativity and flexibility is limited.

3 The goal oriented approach

In the goal oriented approach, ordering of activities is a function of stated objectives, i.e. during process modelling, we describe the objectives that must be satisfied (the *what*) [Thomas 1989]. The environments based on this approach are called *proscriptive* [Heimbigner 1990] to indicate that the process model and the enactment engine only proscribe inappropriate performers activities. They do not impose the means and order in which activities have to be performed. These are a function of the process goal.

---

[1] In general, prescriptive environments do not provide a total order of activities, partial orders are often possible.

Advantages

In this approach, i.e. in a proscriptive environment, modelling a software process requires to describe *what* the results should be when performing a process activity, i.e. to describe the activity's goal. When such a process model is enacted, the proscriptive environment suggests all sequences of activities that lead to the process goal, while taking into account the process state and the performers needs. Ordering of activities is built as the process model enactment proceeds and there is not a pre-established ordering of activities. This approach succeeds where the activity oriented approach fails, its main advantages are:

— Modelling software processes in the goal oriented approach does not require the knowledge of all the activities of a process or of all possible orderings. Indeed, the process engineer has not to describe *how* process activities have to be carried out.
— In a goal oriented approach, unforeseen situations can easily be handled by a proscriptive environment without requiring their description in advance into the process model.
— Performance support in proscriptive environments is not restrictive. As the scheduling of the activities is built during enactment time, enactment is no more controlled only by the environment but by both the environment and the user performer. Process performers are no longer limited on how to do their work, they cooperate with the environment by providing to the enactment engine process performance feedbacks and by doing their work in the best way.

Drawbacks

The goal oriented approach drawbacks are:

— The process models that are built following a goal oriented approach are more difficult to understand as they do not represent a detailed description of the ordering of process activities. Enacting and monitoring such models is also more difficult and the enactment engine has often to handle the problem of multiple choices, i.e. when there are several solutions that lead to a given goal.
— The software process performance support that is provided by the proscriptive environment is for some cases of performance too loose. For example, performers may hope that the enactment engine take away the control for some process steps. It is also more advisable that a novice performer have a more restrictive process performance support for following a software process model.

4 Related work

Most of the systems presented in the literature follow an activity oriented approach where scheduling is static. The ARCADIA [Taylor et al. 1988] project is an example where activity ordering is governed by procedural language control structures. ARCADIA-APPL/A is one of the systems that is strongly prescriptive. Even though control structures are less rigid in other proposals, the scheduling remains static.

This is the case for Petri nets based systems like MELMAC [Deiters & Gruhn 1990], PRISM [Madhavji & Gruhn 1990], and ProcessWeaver [Fernstrom 1993]. There are other systems that can be considered as being weakly prescriptive. Indeed in their process modelling formalisms there exist no control structures that govern ordering of activities. This is the case for MARVEL [Kaiser & Feiler 1987], HFSP [Katayama 1989] and ADELE/TEMPO [Belkhatir et al. 1993] where ordering of activities is respectively determined by the pre and postconditions, the inputs and outputs, and trigger rules. Nevertheless, these systems do not provide some of the proscriptive environment's advantages such as exception handling.

Two systems follow a goal oriented approach, they are GRAPPLE [Huff 1989] and the system that we have developed, PEACE [Arbaoui & Oquendo 1993a], [Arbaoui 1993]. The goal oriented approach was realised by using planning technics in GRAPPLE and a logic based formalism in PEACE. In these systems, modelling a process step requires the specification of its goal and enacting a process model fragment requires the achievement of its goal, i.e. by using planning in GRAPPLE and reasoning in PEACE. These two systems are proscriptive, they support dynamic ordering of process activities and exception handling.

5 The mixed approach: goal and activity oriented

We can conclude from the analysis of advantages and drawbacks that the goal oriented approach is more appropriate to handle dynamic ordering of software processes activities. However the activity oriented approach is more appropriate to enforce possible orderings of software process activities.

The two approaches are in fact complementary, i.e. prescriptive environments fail where proscriptive environments succeed and vice versa. The advantages of both approaches may lead to process definitions that may range from statically defined to dynamically computed orderings of process activities. This conclusion suggests that Process Sensitive Environments must support both approaches.

Our previous work on software process has investigated the two approaches. The ALF/MASP process modelling formalism [Oquendo et al. 1991] provides an activity oriented approach where activities (called operator types) are described in terms of pre and postconditions and orderings may be expressed to define possible sequences of operator types (those that are designated in the orderings). The PEACE process modelling formalism as cited so far is goal-oriented. Activities are described in terms of goals that must be achieved by their sub-activities and so on. An inference engine constructs plans of possible sequences of activities according to the activities' goals and the process state.

The next step on our work will be to investigate how to combine the two approaches. Among the advantages that a mixed approach can provide, we can mention the following ones:

- Software process modelling using a mixed approach will result in understandable and more complete process models. Indeed, both goal and activities will be explicitly described as well as their interrelationships. The activity oriented approach will be used for modelling process steps if the process engineer needs to enforce ordering of activities (this will be probably the case for large grain process models where the process model is also a function of the organisation structure and resource constraints). The goal oriented approach will be used for modelling process steps if the process engineer does not need to constrain ordering of activities, however the goal of the activities needs to be precisely identified (this will be probably the case for finer grain process models, e.g. at the individual level or at the interaction level).

— Software process enactment following the mixed approach will provide several kinds of assistance. For example, if the project manager decides that some process activities have to be performed according to a predetermined ordering, then the corresponding process model fragment must be enacted following an activity oriented approach. Otherwise, a performer may request to the environment how to satisfy the activity goal.

Our proposal is to enhance PEACE with a three-level process modelling formalism. The extended PEACE environment will provide a formalism for describing process models according to three levels:

— The strategic level: a process model is described in terms of a directed acyclic graph of goals;
— The tactic level: if there is a strategic level, each goal is associated to a set of activities that may be used to satisfy it; if not, activities are associated to activities, called its sub-activities.
— The operational level: a set of ordering constraints may be specified to each set of activities, thereby enforcing ordering of activities.

The mapping among these three levels will be supported by the PEACE process enactment engine that will enact the process models according to their degrees of definition.

Using the three-level process modelling formalism a process model may be described according to:

— a pure goal oriented approach: the strategic and tactic levels are defined, no operational level is provided;
— a pure activity oriented approach: the tactic and operational levels are defined, no strategic level is provided;
— a mixed approach: the strategic and tactic levels are defined, and some operational levels are provided.

It is worth to note that in this mixed approach the goal oriented paradigm will be the basis for process definition; the activity oriented paradigm may be seen as enforced plans for reaching defined goals.

Acknowledgements

We wish to thank all the members of the GPG (*Grenoble Process Group*) for useful discussions and for their contributions to the ideas presented in this paper. The Grenoble Process Group (GPG) is composed by members of the following organisations: Cap Gemini Innovation, CRISS (Université Pierre Mendès France) and LGI (Université Joseph Fourier).

References

[Arbaoui 1993] Arbaoui, S., "PEACE : Un formalisme fondé sur une logique modale pour la modélisation des processus logiciels évolutifs et non-monotones", *Thèse de Doctorat*, Université Pierre Mendès France, Grenoble, France, July 1993 (in French).

[Arbaoui & Oquendo 1991] Arbaoui, S. and Oquendo, F., "Où en est la modélisation du processus de production du logiciel?", *Proceedings of the 4th International Conference on Software Engineering and its Applications*, Toulouse, France, 1991 (in French).

[Arbaoui & Oquendo 1993a] Arbaoui, S. and Oquendo, F., "The PEACE Project: Goal Oriented Approach and Nonmonotonic Process Modelling", in *Advances in Software Process Technology*, Research Studies Press (J. Wiley) (book to appear in 1994).

[Arbaoui & Oquendo 1993b] Arbaoui, S. and Oquendo, F., "Managing Inconsistencies between Process Enactment and Process Performance States", *Proceedings of the 8th International Software Process Workshop (ISPW-8)*, Dagstuhl, Germany, March 1993.

[Belkhatir et al. 1993] Belkhatir, N., Estublier, J., Melo, W. L., "Software Process Model and Work Space Control in the Adele System" *Proceedings of the 2nd International Conference on the Software Process*, Berlin, Germany, February, 1993.

[Deiters & Gruhn 1990] Deiters, W., Gruhn, V., "Managing Software Processes in the Environment MELMAC", *Proceedings of the fourth ACM SIGSOFT Symposium on Software Development Environments*, Irvine, California, December 1990.

[Dowson 1992] Dowson, M., "Consistency Maintenance in Process Sensitive Environments", *Proceedings of the Process Sensitive SEE Architectures Workshop*, Boulder, September 1992.

[Fernstrom 1993] Fernstrom, C., "PROCESS WEAVER: Adding Process Support to UNIX", *Proceedings of the 2nd International Conference on the Software Process*, Berlin, Germany, February, 1993.

[Heimbigner 1990] Heimbigner, D., "Proscription versus Prescription in Process-Centered Environments", *Proceedings of the 6th International Software Process Workshop*, Hakodate, Japon, October 1990.

[Huff 1989] Huff, K. E., "Plan-Based Intelligent Assistance: An approach to supporting the software development process", *Ph.D. Thesis*, Department of Computer and Information Science, University of Massachusetts, September 1989.

[Kaiser & Feiler 1987] Kaiser, G. E. and Feiler, P. H., "An architecture for intelligent assistance in software development", *Proceedings of the 9th International Conference on Software Engineering*, Monterey, March 1987.

[Katayama 1989] Katayama, T., "A Hierarchical and Functional Approach to Software Process Description", *Proceedings of the 4th International Software Process Workshop*, ACM Software Engineering Notes. Vol. 14, No. 4, June 1989.

[Madhavji & Gruhn 1990] Madhavji, N. H., et Gruhn, V., "PRISM = Methodology + Process-Oriented Environment", *Proceeding of 12th conference on Software Engineering*, Nice, France, 1990.

[Oquendo et al. 1991] Oquendo, F., Zucker, J-D., Griffiths, Ph., "The MASP Approach to Software Process Description, Instantiation and Enaction", *Proceedings of the First European Workshop on Software Process Modelling*, Milan, Italy, May 1991.

[Taylor et al. 1988] Taylor, R. N., Belz, F. C., Clarke, L. A., Osterweill, L., Selby, R. W., Wileden, J. C., Wolf, A. L., Young, M., "Foundations for the Arcadia Environment Architecture", *Proceedings of the 3rd ACM Software Engineering Symposium on Practical Software Development Environments*, Boston, Massachusetts, November 1988.

[Thomas 1989] Thomas, I., "The Software Process as a Goal-directed Activity", *Proceedings of the 5th International Software Process Workshop*, September 1989.

Software Process Design Based on Products and the Object Oriented Paradigm

Joachim Tankoano[1] , Jean-Claude Derniame[2] and Ali B. Kaba[2]

[1] Université de Ouagadougou (ESI) - 03 B.P. 7021 Ouagadougou 03 - Burkina Faso
[2] CRIN-Bâtiment Loria BP 239 - 54506 Vandoeuvre-Les-Nancy - France

Abstract. In the object oriented paradigm, the class concept allows us to abstract a collection of objects sharing the same structural and behavioral knowledge. Structural knowledge describes the static structure of objects and behavioral knowledge describes messages that can be processed by objects. This article proposes a new kind of knowledge which describes construction process of complex and composite objects, in addition to the structural and behavioral knowledge of classes. This knowledge is called genetic knowledge and is introduced to allow a software process modeling based on products and the object oriented paradigm.

1 Introduction

In the previous process modeling works, the approaches relying on activities have been privileged. In these approaches, the description of development objects and activities is based either on multiparadigm formalisms [Chr 93] [Der 92] [Peu 92] [Kat 89], or on a unique object centered formalism [Sno 92] [Con 92]. This orientation has been positively influenced by activity-based approaches normally used for applications design in industrial process control field and by some important similarities between these two classes of problems. In this paper, we discuss about some noticeable differences between the both classes of problems, to justify the exploration of another approach for software process modeling:

- Industrial processes are indeed characterized by a very few volume of persistent data and by the simultaneous production of a great number of instances of a same product. On the opposite, software processes generate a great number of complex and multiform persistent data and are used by one or many persons in a collaborative manner, to produce only one instance of a product.
- Corollary, in process control applications, the main problem can be reduced to the maintenance of an ordering relation between entry and exit events. Products are not of great interest. They are of interest only through some events noting their state evolution. In these applications, it is mainly the environment view (i.e. the machines, robots, trucks, atmospheric conditions,...) that has the first order role. For software processes, the main problem is somewhat different. It can be reduced to the definition of a scenario to organize the activities for building or modifying the components of a product, using if necessary other products and resources. As a consequence, the view of products is more important and is of more interest than the view of

activities. Indeed, the view of products structure seems to be more stable than the activities organization which can be adapted or replaced depending on criteria such as project size, partners expertise, applications class, etc... Moreover, the activities are firstly defined according to the products characteristics[Huf 90]. In fact, it seems more instructive to bring the software process issues closer to those of biological development. The section 7 highlights this metaphor.

On the other hand, it is fundamental to be able to reuse, adapt and enhance a software process. In the other classes of problems having this requirements, the object centered approaches provide good solutions [Nar 88].

So, we will consider an approach for software development process modeling that relies on two fundamental points :

- First, the process model designer has to pay more attention to the view of products than to the view of activities. As a consequence, he has to regard a product as something characterized by its *sub-products* and by *decisions*, both implying activities to be arranged. In other words, he has to think about the activities only through the results he pursues.
- Next, he has to integrate *structural*, *behavioral* and also *genetic* knowledge in a uniform framework which is centered on object. That will give to the system a reflective capacity and a support for dynamic evolution. This knowledge is essentially used to characterize respectively the *products structure*, their *applicable tools* and their *development process*.

In the recent works, some authors have also proposed an exploration of approaches which are not activity-based ones [Fut 89] [Nak 89] [Tho 89].

This paper presents basic concepts chosen to define software process in our approach, an outline of the representation of these concepts using frames, an overview of how to use these concepts, some extensions to knowledge representation languages based on frames related to genetic knowledge requisition and to implementation features, finally, the main advantages of this approach.

2 Basic Concepts

They are the concepts of meta-model, model and instance which are very closed to those of meta-class, class and instance of the object oriented paradigm [Mas 91].

Model: The concept of model is used to abstract structural, behavioral and genetic knowledge units, related to concepts of a reference universe, in which we can find out:

- products types of large and fine granularity (ex : the concept of requirements set, the concept of module, the concept of entity in E/R model, the concept of control point report,...),
- tools,

- concepts from the environment enacting the process (ex : role, resource, processor, directory,...),
- or concepts used when formalizing knowledge described in meta-model, models and instances (ex : attributes, facets).

One of the main particularities of the model concept against the class concept is that classes don't have genetic knowledge. The representation of this knowledge through the model concept is investigated in the section 6.

The software process designer expresses its process essentially in terms of products models. He can complete these products models with the models of concepts from the enactment environment, in order to consider organizational rules related to the cooperative work and to the project management.

Instance: End users of a software process model define their products in terms of instances. The role of the models is to help users for creating these instances, using knowledge they hold on their structure, on their behavior and, may be, on their development process. Instances built from a model have an identical structure, derived from the model. Instances cannot be used to generate other instances.

Meta-Model: The meta-model is predefined. It is used by the software process model designer to create his models. It encompasses knowledge on the structure and the behavior of each model.

3 The Representation of Basic Concepts

Meta-model, models and instances are objects, represented in the enactment environment using the concept of frame [Mas 91] [Min 75]. This generic concept, which has already raised an interest for descriptive knowledge representation in AI., permits to implement a reflective environment by defining each of theses objects by means of a list of couples (attribute-value), where each attribute is represented by an object (instance of the model "attribute-model") and each value is represented by an object (instance of the model "value-model").

The attributes of a frame representing an attribute are the facets of this attribute. The facets are used for associating to this attribute different characteristics such as its type, its default value, the mean to infer its value, the assertion that has to be always verified by its value,...

Likewise, the attributes of a frame representing a value are used for characterizing the value of an attribute with its ancient versions, its creation date,...

The main advantages of this representation are mentioned in section 7.

4 Objects Base Organization

The organization model of the objects base bears some similarities with ObjVlisp Model [Coi 87].

Indeed, the objects (meta-model, models, instances) form an instantiation tree. The root of this tree is the predefined object "meta-model", which is also its own instance (c.f. fig.1). So, each object is an instance of another which holds knowledge on its structure, on its behavior and possibly on its manufacturing process.

In another way, the object "meta-model" and the objects "models" constitute an inheritance tree. The root of this tree is a predefined model called *basic-model* (c.f. fig.1). The basic-model contains properties which can be inherited by the meta-model and by any model. Every model inherits especially the capability of creating instances from the basic-model. In the following, models from which a model inherits its properties will be called *super-models*. According to the frame theory, the attributes of a model define only the points which distinguish it from its super-models. They can be new attributes, or redefined attributes. Each model dynamically inherits[3] the attributes from its super-models.

In addition, instances of the models that define a software process and its environment can be bound by more specific semantics links described in these models (composition link, derivation link, ...)

5   Principles for the Software Process Modeling Approach

The definition of a development process with the concept of model can be done indifferently following a top-down, a bottom-up or a mixed approach.

In a top-down approach, the starting point has to be the definition of an "embryo" model of product. The purpose of this model is to allow the creation of instances without particular genetic knowledge. As a consequence, its structure has always to be simple. Particulary, it has to have only one sub-product which is the product to elaborate. Obviously, genetic knowledge on how to build it has to be in the embryo. From this point, the process designer has to define the model of the product to build by defining its structure in a high level of abstraction, its behavior and the development process of its sub-products. This refinement process is recursively repeated for each identified sub-product, until all sub-product are terminals (i.e. such that there exists a predefined process or tool to build their instances).

In a bottom-up approach, the process designer defines new products models combining already defined ones.

Practically, software process modeling is never linear but follows a mixed approach, i.e. by means of decomposition and integration.

---

[3] With the class concept, the inheritance is static in a sense that each instance of a class contains, as its own attributes, the attributes defined by its class and those defined in and automatically inherited from its super-classes. On the other hand, with the frame concept, each instance of a frame contains, as its own attributes, only the attributes defined by its frame and those inherited from its super-frames but redefined in its frame. Others attributes of its super-frames are dynamically inherited, when necessary.

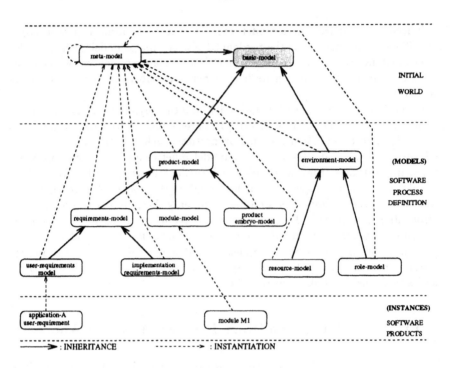

Fig. 1. Objets inheritance and instantiation trees

6 Extensions of Frame-based Knowledge Representation Languages

6.1 Facets

The facets supported by a knowledge representation language based on frames depend on the class of considered applications and change from one language to another. Here, for the representation of meta-model, models and instances using frames, we need facets of general usage, such as :

- facets for typing ($is-a, $list-of, $domain, $range, $cardinality, $default, $value,...),
- daemon facets ($if-needed, $require, $if-success, $if-failure, $if-added, $if-removed,...)

and also more specific facets. We will limit this presentation to new facets directly related to software process modeling.

The facets $new-ordering and $additive-ordering: These facets permit to associate to an attribute designating a sub-product, some ordering constraints on the activities related to the manufacture or to the modification of this sub-product. *These facets and usual daemon facets allow to define the genetic knowl-*

edge of a sub-product. In the case of the $additive-ordering facet, when the concerned attribute is inherited, the introduced ordering constraints are added to the inherited ones. But, with the $new-ordering facet, the inherited constraints are overriden.

The facet $init-params: It allows the process designer to associate to an attribute designating a sub-product, the definition of the parameters which will have to be provided by the end user, before triggering the activity linked to this sub-product. For instance, these parameters can specify the person(s) responsible of the activity and the other resources allocation.

An example: The following example illustrates how the models could be described. It contains the definition of two models. The first model (module-embryo-model) is an embryo model. Its attribute named "product" designates the product to build. The $is-a facet of this attribute indicates that this product must be an instance of the second model named "module-model". The $init-params facet specifies the informations to be provided before triggering the construction activity of the required module. These informations include the responsible person of this activity who has to play the project manager role, the members of the team who must be engineers, the due in date and due out date of the activity. Finally, the $new-ordering facet specifies the genetic knowledge associated with the required module. This knowledge is given by a path expression which indicates an order to elaborate the sub-products of the required module (i.e. module requirements, module design, design review, program and user test report).

The model "module-model" describes in the same way the components of a module.

```
(module-embryo-model
  (super-model
    ($value product-embryo-model))
  (product
    ($is-a module-model)
    ($init-params
      (leader(project-manager), team(+ engineer),
       duein(date), dueout(date))
    ($new-ordering
      (requirements, + (design || review),
                      + (program, userTestReport)))
  (view
    ($is-a method)))

(module-model
  (super-model
    ($value product-model))
  (initDate
```

```
    ($is-a date)
(completionDate
    ($is-a date)
(currentState
    ($domain (initializing, building, completed, modifying)
    ($default initializing)
(requirements
    ($is-a module-req-model)
    ($init-params
        (leader(req-engineer), team(+ engineer),
         duein(date), dueout(date))
    ($new-ordering
        (-- def ordering of requirement definition tasks ---))
    ($require
        (-- leader must be in team declared by project-manager)
    ($if-success
        (-- informs project manager and programmer -- ))
(design   ........ )
(review   ........ )
(program  ........ )
(userTestReport   ........ )
(view
    ($is-a method))
(print
    ($is-a method)))
```

6.2   Enactment Environment Features

Among other extensions brought to knowledge representation languages based on frames, the most important are the functionalities of the enactment environment. Here, we will limit ourselves to some general principles related to the instantiation mechanism for the models. This mechanism is another important specificity of the model concept against the class concept.

A development project has to begin with the instantiation of an embryo model. During this operation, the project initiator must provide some informations by means of the facet $init-params associated (insight the embryo) to the attribute designating a product to construct. As in the example of the last subsection, the name of the project manager has to be provided here. As a result of this instantiation, an activity must be started in the workspace of the project manager. On his turn, the manager will be able to start other activities which will run in the workspaces of the team members. All these activities are long transactions [God 93], which can be stopped only when the corresponding sub-products will be realized. So, at any time, each team member has the activities he has to pursue in his workspace.

To implement this general principle, it requires some functionalities from the enactment environment. Among them are : concurrent and parallel tasks management, long transactions management, convivial user interface (multiwindows, windows iconification,...).

Obviously, the system interpreter must also know all the rules for using the knowledge described in the models (rules of planning, control, guidance, concurrency arbitration, etc...).

7 Some Advantages of the Approach

From a general point of view, one of the merits of this approach is to provide, through an analogy, a seductive anchorage point to the gestation phase of the software life cycle. This analogy, which brings software process issues closer to those of biological development, relies on two points:

- First, software products and living organisms are both constituted of a great number of elementary components (products of fine granularity for software and biological cells for living organisms) which are also software products and living organisms. These elementary components bear some similarities. Like products, biological cells are also characterized by their (chemical) structure, by their behavior with their environment and by some genes, which govern the synthesis of their (chemical) components.
- Next, in both cases, the life cycle begins with an embryo which grows progressively, getting more and more complexity in its structure and in its functionalities, following a predefined plan.

In other respects, this approach provides a framework for tackling actual problems of software process definition and enactment, in a proper and uniform way. Effectively, the frame formalism is flexible enough to allow a structured and incremental description of knowledge, in general incomplete, changing and in multiforms. It's the type of knowledge that characterizes products and development process in software industry (multiform semantic links, descriptive knowledge, procedural knowledge, various cooperative points of view ...).

- For instance, orthogonal definition of complementary points of view on a product development can be achieved very simply. Indeed, to define the quality engineer's point of view and the project manager's one on a product development process, it is sufficient to define firstly a model for that product without these two views and to specialize further this model taking into account the project manager's point of view and to specialize again the obtained model taking into account the quality engineer's point of view (obviously, the order of this specialization is of first importance, the same as in any object oriented approach).
- Similarly, products and sub-products representation (and their successive versions and variants), roles and resource representations can be achieved in a uniform framework, which can simplify the assistance in configuration management, in version management, in cooperation arbitration, in planning and in project management.

– Daemon facets which can be associated to frames attributes provide an elegant inference mean to implement some forms of system initiatives.

Moreover, the reflective capacity of the proposed representation model simplifies evolution problems. Since models are represented by means of frames which support a dynamic inheritance mechanism, it is possible at any time to make their structure evolve, by modifying, adding or deleting attributes, with a minimum of effects on the hierarchy of models and on their instances [Nar 88].

We are actually exploring more deeply these interesting features of the approach.

References

[Chr 93] **Christie A. M.** *Process Centered Development Environments: An exploration of issues* Technical Report CMU/SEI-93-TR-4.

[Con 92] **Conradi M. & al** *Design, Use and Implementation of SPELL, a Langage for Software Process Modeling and Evolution* in Derniame J. C Software Process Technology. LNCS No 635. Springer-Verlag. Sept. 92.

[Der 92] **Derniame J. C. & al** *Process Centered IPSE's in ALF.* Proc. 5th CASE Workshop. Montréal July 92.

[Fut 89] **Futatsugi K.** *Products Centered Process Description = Algebraic Specification of Environments* ISPW6, Hakodate, Jap., 10/1990.

[God 93] **Godart C.** *COO: A transaction model to support cooperating developers coordination.* 4th ESEC GARMISCH.

[Huf 90] **Huff K. E.** *On the relationship between software processes and software products.* ISPW6, Hakodate, Jap., 10/1990.

[Kat 89] **Katayama T.** *A Hierarchical and Functional Software Process Description and its Enaction.* Proc. of the 11th ICSE, p 343-352 A.C.M 1989.

[Mas 91] **Masini G. & al,** *Object-Oriented Languages,* Academic Press, London, 1991.

[Min 75] **Minsky M.** *A framework for representing knowledge,* In P. Winston , editor, The Psychology of Computer Vision pages 211-281, Mc Graw-Hill, New-York, 1975.

[Nak 89] **Nakagawa A. T., Futatsugi K.** *Products Based Process Models.* Proc. ISPW5,Kennebunkport, Maine, USA, 9/1989.

[Nar 88] **Narayanaswamy K., Bapa Rao K. V.** *An Incremental Mechanism for Schema Evolution in Engineering Domains* Proc. of the Data Engineering, p. 294-301, IEEE, 1988.

[Coi 87] **Cointe P.** *Metaclasses are First Class: The OblVlisp Model.* Proc. of OOPSLA'87. 1987.

[Peu 92] **Peuschel B., Schäfer W.** *Concepts and Implementation of Rule-Based Process Engine* Proc. of 14th ICSE-Melbourne May 92, p 257-276.

[Sno 92] **Snowdon R.** *An Example of Process change* in Derniame J. C Software Process Technology. LNCS No 635. Springer-Verlag. Sept. 92.

[Tho 89] **Thomas Ian** *The Software Process as a Goal-Directed Activity* Proc. ISPW5,Kennebunkport, Maine, USA, 9/1989.

Experiences with software process technology

Department of Computing,
Lancaster University,
Lancaster LA1 4YR,
United Kingdom.

Software process technology has now reached the stage where it can be used across a range of different projects. This session is concerned with a description of some practical experiences of using process technology. These include quite different experiments from the evaluation of a commercial product using a shared, well-understood example, through applications outside of software engineering to practical experiences of the use of a process modelling product in a large software development project.

The paper by Robertson is based on the common example proposed at the 6th International Process Workshop. He has taken a commercial process modelling product and applied it to this application. His evaluation suggests that this relatively simple example is sufficiently complex to act as a vehicle for comparing different technologies. He also reveals omissions in the example and in the ProcessWise tools.

By contrast, the paper by Kramer and Dinler has taken software process technology and applied it to the hardware design process. Not surprisingly, the technology transferred quite easily and they suggest that the hardware CAD community could benefit by taking account of research in software process technology.

The paper by Ambriola *et al.* is a complete contrast to these in that the objective of the work is not about experiences with a specific process technology. Rather, it is concerned with the general issues of process and product measurement and the use of these measurements to make judgements on process improvements. Their experiment is based on student group projects. They make the points that introducing metrics not only changes the nature of the process but also makes that process more akin to that used for industrial development. They conclude that their work is not only relevant in an educational context but that measurement is important if the intent is to create a high-quality process.

Finally, the paper by Aumaitre and Muller describe an experiment in using process technology in a large-scale software production environment. They have modelled part of the European Space Agency process using Process Weaver. Their conclusions from this large scale experiment are that the technology was very useful but that we need much better methods and tools for process understanding and capture and that process model validation is a critical issue.

An Implementation of the ISPW-6 Process Example

Ian Robertson
email: ir@cs.man.ac.uk

Department of Computer Science
University of Manchester M13 9PL

Abstract. This paper documents some of the work involved in describing the ISPW-6 process example in terms of graphical models and in terms of a modelling and enactment language PML. It further describes experiences in instantiating this model in ICL's Processwise Integrator support system, and outlines the lessons learnt and directions for future work.

1 Introduction

There are numerous technologies, in various states of development, which attempt to support the software process. It is not an easy matter to make comparisons between technologies; not only because of the variety of approaches but also lack of a familiar and comprehensive model on which to base comparisons. In order to remedy this state of affairs, the ISPW-6 [7] example process was formulated. This was developed at the 6th International Software Process Workshop, and hereinafter will be referred to as the ISPW-6 Example, or simply as the example process.

After a very brief introduction to the enactment technology, the work of modelling the process example is described: both in terms of the different models needed and in terms of the process of modelling. At the end of Section 3 there is a description of the instantiation of the model and its enactment. The lessons learnt are discussed in Section 4 with Conclusions addressed in Section 5.

2 The Processwise system

ICL Processwise comprises a suite of services designed to support organisational process activity in a number of ways. The 'Business Modeller's Workbench' offers a tool to model and to simulate process behaviour; the 'Integrator' is a process integration and enactment system; and the 'Guide' describes a particular methodology designed to exploit the features of these technologies. The technology of immediate interest is Processwise Integrator (PW Int) [1].

The system originated in the Alvey IPSE 2.5 project which concluded in 1989. ICL subsequently took up the software rights, hardened the system, and implemented the Process Control Engine in the Unix environment. As a first step to commercial release it was renamed Process Support System. After STC's sale of ICL to Fujitsu, the development team became known as the Process Support Centre and the technology was further developed and became a part of the Business Process Re-engineering strategy known as Processwise. The PCM was implemented in DRS 6000, and with other changes the Process Control Engine (PCE) became the Process Control Manager (PCM), and the language Process Modelling Language (PML) became Process Management Language. The current release of the system is ProcessWise Integrator 2.

Liu and Conradi [3] report that the paradigm of PW Int is closest to that of Arcadia [13]. The semantic model is the process programming language, there being no generic model, and the application-specific model is defined as a program in that language. The system takes the role/activity/interaction notion of defining the mechanism for causing transformation events and provides for their enactment in the same context. It provides a framework within which tools can be effectively coordinated to service a process representation of an information systems development methodology.

It is thus a process-centred environment comprising three elements: the PCM , the UI Servers, and the Applications Servers.

The environment holds a model of the process network described in PML [9, 10]. The language identifies four principal classes: entities (records), activities (procedures), roles (encapsulations of data and behaviour) and interactions (corresponding uni-directional communications channels). These principal classes, along with numerous primitive classes, can be used to define the process network. There are three language interfaces which together control the evolution of the model: they allow a class definition to be compiled into a class value, a new instance of a role class to be created, and a role class value to be re-defined.

The heart of the system is the PCM; that component which identifies, locates, and schedules activities which can be executed. It does this by scrutinising each role in turn and examining the guard property of each action which determines *when* that action is allowed to be executed.

Process participants communicate with roles through the medium of a 'pseudo role' known as user agent. The User Interface representation is hierarchic, offering, at the highest level, an agenda of the roles bound to a participant's user agent. Each of these opens into an action agenda allowing selection by the user. This is shown in Figure 5 and described more fully in Section 3.8.

Application integration comprises the ability to pass data as byte string or object to an application running in another environment, to interact with it, and to obtain outputs.

3 Implementing ISPW-6 in PML

3.1 Overview of model architecture

The process example is of a nominally generic process commonly found in organisations concerned with the development and maintenance of software systems. It focusses on activities associated with making planned changes to single specific modules or units which comprise a single software system. No information is provided about participant skill levels, whether the enactment should cater for novice or expert or both, of the software system itself, or of volumes. The process is described clearly and concisely in narrative form as a list of activities defined with inputs, outputs, purpose, and responsibility. This effective statement of requirements corresponds to Feiler and Humphrey's [5] Process Definition level of abstraction, and to the PM2/PM3 meta-process level of Conradi et al [2].

A number of writers confirm the difficulty of representing process activity in a meaningful and concise manner. Curtis [4] confirms the four perspectives widely accepted as being needed to describe a process: organisational, functional, behavioural, and informational, but it is not an easy matter to obtain clean abstractions of these perspectives with the tools currently at our disposal. Conradi et al take a rather more pragmatic approach and recognise at least five sub-models:

1. Activity model. This is the executable model.
2. User model. Describing the service provided to the process participants by the system, and the corresponding obligations placed on them.
3. Organisation model. The model of organisation role structure and functional relationships which associate these roles.
4. Product model. The data structure and relationships.
5. Tool model. Description of tool architecture.

This latter was considered more appropriate as a framework in which to describe the different facets of the subject process and the models needed were not exactly as postulated in [2]: the nature of the process is such that there was no need for a tool model, and, because of the focus on enactment, there was a distinct need for a model of the work infrastructure or environment appropriate for participants; this was called the Environment model.

3.2 Methods and tools

The work described herein does not fall neatly into the phases of the PM1-5 meta-model [2], as the focus of the ISPW-6 example is on the implementation of a model already fairly well-defined in narrative form, with adequate information to begin the PM3 Customisation phase. PADM (Process Analysis and Design Methodology [16]) provides a coherent strategy and techniques for much of the area of PM1 through to PM4, and indeed outside of this framework, identifying the need for a 'baseline' model, stressing that once a 'target' process (or even processes) has or have been identified, the implementation route will of necessity be from 'what is' to 'what ought to be'. The ISPW-6 example assumes a 'green field' implementation, i.e. there is no need to take into account current work practice and cultural influence.

Certain of the representation methods advocated by PADM were also used in this study: the first using the role-interaction paradigm of process [6] to identify user roles (i.e. sociological roles within the organisation, commonly aligned to job descriptions), to map tasks or activities to these roles, and to identify at a coarse grained level discrete states and associated events of the process. The resulting diagrams are known as RADs [8]. The second was the use of the activity diagram (AD) to map activities independently of roles [1]. There is another type of diagram in

---

[1] A PC modelling tool RADitor is available for role-activity diagrams (developed by Co-Ordination Systems), and the activity diagramming tool is a component of Process Modeller's Workbench being developed by the Informatics Process Group.

PADM known as dependency diagram (DD) which provides a high level abstraction of the essence of complex processes. This was not required in this simple example. The Methodology does as yet provide no guidance for implementation or for selection of support platforms.

3.3 The User Model

In this study the model took two forms. The first was a RAD model of roles, tasks and artifacts shown in Figure 1. It provided a very concise representation of the process, however the greater detail needed to structure an implementation was provided by the second form: it was much more fine-grained, and comprised narrative lists of user activities which might be ascribed to these roles. For example a designer would want to be notified of an impending task, to be made aware that documents were ready and available for use, to be able to work possibly at intermittent intervals, to dispatch the work item and finally to be notified if re-work was necessary or if the item had received approval. We would assume that the task would not be complete until the design had been approved in review, so the facility to iterate would be necessary.

Role activity Diagrams define the scope of role behaviour. When considering organisation roles, they indicate the different activities which can take place and the dependencies which exist between them.

The meaning of the diagram can be clarified by taking the example of the organisation role of Design Engineer.

Once notified of a task, the Design Enginer can work on either Modify Design, or Modify Source Code. Once the code has been modified and passed to Design Review, the activity goes into a 'waiting' state (identified by the tail). If the code is approved, the activity Modify Design is completed and ceases to exist. If Code Feedback arrives, the activity can be re-invoked by the Design Engineer to address the feedback issues. Another kind of dependency is illustrated at completion of Modify Source Code. Here, the Source Code cannot be despatched to QA Engineer until the Approved Design is available.

The only significant departure from the example process is that joint responsibilites have been re-interpreted into unitary responsibilites. The implementation technology has, as yet, no mechanism for interpreting joint responsibility in terms Processwise Integrator technology.

It should be emphasised from the outset that we are dealing with two distinct types of 'role'. There is the organisation role referred to here, which can be conveniently referred to as the user role; and the unique definition of role in ProcessWise (single threaded, defining scope of entities, forming the basis of the user interface, unit of change) which can be called a system role, or in PW Int terminology, an on-line role.

An example of the activity list is provided in the description of the application model for the Modify Code task on page 8.

3.4 The Environment Model

The process example was well defined, but to make the enactment meaningful in the context of an organisation some attention had to be paid to the support or infras-

Organisation Roles, Activities, and Interactions

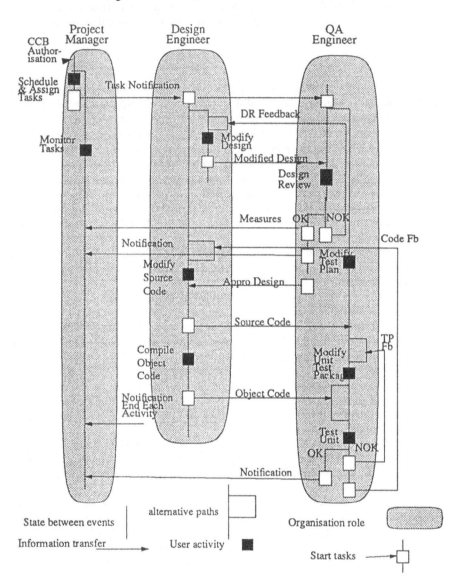

Fig. 1. The User Model

tructure necessary for the process to be enacted. This helped ensure a reasonably realistic implementation for participants, and assisted in throwing light on some of the issues which could arise in a real-world implementation.

It was found helpful to encapsulate certain 'housekeeping' activities into system roles which were permanently bound to participants . These roles supported service activity rather than task activity and were referred to as Admin roles. They are discussed on page 13.

The environmental aspect which was selected for inclusion in this implementation was that of the library service. To be effective a process enactment system would have to interact with the library facilities used to hold these data items, and this is represented in Figure 2.

3.5 The Organisation Model

This was a simple reporting hierarchy with a single manager having responsibility for and control over a group of software engineering staff who could be identified as primarily either design engineers or QA engineers. It clearly indicates that as the process spans only a single group of users, the PM is responsible for controlling both the working of the process and the evolution of the process. The other significant concern in the organisation, the mapping of role sets [12] of group responsibilities such as the Design Review team to the organisation structure, was not addressed. Delegation issues were not present in the process example.

3.6 The Product Model

As product is not the primary concern in this study, this model is trivial. The process example only considers a single system whichyou comment o comprises unidentified modules or units each of which is composed of design, object code, source code, test plans, unit test packages under version control. This control was modelled in the library service.

Notwithstanding this simplistic situation, the issues surrounding this kind of model and its relationship to the associated process model are current research topics.

3.7 The Activity or Application Model

The use of the term 'application' is preferred in the context of the executable model as it clearly refers to a system model, whereas 'activity' might be either real-world activity, or system activity and can also get confused with activity diagrams which are useful for structuring real-world activities.

This is the model which is ultimately enacted, and in its final form is expressed in the process definition language[2] PML for execution in ProcessWise Integrator system. The development of the model, of what is in essence a process management

---

[2] The term 'process definition language' is possibly more appropriate than 'process modelling language' in that it reflects more accurately the departure from the original ideals of the language.

The interaction relationship between system roles

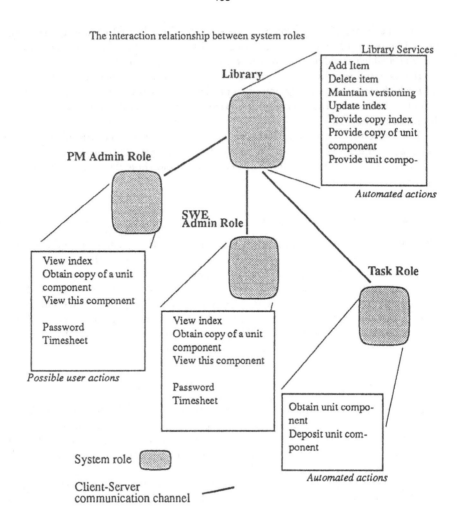

Fig. 2. The Environment model

system, was driven by the nature of PML and the properties of the support system. Of paramount importance in PW Int is the need to identify from the outset the appropriate system roles and granularity appropriate for the application. It is not impossible (but highly unlikely) that system roles could map directly on to user roles, and at the other end of the spectrum a role might represent but a single activity. However the most likely situation is that the behaviour will somewhere between these two extremes. Key considerations in defining system roles are:

- Need for run-time concurrency
- Scope of data entities
- Requirements of user interface
- Desired scope of change

The user model has been transformed to reflect these criteria and this is shown in Figure 3 as Application Model 1. There is a small extension to the Requirements to better illustrate the receiving of a modified design. Review system roles are provided to enable users to participate in the review process prior to a review meeting at which decisions might be made. On the other hand, CCB was not modelled as a system role because it increased complexity without contributing to understanding. The control process for the application model, really a component of the meta-process itself, is shown in Figure 4.

These diagrams formed the basis of describing the process in PML. The system roles were constructed of three basic overlays utilising the inheritance properties of the language. The essential behaviour of *all* task roles is defined in *WPRole*; these were : to maintain and display when required certain task information (identified as *a_scheduleDates* below, information is bound on instantiation and subsequently changed by a Re-scheduling action); to provide a facility to display a message when and if the task was changed by higher authority such as the PM (identified by *displayMessage* changed by a Hold/Restart/Cancel action), and to dispatch a message to PM on conclusion of the task (*sendIt*). The PML for this behaviour is illustrated below by the definition of *WPRole* as a sub-class of the pre-defined PML role class *Role*.

```
WPRole isa Role with
classes
assocs
        doneGP    :giveport DonEnt
resources
        wpEnt    : WPEnt
        thisRole:String
        whoiam   : String := ''
        doneEnt : DonEnt
        kill     : Bool := false
        schedFormat : collof UIField:=collof UIField(
                UIField(name='startDate', label='Schedule Start'),
                UIField(name='duration', label='Duration'),
                UIText(name='requirements', label='Requirements'),
                UIField(name='notes', label='Note'))
```

```
        seeMessage      : Bool := false
        onHold          : Bool := false
        messageString   : String :='New Scheduling Information '
actions
        a_scheduleDates:{
                UserAction(agendaLabel='Task Information');
                ModifyNow
                        (agendaLabel='Task Information',
                        object = wpEnt, readOnly=true,
                        format=schedFormat)
                        }

        displayMessage:{
                ViewResourceNow
                (agendaLabel=' Message', object=messageString,
                label=whoiam);
                seeMessage:=false
                        }
        when seeMessage

        sendIt:{
                Assign(from=whoiam, to=doneEnt.task);
                Give(interaction=doneGP, gram = doneEnt);
                kill:=true
                }
        when nonnil doneEnt


termconds  kill
end with
```

The specialisations appropriate for each particular kind of task were then defined as sub-classes: for example the Modify Code task role (*MSCRole*) is a sub-class of *WPRole* which incorporates the following behaviour:

– Create an object *scEnt* to represent source code.
– Allow modification *scEnt* using a text editor.
– Allow dispatch of a copy of this code to Modify Unit Test Package role only after the approved modified design has been received by Modify Code role from Review Design.
– Simulate compilation of the code in *scEnt* into object code.
– Allow dispatch of this object code to Test Unit task role.
– Provide for handling of feedback from Test Unit task role.
– Provide status messages.

Finally, the definitions of the library service client were instantiated as a sub-class of *MSCRole*, called *MSCLibRole*.

The implementation of the library facility shows how a network of roles and interactions can be constructed to work in a client server manner. The library is the server. It understands a number of library requests which are sent to it using

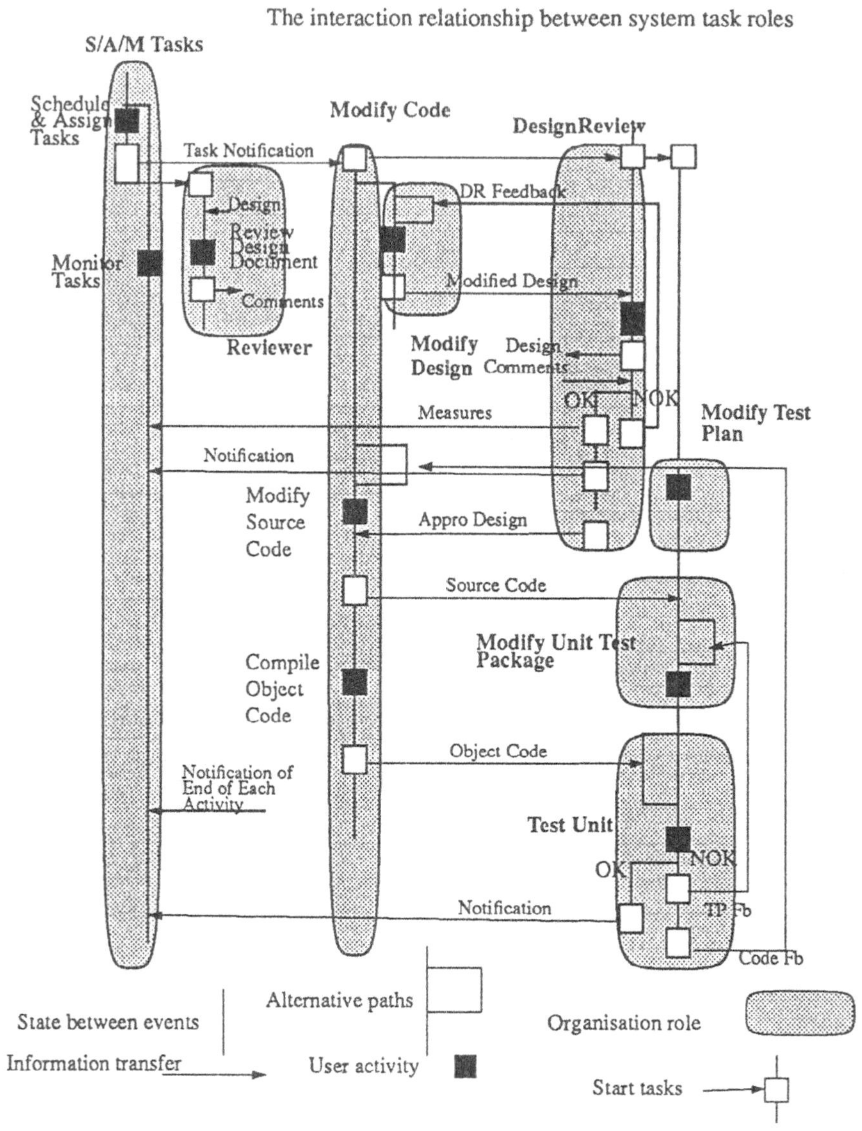

The interaction relationship between system task roles

Fig. 3. Application Model 1

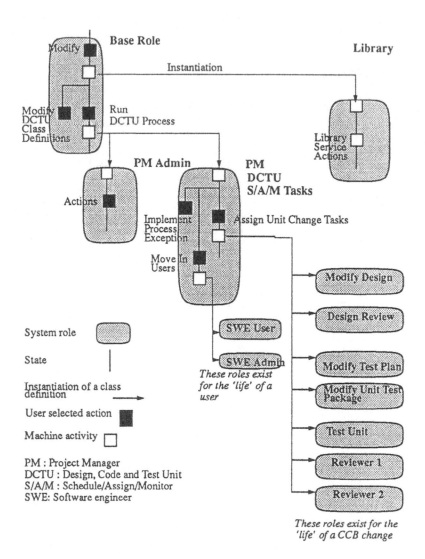

Fig. 4. Application Model 2

an interaction. All roles which use the library can give requests to this interaction, only the library will read them. Each role which uses the library is a client. When it sends a request to the library it includes the giveport of the interaction which the library will use for the reply. The client role will subsequently receive the library's reply on the interaction's takeport.

With this well defined interface, the system roles which use the library do not need to know any details of its implementation. They only have an interaction giveport to which they give library requests. (To be a library using role it will either be given this giveport on starting or at least before its first request.) Indeed they cannot tell if the library is implemented by one role, a collection of roles, or one, or more, roles interfaced to some external tools. The current implementation has the library as a single role which handles requests one at a time.

The data held in the library is identified by its unit name, a part within that unit, 'design', 'source code', 'unit test pack' etc., and where relevant a version number. The library using roles are divided into two types: browsing and updating. A library browsing role can get a copy of any item in the library, but cannot do any updating. A library updating role is able to retrieve items from the library and subsequently send back the item to be stored in the library as a new version.

In this example the admin roles, *PM Admin* and *SWE Admin* have library browsing facilities. The task roles are library updating roles. However, they are specialised library updating roles in that they only retrieve and update one item. For example *MUTP* role which has been created for a change on unit 'scanner' will retrieve and update only the 'unit test pack' part of unit 'scanner'. Figure 2 gives an overview of this architecture of the library system roles.

In the current version of the system, the task roles will obtain the relevant item from the library during an initialisation stage, and will replace the new version just prior to the role terminating. This could be changed if it was decided that the latest working versions of components should be available to others through their Admin roles.

3.8 The Meta-process: the development of the application model

This section describes the evolution of the application from narrative requirements through to implementation and evolution. To facilitate this phase, the narrative description was transformed at a slightly higher level of abstraction into two forms: one a representation of activities in an Activity Diagram, the other to a RAD to allow a more succinct description of the overall process (on a single A4 sheet). The Activity Diagram had elsewhere been found to be a useful tool to map activity independently of role responsibility, but in this more simple case its use was as a quick reference to the requirements. The Role Activity Diagram initially incorporated knowledge of the support system, however this inclusion was subsequently judged to be an unwarranted complexity and was removed. To all intents and purposes, this initial phase was the preparation of the User Model in Figure 1.

When considering the needs of a potential software engineer user it quickly became clear that it would be necessary to include in the implementation certain further behaviour not referred to in the ISPW-6 example description; activities which would be required in any proposed enactment to allow participants to function effectively in their organisation and system environment. Such activities were listed and initially mapped to user roles: those identified in the User Model. These were in effect the requirements for the environment, the Environment Model (Figure 2)

At this point the next major transformation was to scope the identified activities into system roles, to identify precisely what would be required from the support system. Apart from PW Int considerations identified, the needs of the 'participants' had to be considered, particularly how a participant might wish to navigate among and through activities, and how a participant's organisational responsibilities might be expressed through the user interface. It appeared to be a very subjective consideration; in this development a principle of 'Least Effort' was adopted, i.e. make the work of finding a work item by navigating among activities as easy as possible. In the application only one interpretation has been included; ideally a participant ought to be able to structure activities at will (constrained only by high-level process and system considerations). It became clear that was there were two distinct types of activity: those which ought to be permanently available for the participant, and those which were contextual and which ought to have transient existence. These former were scoped into Service system roles, labelled Admin, the latter into Task system roles. The mapping of these system roles to user roles is the first (diagrammatic) phase of the Application Model 1 as a RAD.

The correct establishment of interactions between system roles is critical to the success of a PW Int application, and this need drove subsequent work. To ensure smooth development an Interaction Map was prepared showing precisely the nature and function of the minimum necessary set of interactions, and when they had to exist. This was used to write the first phase of the application model; to allow instantiation of the task roles, comprising absolute minimum of functionality, in correct sequence and with correct links in place.

Subsequent development of the Application Model 1 was concerned with specialising these class definitions incorporating the information contained in the Organisation, Product and User models, and in extending the fine grained functionality of the task roles. There is wide freedom in PML to define the guards for actions to implement behaviour via the intra-role scheduler (part of the PCM), however this freedom means that guards become very complex very quickly, and even in this simple model it was not easy to implement desired changes to some behaviours.

One portion of the meta-process was implemented in PW Int as the first specialisation of the system *Base* role. This provides a number of functions: to bootstrap the application, to provide a harness within which the application can be executed, to provide services that can usefully exist at a higher level than the application itself, and, most importantly, to provide that portion of the feedback mechanism which allows external change of the application model. One can imagine the cycle of monitoring of process performance, taking a view on the changes needed to effect improvements, and effecting such improvements by dynamically changing either class definitions, enacting instantiations, or both. This process component was modelled as Application Model 2 (Figure 4).

The development of the *Library* service role was a significant effort done in parallel with the task role development in the application model. This service was implemented as a specialisation of the basic application model: the library class definitions were introduced and task roles subclassed to incorporate functionality allowing access to the library service.

3.9 Enacting the process

There are three separate contexts for instantiation of the different components of this implementation. All of them are 'dynamic' [5]. The first comprises the application models 1 and 2, loaded into the basic PW Int persistent store containing initially an instance of class *Base* role. During the execution of the process itself, a userAgent system role and Admin system role (either *PM Admin* or *SWE Admin*) are created for each participant brought within the scope of the system. Lastly, an assignment of a particular CCB change (through invocation of the action Assign Unit Change Tasks, see Figure 5) creates specific instances of task roles bound to selected participants.

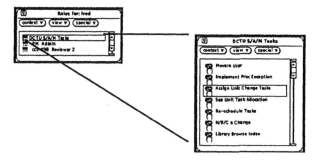

Fig. 5. UI Representation

In the PW Int support system, all implementations use a specific persistent store containing an initial specialisation of system role *Role* as *Base* incorporating functionality to change itself. This facility is used to load the code for both application models. At the conclusion of this loading, the library service is started automatically and an action in *Base* offers the action 'Run DCTU Process' and, on its selection, a prompt requests the user name of PM and proceeds to instantiate one *DCTU S/A/M Tasks* role (Schedule/Assign/Monitor), and one *PMAdmin* role, both bound to PM's user name. Figure 5 illustrates a typical role agenda for a PM whose username is 'fred', and an action agenda for *DCTU S/A/M Tasks*. In the example shown, it can be seen that fred is also the second reviewer for change reference ccb # 98. This bootstrap activity can be followed quite clearly on the role activity diagram Figure 4.

An essential precursor to the demonstration is for PM to 'Move In' a number of users, identified as QAE or DE. The ISPW-6 process enactment starts by PM selecting 'Assign Unit Change Tasks'. This allows identification of unit to be changed, choice of DE, QAE, and Reviewers for that particular change.

The implemented process was enacted using ProcessWise Integrator 1.1, the Process Control Manager component available both in Unix on a SUN server, and in ICL VME [14] on an Estriel mainframe located at Manchester. The user interfaces ran on SUN workstations, usually at Manchester but not infrequently at Southampton, Bristol, and Durham using the X400 protocol on the JANET network.

The system supporting the ISPW-6 example process normally runs continuously, being stopped only once per week at a convenient time for a brief garbage collection. Thus it is always available for demonstration with access from Manchester or from elsewhere.

4 Lessons Learned

4.1 Scheduling

This is a prime concern of a typical manager and careful thought was given to the extent to which it ought to be supported in the implementation. 'Scheduling' means the preparation of a plan to accomplish a piece of work in a certain time period. In order that this can be done, the manager needs to know the sequence in which discrete activities can occur, whether or not concurrency can be exploited, other constraints on the activities, and lastly, what human and machine and other resources (such as office space) are available.

Resources were not available to provide any degree of detailed implementation to support this kind of managerial activity. Many excellent software packages exist which can do this and the facility of ProcessWise Integrator to integrate a tool would be the normal way of incorporating the facility. The place for PW Int in this context is in the linking of knowledge of current activity state through 'Monitoring' to 'Scheduling' and 'Rescheduling'. In a normal design environment common obligation on designers is to complete a daily time sheet as an indication of how their time was allocated between workpackages. It would seem sensible to allow this information to be collated automatically and used for again automatic updating of records of work done and work remaining to be done in a scheduling tool. PW Int provides the necessary envelope within which this kind of activity could sensibly be provided.

Other task related information can be abstracted, e.g. when activities have been commenced, However it is not easy to abstract this information from the system in a sensible and reliable way (the system has no understanding of the data) , and recourse would likely be made to participant-provided 'time sheets'. The manager then has the current information needed: how much has been done; what has finished; when current tasks likely to finish; what should have started and hasn't.

4.2 User interface

It is necessary to visualise just how a user might want to navigate among tasks and services available. With PW Int as a support enactment system we have the opportunity to 'parcel' the behaviour with an entity and refer to it as a system role, or to provide a system role with appropriate 'tools' for holding and for manipulating entities, or some combination of the two. Criteria for choice would include just how routine the activity is, what to see if there is no work to do, volume of products, preference of users.

Certain activities were context-free, for example certain library access functions; others, such as tasks, were very context-dependent. Relevant here for example was what the screen ought to display when there were no process tasks to perform.

In addition, of course the constraints of the PW Int user interface restrict opportunity. Screen representation can be very much an area of individual preference and ideally therefore ought to have defaults accessible by the user. However as the architecture of the application model is heavily dependent on this choice, certain decisions had to be made and closed at an early stage. One of the more obvious examples of this is the location of activities. It may not be at all clear to the process designer which role is the most appropriate for a particular activity, but the choice cannot be left to the user because it may not be an easy matter to move an action between system roles, particularly if performance is an issue.

4.3 Process control

The organisation chart defines who controls which roles. Thus it is clear that PM controls the activities of Software engineers. What does this entail? Essentially it is the ability to allocate resources and to assign tasks, and the responsibility to ensure tasks are completed according to schedule. However it also includes the ability to make changes in the process. The essence of improved process performance is a clear identification of the mechanism whereby the process can be changed. This implies the existence of another 'orthogonal' process: not concerned with the day-to-day activities or performance, but the performance of the process as a whole. A process component has been written in PML called the Process Model for Management Support [15]. It provides a context for delegating objectives, planning, implementing, monitoring and re-planning process models and will be incorporated into the implementation in future.

A well-known feature of PW Int is the ability to make change 'on the fly'. This is modelled in this example process so far in only one way: to modify an existing instance of Design Review to bypass reviewers. It is accomplished by the PM selecting the appropriate action which offers a choice of CCB Changes to target, to select the appropriate modification, and to identify the target system role in which the modification is to be implemented. Other aspects of the ISPW-7 'Change' extensions will eventually be incorporated.

However behaviour changes usually involve action sequencing, and difficulty was encountered in determining process flow from action guard definitions in PML. This could be problematic in live enactments and some formalism is needed to guide the determination and testing of guard statements.

4.4 Guidance and enforcement

The paradigm of PW Int is essentially one of prescription and the work available is defined in the system and the facilities available are prescribed in the system.

It attempts to support the behaviour of the software engineer rather than merely indicate what task has to be done next. However just how much freedom participants are given is ultimately the choice of the process owner.

This will be an ongoing debate and we have yet to understand if one way is better than another, or under what circumstances one is better than another. Is automating of procedures adequate? Taylorism co-ordinated the work of craftsmen and re-structured the activities to improve productivity. It is not yet possible to co-ordinate the intellectual effort of knowledge workers in the same way.

4.5   Co-operative work

PW Int does not at present support multi-user access to system roles and thus there is no means of representing joint responsibility. Group responsibility can only be represented by decomposing the process into more elementary activities which can be assigned as roles to single users in a 1:1 relationship. In this model such difficulties were experienced in 'Review Design' and 'Test Unit', which are both joint responsibilities. To support the notion of joint responsibility a separate role would have to be created to allow identification of decisions and concurrence with or rejection of them, together with a framework for negotiation.

It is not yet possible to adequately represent the mapping of roles in organisations between groups and individuals. Singh [12] has recently made progress and uses the term role sets to represent group responsibility however they are difficult to manipulate and do not yet adequately cope with the dynamics of responsibility transfer, delegation and subsumption.

4.6   Knowledge of state

Difficulty was found in communicating to the participants knowledge of current system state, in the sense 'what can happen next and why isn't it happening'. A device was adopted through the use of dummy actions to convey this information, but a suitable mailserver to support communication in the context of the process would be useful.

4.7   Meta-model and Methodology

The work of developing these models has made a small contribution to our knowledge of how to go about implementing a particular (simple!) process description. Although PADM is primarily concerned with mapping and interpreting real-world processes, it played a part in addressing many user-centred issues, particularly those around choice of a suitable system roles and working environment. In addition the diagramming tools were useful.

It must be borne in mind that this example process is in many ways quite unlike real-world processes in the clear definition provided, the absence of cultural influences and absence of any need to consider the transition to the supported process. It also may represent only a tiny portion of the spectrum of process activity which might be considered for process support.

The ISPW-6 example is coarse-grained and represents a typical description of 'what ought to be' rather than 'what is'. There is no reference in the PM1 stage of the meta-process to establishing the 'what is' process as a basis for planning the transition to the 'what ought to be' process, but, as White mentions [16], in the real world this transition may well be the biggest problem to be dealt with.

This issue is very pertinent when considering the impacts of context and skill. The activities that are performed and the way that they are performed are frequently heavily dependent on the nature of the information to be handled, and on the skill and experience of the individual participants.

5 Conclusions and future work

The process example may well be a useful vehicle with which to appraise alternative technologies. It encompasses most kinds of purposeful behaviour and only one kind of process seems to have been omitted: that of a management control. Together with the extensions, there appears to be adequate scope for investigation into the strengths and shortcomings of technologies.

As well as offering a demonstrator for critical appraisal, this work also contributed to PADM as an example of a modelling and instantiation route into this specific enactment technology. More implementation work in Processwise and other systems will enable some guidance to be provided for those seeking to implement modelled processes.

Mention has been made (Section 4.3) of the difficulty of scheduling activity which is even of only moderate complexity. One possible solution to this problem lies in the use of OBM (Organisational Base Modelling) [11] to rigorously specify a process prior to implementation. OBM's use of operation patterns to express the often complex logic of activity behaviour may lead to a relatively simple method of defining guard statements of actions in PML. If this is successful then the way is clear to make use of requirements validation through process simulation.

It is intended that development of the implementation described herein should continue as resources permit, to eventually address in full the issues raised in the extension to ISPW-6. In particular, the integration issue has to be brought to the forefront. It may be opportune to model the example process as a pattern of constrained invocations of tools rather than making use of the rather primitive graphics of the User Interface. This may well be most appropriate application domain of PW Integrator technology. In addition, we feel that the instantiation of a coherent 'managing' process, to support planning, implementation, monitoring and re-planning, would significantly extend the scope and interest of the example.

One concern is that, as a demonstrator, the full process example is already quite complex and we anticipate different versions of the implementation to focus on different specific issues.

A notable omission from the process example, understandable in one of such simplicity, is consideration of how the process might change depending on the kinds of modules being changed. There is concern in software engineering circles that 'context' of the process activity, or the products being developed or being produced by the activity, may well have a profound influence on the process under which they are produced. A SERC funded project 'Evolution of Large Software Systems' will start in Manchester and Southampton in late 1993, investigating the means to control the evolution of systems within the context of a system architecture definition and architectural process.

The work bearing fruit in PADM will continue in another proposed SERC funded project 'Process Engineering Framework' of which the Methodology component will complement and extend earlier work under the IOPT project. Of particular interest will be the development of process theory, process taxonomies, and process engineering practice and techniques.

It is of particular interest for us to understand the extent to which the ISPW-6 process may be considered generic. There is a plan to model real world software processes using PADM to determine the extent to which they may be 'subclasses' of the process example, and if so, how specialisation might be brought about.

Ongoing action research with industry will continue to be a valuable source of real-world knowledge and a proving ground for ideas, theories and tools.

6 Acknowledgements

I would like to thank Mark Greenwood of Southampton University for his perceptive ideas and criticism and also for his substantial direct contribution to this implementation.

References

1. R.F. Bruynoghe, J.M. Parker, and J.S. Rowles. PSS:A system for Process Enactment. In *Proceedings of the first International Conference on the Software Process, Manufacturing Complex Systems*. IEEE Computer Society Press, 1991.
2. R. Conradi, C. Fernström, A. Fuggetta, and R. Snowdon. Towards a Reference Framework for Process Concepts. In *Proceedings EWSPT'92*, volume 635 of *Lecture Notes in Computer Science*. Springer Verlag, 1992.
3. R. Conradi and C. Liu. Process Modelling Paradigms: An Evaluation. In *Proceedings of the First European Workshop on Software Process Modeling*, Milan, 1991.
4. R. Curtis, M. I. Kellner, and J. Over. Process Modelling. *Comms. of A. C. M.*, 35(9), September 1992.
5. P.H. Feiler and W.S. Humphrey. Software Process Development And Enactment: Concepts And Definitions. In *Proceedings of the Second International Conference on the Software Process*. IEEE Computer Society Press, 1993.
6. A.W. Holt, H.R. Ramsey, and J.D. Grimes. Coordination System Technology as the Basis for a Programming Environment. *Electrical Communication*, 57(4), 1983.
7. M. Kellner, P. Feiler, A. Finkelstein, T. Katayama, L. Osterweil, M. Penedo, and H.D.Rombach. ISPW-6 Software Process Example. In *Proceedings of the First International Conference on Software Process*, Washington, 1991. IEEE Computer Society Press.
8. M.A. Ould and C. Roberts. Defining Formal Models of the Software Development Process. In Pearl Brereton, editor, *Software Engineering Environments*. Ellis Horwood, 1987.
9. C. Roberts. Describing and Acting Process Models with PML. In *Proceedings of 4th International Software Process Workshop*, Moretonhampstead, 1988.

10. C. Roberts and A. Jones. Dynamics of Process Models in PML. In *Proceedings of 5th International Software Process Workshop*, Kennebunkport, 1989.

11. J. Sa, B.C. Warboys, and J.A. Keane. OBM: A Specification Method for Modelling Organisational Process. In *Proceedings of the Workshop on Constraint Processing at the International Congress on Computer Systems and Applied Mathematics (CSAM'93)*, St. Petersburg, 1993.

12. B. Singh. Interconnected Roles (IR): A Coordination Model. Technical Report CT-084-92, MCC, 1992.

13. R.N. Taylor et al. Foundations for the Arcadia Environment Architecture. In Peter B. Henderson, editor, *Proceedings of 3d ACM SIGSOFT/SIGPLAN Software Engineering Symposium on Practical Software Development Environments*. In SIGSOFT Software Engineering Notes 13(5) pages 1–13 November 1988, ACM SIGPLAN Notices 24(2) February 1989.

14. B.C. Warboys. VME nodal architecture: a model for the realisation of a distributed system concept. *ICL Technical Journal*, 4(3), 1985.

15. B.C. Warboys. The IPSE 2.5 Project: Process Modelling as a basis for a support environment. In *Proceedings of the First International Conference on Software Development, Environments, and Factories*, Berlin, 1989.

16. P. White. Report on the Process Analysis and Design Methodology. Technical Report 142, IOPT, 1993.

Applying a Metric Framework to the Software Process: an Experiment

V.Ambriola, R. Di Meglio, V. Gervasi, B. Mercurio

Dipartimento di Informatica - Università di Pisa

Abstract. In this paper, we describe an experiment in process management techniques and software product metrics. The starting point is the definition of a complete metric framework for process and products, on the basis of a detailed definition of the entities involved in the process, their relationships and of the documents produced. We then investigate the effects of introducing an organized process in an academic environment, as well as the relationship between process and product metrics. Our goal is to verify how such a metric framework may be used to optimize the process, in order to raise product quality.

1 Introduction

Finding exact ways of measuring the software process and its products is a very important goal for the whole software industry; a coherent framework of measurements which includes all the phases of the software life-cycle is a primary need for those companies, such as the E.S.A. [1], which develop mission critical systems.

It is true as well that many important experiences in the study of software metrics (e.g. [2]) have been produced in an academic environment, thanks to the opportunities provided by comparing the systems designed by several groups of students, working on the same set of requisites: experiments of this kind would be unreasonably expensive in a corporate environment. To give an example of this costs, we have estimated that a one-semester course with 100 students, if the working hours devoted to the project developed in the course would be paid with an average programmer's salary, would cost more than a million dollars.

In many cases, however, the kind of software process implemented in Software Engineering courses is only vaguely reminiscent of the process actually required to develop a large information system. Most often, the project team in a didactic project is not organized, or is organized in a very loose way, and there is no definition of roles within the team. Often there is no definite process structure and data collection is not implemented in a rigorous way, so that the effectiveness of the measurements is seriously impaired. The organization of these kind of projects is, in fact, corresponding to that of an *initial process* [3].

The goal of the experiment described in this paper is studying the effect of introducing process management techniques and software product metrics in the project assigned to the students in the undergraduate and graduate course of Software Engineering of the Università di Pisa [4]. We are particularly interested in:

- formalizing a model of the optimal structure for our project, on the basis of our previous experiences, in order to provide the students with a clear framework of their activities;
- defining process metrics which, when properly employed, enable the teams to monitor and optimize their work;
- defining product metrics for the documents and objects produced during the project, using them to enhance product quality and to validate the subjective metrics typically employed to grade the students;
- verifying the effect of introducing an organized process on the quality of the students' efforts, to define further improvements to the process quality and hence to the quality of the teaching;
- studying, using well-established psychology techniques, the behaviour of the teams, verifying the correlation between the internal organization of a team and its results.

Much of the elaboration and validation of these results is still in progress, and in this paper we introduce the motivations of our research, describe the experiment, provide details of the metrics we used and/or defined and hint at some of the preliminary results obtained from the study of the data we collected. We also want to show the benefits we obtained from introducing a well-defined organization for projects in the course, not only from a didactic point of view, but also from the feedback and insights such an experiment may provide to software industry.

2   Teaching Software Engineering

In teaching Software Engineering, several different approaches are possible [5]. Basically, the difference is in the balance between lectures, discussion and project, and in the nature and size of the project chosen. In our course, we put a strong emphasis on the practical experience provided by a large project effort. The lectures (about 60 hours) provide the students with the basic notions of software life cycle, metrics, formal specification languages, and so on: these notions are required for the project, and most of them are immediately translated to a practical experience.

We give a lot of attention to the choice of the project assigned to the students: the requirements of the system are usually provided by an external client (for example, during the last two years the clients were ENEL, the Italian electric company, and the Bank of Italy). While the characteristics of the systems vary widely (recent projects were concerned with designing a system for the remote control of a robot in a satellite, the coordinator of an hydroelectric plant, a system for managing the National roll of Credit Institutes, etc.), all of them have some common features, which have consequences on the way we organize the process:

- the systems are *large*, so that the students have to deal with problems of modularization, refinement, etc. Systems of this size cannot be fully coded in 4 months by a small team, so we have decided to end the project with the design phase;

- the systems interact with a *complex, real-world domain*: when using toy problems, most of the difficulties of the analysis phase (understanding technical documentation, understanding the requirements of the client, and so on) just disappear, as the system is fully defined by the problem definition. Our students must instead overcome these problems during the analysis phase, and a good part of the course is devoted to defining the User Requirements Document (URD) and the formal specification of the system.

2.1 Previous Experiences

In the last few years, we have put a growing emphasis in our course on:

- using state-of-the-art languages and CASE tools (vs. "traditional" programming languages or informal analysis/specification methods);
- dealing with real-world systems and problems (vs. using toy problems in the project);
- following a well-defined process with document writing guidelines, delivery deadlines, etc. (vs. loosely organized process, with final grading only).

We have obtained very satisfying results: the students, often completely without experience in large system design, have been able to tackle with complex, real world situations, have learned how to evaluate their own work, and overall have shown a significant increase in their understanding of the problems involved with large scale software projects. At the same time, however, we have found that the usual, subjective ways for grading the students are not adequate to evaluate in a satisfactory way the systems designed by the teams of students. The search for more objective ways of evaluating product quality is one of the reasons which encouraged us to merge the study of process management, metrics and teaching in a unitary framework.

It is often said that you can't control what you can't measure, and we have experienced ourselves the truth of this statement: whenever measuring and evaluating the students' work was difficult or complicated, we realized that the real problem was the bad organization of the underlying process. On the other hand, we needed well defined metrics to understand and control our software process. Our goal, then, became creating a cycle of process definition/metrics definition/metrics validation/process definition, in order to raise the quality of the process and its products.

2.2 Learning in an Organized Framework

The validity of an experiment in metrics is closely dependent on how the context of the experiment is organized: we need to decide clearly, at the beginning of the process, how the project must be managed, which form the documents must have and the evaluation criteria in order to have a repeatable experiment, which provides results which may be valid in similar contexts as well. Furthermore, it is impossible to measure *all* the aspects of the process and the products: only with a clear model of the process and of the document format it is possible to define which characteristics are the most important ones to measure.

On the basis of these considerations, along with the didactic goals we mentioned earlier, we decided to supply the students, at the beginning of the course, with a full set of rules to follow during the process: which formal roles must be assigned to members of a team, how to monitor and report working time and activities, which form the documents must have, and so on. While this is an unusual experience for most students, following these rules quickly becomes natural for them and the students soon realize their importance if they want to succeed in their project work. These rules are provided to the students in written form, as a sort of "manual", which must be studied at the beginning of the process.

Using a well-defined process is also interesting from the client's point of view: while, in general, it is not possible to have a direct transfer of the system design to the corporation which provided the project, the client has a chance to examine the process and gets many useful insights on the problems which could arise when the system will be developed following the corporate process rules (as the information system designed by the students are very often chosen among the systems which the client has to design in the near future). Without a well-defined process, the experiment would not be very useful to the client, as its characteristics would be too different from an industrial design effort.

In deciding how to model the organization of the process, we were very concerned with balancing *competition* and *cooperation* between the students. While competition is useful to encourage the teams to produce a high quality work, too much competition is harmful, both from a psychological point of view and as it precludes any form of *knowledge transfer* between the teams, even when a transfer could be useful (e.g. when learning to use CASE tools).

In order to encourage cooperation, a *committee* is included in the process. One member of each team participates to the activity of this committee, which provides some "services" to the teams in each phase of the project life-cycle. This activity stimulates cooperation: if the committee performs well its functions, this is beneficial to every team.

Another entity, the *council*, made up of the team leaders, is in charge of defining *process changes* and of managing the *resources* (time, computing facilities, etc.). This activity, however, is not cooperative in a strict sense; rather, it implements a form of *controlled competition* to access resources: the competition is controlled as the activity of the council is monitored by the teacher of the course.

3   The Process and the Products

The project basically follows a *waterfall* process model, which ends with the architectural design phase: it is not possible to develop and integrate the code in a 4 months course and, furthermore, programming experiences are already included in other courses in the students' curricula.

The teams are made up of 5 students, one of which takes the role of *project leader*. Another member of the team is designated as *representative* of the team in the committee. While no other roles are formally defined, subdivision of tasks and specialization within a team are encouraged, considering the amount of work to be done and the number of new skills which have to be developed by the students during the course.

The first week of the course is devoted to the organization of the teams and the study of the manual with the process guidelines. The documents with the informal description of the system requirements and the technical documentation on the system domain are immediately given to the students.

The study of the domain and the definition of a User's Requirement Document, which must include a non-ambiguous, non-redundant description of the system requirements (written in natural language) takes up the following 4 weeks. While this is a large part of the course, an in-depth work during this phase is the foundation on which a good formal specification and, later, a good design, may be built.

As soon as the URD has been defined (a single one is selected among all the URDs produced by the teams), the formal specification of the system begins. We have decided that formal languages with well defined semantics, such as LOTOS, should be used in this phase, rather than semi-formal specification techniques. The requirements in the URD must be traced to the specification, and the interaction between the specification and the system environment must comply with a standard interface defined by the committee. The specification must be *executable* and must pass a testing phase in order to be approved.

In parallel with the development of the formal specification, each team must design and prepare a demonstration of the *user interface* of the system. The UI must be consistent with the URD requirements and with the formal specification.

The project ends with the *architectural design* phase, where each team, using its own specification as a starting point, produces a design of the system using HOOD (Hierarchical Object Oriented Design) [6], a formal language particularly suited to the design of systems which must be programmed using Ada. The specification and design phase have a duration of approximately 6 weeks each.

In the following sections, we will provide an overview of the structure of each phase, in order to show more clearly the relationship between the process and the metrics we used, which are described in section 4.

3.1 Definition of the URD

The definition of the user's requirements is perhaps the most unusual (for the students) of the phases in the project life-cycle, and it is probably the most competitive as well (as only one of the URDs is chosen at the end of the phase, so there is a "winning" team). This two factors, together with the need of mastering a complex domain, make the required effort much harder than it would seem at a first sight.

From our experience, we have got a very clear idea of the way a document in this phase should be written, in order to be useful both as a reference to the client (who needs to be sure that his requirements have been understood) and to the people who develop the formal specification (who need clearly defined requisites which are easily traceable to a formal document):

- the URD must be concise, unambiguous, terminologically correct and consistent (internally and with respect to the user's requirements); '
- the information about the *domain* and the information about the *system* must be clearly separated;
- it must be written in a natural language, but it has to be as *structured* as possible.

To ease the work of the students in writing a document with these characteristics, the URD is divided in two parts:

- a *glossary*, which includes all the definitions required to understand the URD, providing in fact an abstract model of the system's domain; the glossary is further divided into two parts:
  - a *public* glossary, produced by the committee;
  - a *private* glossary, produced by each team to complement the public glossary if the definitions included in the latter are not sufficient for the team's URD;
- the *URD* proper, which includes the description of the system's requirements and constraints.

Obviously, in an ideal case the public glossary should include only and all the definitions required by the URD, and the private glossary would not be necessary.

By enforcing a strict division between the system and its domain, producing an URD with the desired characteristics becomes much easier for the students, and evaluating the documents becomes easier as well.

As the documents are written in a natural language, evaluating them requires a good measure of subjective judgment. To avoid a completely arbitrary approach to this evaluation, we have two *quality controls* (QC) on each of the URDs (each team controls the quality of two of the URDs produced by other teams); the quality controls must check the presence of *ambiguities, redundancies, internal inconsistencies* and *terminological errors* (A.R.I.T. errors).

At the same time, a *judge* evaluates the *style* of the document and its *consistency* with the users' requirements.

At this point, the QC teams discuss the error they have found together with the team who produced the URD and the judge; after this discussion, the judge decides if the errors found by the QC teams are to be considered real errors, or if the QC teams were wrong.

The approved A.R.I.T. errors and the judge's rulings are used to evaluate the URDs. The quality control efforts are evaluated as well: a good quality control must find *all* and *only* the errors in the URD, so that there are penalties for errors found but not approved and errors not found by a quality control team. These evaluation criteria also ensure that a quality control team does not try to undermine another team's effort by revealing more errors than actually present in the URD.

After the evaluation, the best URD is selected, which will be used as a starting point for the formal specification work of each team. The selected URD undergoes another quality control in order to find any error which has not been found during the earlier quality controls. All teams participate to this control and, after this revision, no more changes to the URD are possible. The number of errors found during this latter control also provides an indication of the effectiveness of the former ones.

3.2 Formal Specification

Once the system requirements have been defined in the URD, the specification phase begins. The specification, unlike the URD, is written in a formal language, so that any ambiguity which the URD may still include (which are unavoidable, as it is written in a natural language) may be eliminated before the design of the system begins.

The formal language chosen for the specification phase is LOTOS [7]. LOTOS is well suited to modeling concurrent systems (as most large systems are), as its structure is based on process algebras (such as Milner's CCS [8]), extended with a more powerful representation of data types. A specification of the system using Petri Nets [9] may optionally be included together with the LOTOS description.

Using LOTOS, we may also exploit Lite [10], a CASE tool which allows the syntactical and semantical verification of LOTOS program and the *animation* (i.e. execution) of the specifications. Using this tool, it is possible to *test* the system in a very early stage, ensuring the correctness of its specification.

As we need a unique test plan for all teams, it is necessary to define a standard *interface* for the system, i.e. to define the LOTOS gates which model the interactions between the system and its environment (which includes the user, other information systems, etc.). The committee is in charge of the definition of this interface.

Once the standard gates have been defined, a test plan is prepared by the teacher and made available to the students, so that each team can check its own specification. The plan is not *complete*, i.e. passing the test is a necessary, but not sufficient condition to the correctness of the specification.

Apart from the constraints imposed by the standard interface, each team develops its own specification document, which includes not only the LOTOS description of the system, but also a reasonable complement of graphical and textual parts; these are necessary both to make the evaluation of the specification easier and to ensure that all the people in charge of the design can fully understand the document. This latter requisite is not as important as in a corporate environment, where different teams are in charge of different phases, but has nonetheless some practical relevance, as some of the people in the team may be involved with defining the user interface during the specification phase.

After the specifications are completed, they are validated with a second test plan (unknown to the students); each specification is also subject to a quality control, made by another team; a document is then prepared by the specification team if it does not accept the errors found by the QC as real mistakes. Finally, a judge gives a subjective estimate of a number of characteristics of the specification (e.g. quality of the presentation, efficient use of the expressive power of the formal language, etc.) and, taking into account the results of the QC and the testing, produces the final evaluation.

Unlike the analysis phase, where a single URD was selected, each team uses its own specification as a basis for the design phase, as studying and understanding the specification produced by another team would not be possible in the time available.

3.3 User Interface Design and Demonstration

With GUIs becoming ever more common in recent years, it is now impossible to think of designing software system which does not take adequately into account the interaction between man and machine. From the software engineer's pont of view, an early prototyping of the user interface is useful for two reasons: on the one hand, using the prototype it is possible to show the "look and feel" of the system to the client, reassuring him of the quality of the undergoing work; on the other hand, it is possible to identify defects and misunderstandings in the design of the system (at least as far as user functions are concerned), which could not be immediately evident looking at the URD and the formal specification.

For these reasons, we have decided to include in our process life-cycle a phase where the UI is prototyped and demonstrated to the client; this prototyping is done at the same type as the formal specification. From a didactic point of view, this phase is also useful to show a different approach to the software process, based on *fast prototyping*. The interface demonstration, in a process of this kind, is equivalent to the specification of the system in a "traditional" life-cycle, and this is the reason why the UI design is made in parallel with the formal specification with LOTOS. It comes as no surprise, then, that designing the UI provides useful feedback about the consistency between the formal specification and the system requirements.

It is worth noticing that we don't want from the students simply a *design* of the UI using high-level programming environments; they must also be able to give a *demonstration* of its features, using a multimedia presentation software package. While other approaches to this phase are possible (e.g., designing the interface in such a way that it provides simulated reactions to the user's actions), we believe that putting the emphasis to the demonstration rather then the simulation of activities is more time-effective and provides a very direct way of evaluating the work. The evaluation is based on an evaluation form, compiled each person in the audience of the demo.

The interest of the students for this phase was very high, both because of their interest in learning how to use high level tools and because of their involvement, in a central role, in the evaluation phase.

3.4   Architectural Design

As we have already said, the life-cycle in our project ends with the architectural design phase. The final document produced by each team gives a description of the software architecture of the information system: the components, their functionalities and their interactions are described, without providing a detailed view on how objects and functions are internally coded.

The formalism chosen to support the design phase is HOOD [6], which supports a hierarchical, object-oriented approach to the design. A HOOD design is well suited to being coded using Ada, and for this reason HOOD is an excellent choice for modeling concurrent systems, where a detailed representation the communications and synchronizations within the system is required. Much emphasis is given to the description of the *use* relationships between components, to the control flow and to how functions are provided by objects. For its characteristics, HOOD encourages in a natural way an approach to design based on modularization, decomposition and structuring of the system.

HOOD is also supported by a CASE tool, Adanice [11], which allows syntactical verification, automatic code generation, type checking, etc. Adanice also extracts a number of metrics from the design, such as number of objects, *fan-in* and *fan out* [12], and so on. Some of these metrics have been used in evaluating the design. Adanice also provides support for preparing and formatting the documentation of the design.

During the design phase, the cooperative activity of the committee is centered on providing a description of the objects in the environment of the system, as we want the system interface toward its environment to be defined in a standard way.

We should like to point out that the translation of the LOTOS specification to the HOOD design is not trivial; while both these languages are well suited to describing concurrent systems, they are quite different in their approach. LOTOS is an algebraic, dynamic formalism, while HOOD is object-oriented, hierarchical and gives a static view of the system. Finding a good way of bridging these two formalisms is fundamental for the quality of the design; if the team does not succeed in this translation, it is forced to design the HOOD system from scratch: with only a limited time available, this almost surely implies a low quality of the design.

The design document produced by each team includes:

- an overview of the system architecture;
- a text describing a small number (3-5) of the most important objects in the system;
- a graphical representations of the design tree and of the relationships between objects;
- the design metrics collected by Adanice;
- the HOOD code, formatted using Adanice in order to include only the aspects of the system not included in the graphical representation.

All of these features of the document are used by the teacher of the course to evaluate the design.

4 How to Measure It All?

After detailing the process implemented in the course and describing the documents produced, it is possible to explain the metrics we used and the reasons of our choices. We will give some examples of the results we have found using the metric data we collected and will give some hints concerning the goals we hope to obtain by a more extensive analysis of the data.

Using a complete metric framework to evaluate product quality, to monitor the software process and to find the correlations between process management and organization and product quality is the main characteristic of our software engineering course. While metrics have been collected on SE didactic projects for different kind of research purposes, as far as we know no attempt has been done before in an university to define a set of measurements to cover all phases of the project and to use them in order to optimize the process definition.

Introducing metrics has several important effects on the organization of the process: the entities involved in the process (teams, committee, QC teams, judges, etc.) grow in number and their relationships become more complex, as activities which are often found only in corporate environments (such as quality control, testing and evaluation, standardization of documents, etc.) are introduced. The teams are challenged not only with producing a system design, but with the problems of working in a well defined context, with tight rules on process management and production standards on documents.

This broadening of the didactic scope of the course could be in itself a reason for introducing the metric framework, but there is another interesting effect. A project of this kind becomes a sort of large laboratory where a number of metrics may be introduced, evaluated and compared. As a large number of teams (about 20 in the last two years) are concurrently working on the same set of requirements, a wide range of comparisons on the measurements obtained from the documents are possible, which would be impossible to get in a different context. Our first results are confirming the effectiveness of this "lab" in providing useful insights on the nature of the process and of the project documents.

4.1 Process Metrics

In our process, the teams use a few basic techniques to monitor the workload. The same techniques are also used by the committee to keep track of its activities.

The main characteristics of the process are learned at the beginning of the project by reading the manual, which describes the deadlines, the activities, the entities participating to the project and their roles; on the basis of these guidelines, each team has to define its own internal organization and assign roles to its members.

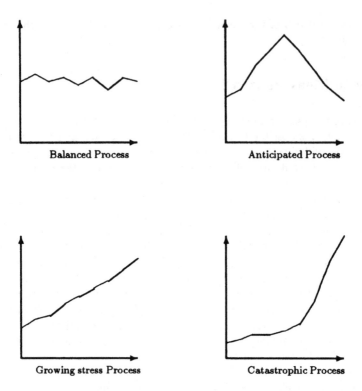

Fig. 1. Calendar Day/Workload Patterns

Each team is required to keep an history of its activities. The book-keeping is made using a pre-defined set of forms, which the leader of each team must compile on a regular basis and which must be delivered to the teacher at the end of each phase. These data are used by the teams to monitor their own workload, using reference patterns (fig. 1) to understand if their efforts are well organized:

- a *balanced process* is the optimal situation: the workload (and team stress) is uniform during the process and the goals are reached at the right time. This is possible only if a good extimate of the workload required is available early in the process;
- an *anticipated process* achieves its goals earlier than required; this is usually fatiguing for the team, however, so that in later phases of the project the team may be negatively influenced;
- a *growing stress process* is the most common case: the initial extimate of the workload is too optimistic; during the process, this mistake is recognized and corrected, but it is necessary to increase the team's efforts. This produces the same problems as the anticipated process; furthermore, sometimes the goals are not achieved in the time available;
- a *catastrophic process* is the worst case: the initial extimate of the workload is

completely wrong and the mistake is recognized only very late in the process. Usually, a process of this kind does *not* achieve its goals, while the people in the team are stressed as much as in the former two cases.

The data is also used to search for correlations between workload patterns and team performances. The forms provided include:

- an *activity-decision sheet*, which must be compiled after every meeting of the team, to provide information on planned, current or completed activities and decisions;
- a *time-activity sheet*, which describes the time spent and the number of people involved in each activity, on a daily basis;
- a *workload form*, which is used to show graphically the total workload (on a weekly basis) and to show the pattern of the workload in each phase and in the whole project

We may define several different kind of observations on this data, including:

- studying the correlation between the workload pattern of a team and its performance (in each phase and in the whole project);
- defining the sub-activities included in each phase; the study of the time spent in the various activities is useful at the team level (to understand the relationship between time spent in the various sub-activities and quality of the documents) and at the project level (to evaluate if the schedule of the process is well organized);
- defining the total (sum of all teams) time spent in each phase, in order to optimize the process, in particular with respect to the definition of the deadlines.

It is worth noticing that this information is *not* used in any way in the *evaluation* of the results, in order to ensure that the data is correctly reported from the students.

4.2 Product Metrics

As we have said earlier, one of the reasons for defining product metrics for the documents produced by the teams is the search for more objective ways of providing a grading for the students. This goal, however, must be balanced against the need of *evaluating* the reliability of the metrics. As a matter of fact, there are very few established metrics for some of the phases (such as the URD phase and the formal specification phase), as most works on metrics usually refer either to project and code metrics or management metrics.

For this reason, we used an hybrid approach to evaluate the documents and providing grades, mixing subjective evaluations from the teacher and various "judges" with objective measurement. We tried to give as much *structure* as possible to the subjective evaluations, asking the judges to provide ratings on a number of well defined parameters of each document. In this way, we are now able to look for correlations between the set of subjective ratings and the set of objective measurements. While we don't believe that subjective evaluations may be completely eliminated, we are quite confident that a much larger number of objective measures than currently used may be substituted to them or used to help the judge in his evaluations.

URD Metrics. The User Requirements Document is written in natural language and, for this reason, is probably the most difficult of the project documents to evaluate using a set of objective metrics. Other characteristics of this document make the evaluation difficult: even the *definition* of the URD itself is quite open to interpretation, both from the point of view of the form the document should have and of its contents (how much detail to provide, how many elements of the system domain introduce in the URD, etc.).

To avoid some of these problems, we have defined the guidelines for writing this document in a very strict way: the URD must not contain any description of the system domain (which is included in the glossary), it must be delivered in several different textual forms (a "standard" text written in Italian, a list of the sentences in the document, a list of the sentences organized using the keywords included in them), and so on. The imposition of these guidelines is helpful to the students for writing the URD, as they make the identification of some problems the document could have easier (e.g. the list organized by keywords is useful to identify if a keyword has been used with more than one meaning, so that ambiguities may be avoided). The guidelines are also useful for the evaluation process, which needs defined standards to ensure that measurements are meaningful.

The evaluation process is divided into three phases, and each phase provides some metrics for the final evaluation of the documents:

1. a *quality control phase* (two teams provide an A.R.I.T. revision on the URD of each team);
2. a *subjective evaluation* from a judge, concerning the *style* and the *correctness and completeness* of the document;
3. a *discussion* to validate the A.R.I.T. quality control, which involves the QC teams, the team who wrote the document and the judge evaluating it.

The A.R.I.T. revisions must follow a very strict form: every error is associated to a single point of the document and must be classified in one of four classes: ambiguities, redundancies, inconsistencies, and terminological errors. Only the errors which the judge approves (after the discussion) are considered by the metric which measures the URD. Each class has an associated *weight* (in descending order, inconsistencies, ambiguities, terminology, redundancies). The weight is used as a multiplier to each approved error, and their sum gives the *A.R.I.T. penalty* of the URD.

In order to establish the effectiveness of the quality control, the errors found and approved are summed (considering the class weight), while each error found but *not* approved in the discussion is subtracted (again, considering the weight) to the evaluation of the QC document. If an error is re-classified, a lesser penalty (which takes into account both the class indicated by the QC team and the class chosen by the judge after the discussion) is applied. By summing up these values, we get the effectiveness rating of a revision.

The subjective evaluation of the URD by the judge is based on grading a number of fixed characteristics of the URD: structure, synthesis, clearness, completeness, language, graphical complements. A small number of bonus points may be assigned for characteristics of the document not included in this list.

The subjective evaluation and the A.R.I.T. penalties are finally normalized and combined, to provide the evaluation of the URD. The rating given to the QC documents produced by a team is taken into account, along with the evaluation of its URD, to grade the overall work of a team in this phase.

While the grading and the choice of the best URD to use for the following phases are based only on the parameters and metrics described up to now (which we call *structured subjective metrics*), we have been able to measure a number of objective characteristics of the URDs and the glossaries, including:

- lexical metrics for the URD: number of propositions, average proposition length, average word length;
- metrics for the glossary: percentage of used terms from the glossary, percentage of terms in the public glossary overridden by terms in private glossaries, number of terms recurring in private glossaries.

The lexical metrics for the URD are meant to provide an objective measure of the readability of the document, on the basis of well known metrics such as the Flesch-Kincaid formula.

The metrics for the glossary evaluate both the *completeness* of the public glossary and its *coverage* of the problem domain: an ideal glossary should include all and only the definitions required by the URDs. In an indirect way, these metrics provide information about the quality of the committee's work.

An example of the metrics used for the glossary is shown in the following table. The first column shows the number of URDs in which a term occurr; the second column shows how many terms have the frequency shown by the first column; the third column shows how many times those terms have been used when the client of the project described it at the teams.

Frequency	# Terms	Freq. Cli. Desc.
9	3	112.3
8	5	43.8
7	3	34.3
6	0	0.0
5	0	0.0
4	1	6.0
3	1	17.0
2	4	5.0
1	3	7.7
0	12	2.9

We see that only 11 out of the 32 terms included in the glossary are used in a significant number of URDs (first three rows), while 12 terms are not used in any of the URDs. This obviously means that the size of the glossary was larger than necessary and implies that the efforts of the committee which produced it were largely wasted.

At the same time, we notice that the "core" set of 11 terms is probably reasonably complete (considering also their frequency in the discussion with the client) with respect to the definition of the domain. A more accurate evaluation of completeness is obtained by studying term utilization in private glossaries.

Objective metrics may be correlated with some of the parameters measured through subjective criteria. For example, the *percentage of glossary terms* used in an URD has been compared to its *completeness* evaluation, showing a meaningful correlation. In a similar way, the lexical metrics may be compared with the subjective evaluations of synthesis, clearness and language. These comparisons are very useful in order to understand if the current subjective criteria provide a meaningful evaluation of the documents.

Specification Metrics. The problems in evaluating the formal specification of the system are very different from those we found in evaluating the URD. Some of the characteristics which were hard to verify in the URD, such as correctness, may be checked in an automatic way on a specification written in a formal language, at least from a syntactical and semantical point of view. This is done using the features of Lite, the programming environment which supports LOTOS, and through extensive *testing* of the specifications, which may be executed in the Lite environment.

However, checking that the specification is formally correct is not sufficient to guarantee its quality. As a matter of fact, the specification must provide the foundation for the *design* of the system, so that it must be easy to understand from the design team: comments in textual and graphical form must be clear and complete, and the formal description itself must be well structured, making good use of the expressive power of the specification language used .

Basically, the evaluation of the formal specification is divided into two phases:

- a *revision* by a single team on each formal specification. The team produces a document, identifying problems and defects in the specification, as far as the *abstraction level* of the specification, its *correctness*, and its *coverage* of the requisites defined by the URD are concerned. The QC document is delivered to the judge, to aid him in his evaluation.
- an *evaluation* from a judge, once again based on structured subjective metrics. This evaluation takes into account the document produced by the QC team. The judge also evaluates the work of the QC team, considering its *usefulness* for his evaluation of the specification.

The evaluation parameters are divided into two classes. Each class includes a number of characteristics, and to each characteristic is assigned a weight, which is used as a multiplier to the rating given by the judge.

- evaluation of *data types* description
  - graphical complements;
  - parameterization in the definition of abstract data types;
  - (informal) use of equations;
  - (formal) use of equations;
  - organization of the data types (coherence with LOTOS specification style);
  - overall readability;
- evaluation of *process* descriptions
  - graphical complements;
  - textual comments;
  - expressiveness of the top level *bex* (Behaviour EXpression);
  - self-containment of processes;
  - granularity of process definitions;
  - use of operators;
  - overall readability.

It is quite clear from this list that much emphasis has been put on evaluating the readability of the document, assuming that its correctness with respect to the URD requirements has already been verified by the QC team and through testing.

As it is quite important that the formal specification is well structured and easy to understand, one of our goals has been searching for objective metrics which could provide information concerning these features. We have been able to define a set of simple software tools that, when applied to a LOTOS specification, measure the *quantity* and *frequency* of the remarks included in the document. The most important result with respect to this phase, however, has been obtained studying a set of specifications written by an ISO committee. This specifications were analyzed, and we determined that it was possible to use the *relative frequency* of the six basic LOTOS operators to define a small number of *paradigms*. These paradigms have been found associating the six-dimensional vector of operator frequencies to each process and looking for *clusters* in this six-dimensional space. Each of these clusters correspond to a different programming style: most well designed LOTOS processes are included in one of these paradigms, while usually a process which does not belong to any of them has some structural problem.

We then analyzed the specifications produced by the students to determine how many of the process included in their specifications were included in one of the paradigms. About 80typical processes, and in some specifications the percentage was 100

We have preliminary results which show that there is a correlation between the rating obtained through the subjective judgment and the percentage of processes of a specification which belong to a paradigm. While there is some sensitivity of the results to the parameters used to define the clusters, this approach seems quite promising.

Using this cluster-based approach, we are able to validate the structured subjective metrics used; at the same time, we are also able to provide the project teams with software tools that help them to verify if their specification is "good" with respect to this metric, hopefully raising the quality of their work.

UI Metrics. During the URD and the specification phases, the output of the team work is a document written in some (natural and/or formal) language, with a well defined structure. For this reason it is possible to define and validate, as we have seen, several objective metrics that may be used to supplement and/or substitute the subjective ones.

The situation is completely different when we are faced with evaluating the user interface of the system. As the value of the interface may be defined by means of its interaction with an user, using subjective evaluation criteria is more a necessity than a choice.

Obviously, first of all we need to verify that the UI is correct with respect to the URD requirements. After checking this, however, we are still faced with the problem of assigning some sort of rating to the quality of the interface.

Our approach to this phase provides a very natural solution to this problem. As the UI is not only *designed*, but *demonstrated* as well, all the teams (or the clients, if possible) may be present to the demo of the UI and asked about their impressions to the interface shown.

The impressions must obviously be collected in a way that ensures that they are well motivated and objective, and for this reason we once again use a structured approach. A form is given to a person chosen from each team; the form includes 14 questions concerning the UI, representing both technical and aesthetic characteristics of the UI: intuitiveness, order, readability, reactivity, coherence and uniformity, documentation, customizability, safety, graduality, programmability and extendibility, cooperativeness, effectiveness.

The evaluation forms provide a significant number of data ($n * (n - 1) * t$, where n is the number of teams and t the number of questions). In the last year, $n = 19$ e $t = 14$, so that we have more than 5000 data available. This means that, rather than simply summing up the ratings obtained from each interface, we are able to apply statistical techniques to reduce the effect of errors and to understand if the evaluations are somehow biased.

Looking at standard deviation and error, we have seen that the set of collected data was basically unbiased (as informally confirmed by the satisfaction of the students for the outcome of the evaluation phase). Anyway, we used factorization methods to provide a correction to the evaluations, increasing the weight of the characteristics proportionally to how "meaningful" they are; this is based on the assumption that the measure of a characteristic is less meaningful if its global mean (i.e. the mean measured on $n * (n - 1)$ ratings) is very far from the global mean of all characteristics (i.e. measured on $n * (n - 1) * t$ ratings). The weighted sum of the evaluations is the rating of the UI.

While the results of this approach have been very interesting, these metrics may be refined. In particular, the list of characteristics to evaluate could be revised, and it is possible that two different kinds of audience ("unskilled" and "experts") will be introduced, each of them responsible for evaluating a different set of characteristics. The unskilled audience would mostly concentrate on evaluating the aesthetics and ergonomicity of the UI, while the second group would concentrate on technical aspects, such as programmability and extendibility.

Design. The process life-cycle ends with the architectural design of the systems, which is delivered by the teams as a document which includes formal parts (project trees, HOOD code) and informal ones (introduction, description of system architecture, informal descriptions of objects). Once again, then, we need evaluation criteria which are based on a mix of subjective and objective metrics.

A lot of work has already been done ([13], [12] et al.) to define metrics which may be applied to a design to determine its complexity and predict future characteristics of the system (e.g. maintainability). Many of these metrics are based on the evaluation of the information flow and of the relationships between objects in the system. The CASE tool used for the design, Adanice, enabled each team to collect some of these metrics, providing some assistance to their design work and to the evaluation process as well. The metrics produced by Adanice from the HOOD design tree are the following ones:

- number of objects;
- number of leaves;
- number of subprojects;
- number of operations provided by the objects;
- number of operations provided by leaf objects;
- average number of sons per node of the design tree;
- maximum number of sons for a node of the design tree;
- average and maximum number of operations provided by the objects;
- average and maximum number of operations provided by leaf objects;
- average *Fan-in* and *Fan-out*;
- maximum *Fan-in* and *Fan-out*.

All these metrics are useful to define the complexity of the design, its refinement level, its degree of modularization, the quality of the decomposition and so on. In general, however, there are no heuristics to know the optimal values for these metrics; usually these data are useful only when compared to data collected on similar systems. Luckily, in our case this is possible, as we have a number of teams working on the same requirements. In this way, we are able to identify whether the measures collected for a team are within a "reasonable distance" from the mean of the measures for the other teams. If the distance is large, this usually means that there is some problem in the design itself.

In our evaluation of the design document, only the number of objects, the number of leaves, the average number of operations per object and per leaf object, and the ratio between these last two values are used; if these values are out of a reasonable interval (i.e. farther from the mean than the standard deviation) a penalty is applied to the document.

As usual, this objective evaluation must be supported by more subjective metrics. A number of features are evaluated by the teacher of the course:the quality of the introduction, the description of objects and HOOD diagrams, how balanced the project tree is, the quality of the HOOD code. All of the collected metrics (objective and subjective ones) are then used to give a final rating to the design documents.

There are no quality controls during the design phase, mainly due to the limited time available.

5 Future Developments

While a lot of work has been done in designing the process, defining and implementing the metric framework and collecting the data, the analysis of their significance has just begun. Our first results are very encouraging: we are finding correlations between data sampled through very different metrics, such as structured subjective evaluations, objective metrics and psycho-sociological testing of the individuals and teams involved in the process.

For example, we have already established some correlations between the workload pattern followed by a team and the ratings of its product; we have seen that many of the objective measurements on the URD correlate quite well with the subjective evaluations; we have found that the clusterization algorithm used to define paradigms for LOTOS processes is very useful in identifying "problem" processes. More results of this kind are coming, and we are confident that in the next year they will be very important to raise the quality of the course.

We are also integrating our effort on process and product metrics with a psychological study of the students; our goal is finding a way to understand the effect of the assignment of people to roles within a team on the team performance, as well as finding ways to define "optimal" psychological profiles for the various roles. This could be helpful for the project teams to optimize their internal organization.

Our final goal is implementing a process where the arbitrary evaluation of the documents and software products created by the project team disappears, and the work is evaluated through advanced techniques which mix structured subjective metrics and objective measurements. Using this approach we want to optimize the process itself, the quality of the documents and, obviously, the value of the students' experience from a didactic point of view - which, after all, is the main goal of the course.

While our experiment has been implemented in an university, we believe that a strong effort on creating a complete metric framework for the whole software process is necessary for everyone who has to create high quality, complex software systems. We have already said that there is a strong feedback between metrics and process organization. With an initial effort in metrics definition, a virtuous cycle starts which may bring to a significant advance in product quality.

References

1. Alcatel Austria and Intecs Sistemi. "Software Metrics Standards for ESA Space Systems". *Studies on ESA Software Metrics Programme Implementation*, April 1992.
2. Sallie Henry and Calvin Selig. "Predicting Source Code Complexity at the Design Stage". In *IEEE Software,*, pp. 36-44, March 1990.
3. Watts S. Humphrey. *Managing the Software Process*. Addison-Wesley, 1989.
4. Vincenzo Ambriola and Tommaso Bolognesi. "The Electric Power of LOTOS". In *FORTE*, 1992
5. Mary Shaw and James E. Tomayko. "Models for Undergraduate Project Courses in Software Engineering". Technical Report CMU/SEI-91-TR-10, Software Engineering Institute, August 1991.
6. ESA/HOOD Technical Group *HOOD Reference Manual - V. 3.1*, July 1991.
7. Ed Brinksma (ed.). *ISO - Information Processing Systems - Open Systems Interconnection - LOTOS - A Formal Description Technique Based on the Temporal Ordering of Observational Behaviour*. Technical Report IS 8807, 1989.
8. Robin Milner. "A Calculus of Communicating Systems". In *Lecture Notes in Computer Science*, no. 92, Springer-Verlag, 1980.
9. W. Reisig. *Petri Nets - An Introduction*. Springer-Verlag, 1985.
10. M. Caneve, E. Salvatori (eds.). *LITE User Manual*. ESPRIT Project 2304 - Loto-Sphere doc. Lo/WP2/N0034/V08, March 1992
11. INTECS Sistemi. *AdaNICE Reference Manual*. Pisa, October 1991.
12. Sallie Henry and Dennis Kafura. "Software Structure Metrics Based on Information Flow". In *IEEE Transactions on Software Engineering*, vol. SE-7, no. 5, September 1991.
13. Thomas J. McCabe and Charles W. Butler. "Design Complexity Measurement and Testing". In *Communications of the ACM*, vol. 32, no. 12, December 1989.

Lessons learned from formalizing and implementing a large Process Model

Jean-Marc Aumaitre - Cap Gemini Innovation

Mark Dowson - Marlstone Software Technology

Del-Raj Harjani - Matra Marconi Space France

Abstract. This paper describes the early results of the PROMESSE project conducted for the European Space Agency, which aims at formalizing and implementing ESA software development processes, and more specifically the lessons learned from this experiment. Following the logic of the study, it presents the lessons learned from the formalization task, then those learned from the implementation. It concludes with a presentation of the method which will be applied for the validation of the implementation (at the time this paper is written, validation is still going on).

1   Introduction

PROMESSE (PROcess Modelling for ESSDE - European Space Software Development Environment) is a project conducted for the European Space Agency (ESA) by Cap Gemini Innovation and Matra Marconi Space, with consultancy support from Mark Dowson of Marlstone Software Technology. The project consists of four main parts:

1. Formalization of the complete ESA software development process in the form of a process model specification.

2. Implementation of an enactable *PROCESS* **WEAVER** [6] process model meeting the specification.

3. Validation of the process model by enacting it in a simulated environment.

4. Integration study (feasibility, strategy) within the ESSDE.

The main purpose of PROMESSE for ESA is to develop a complete model for software development consistent with current ESA software standards and offering a high level of acceptance by the space software developers.

Currently, formalization of the process and implementation of the model are complete, and we are in the validation phase. The work so far, as well as contributing to the objectives of the project, has already taught us a great deal about the process of building process models. In large part this is because of the sheer size of the process being modeled and the detail of the model. Most previous modelling exercises have focused on a fragment of a real or hypothetical process (such as the ISPW-6 Example

Problem [1]), or have abstracted from much of the detail of a complete process. This paper summarizes the approach used in the project, and gives a preliminary description of what we have learned about process modelling.

2 Formalization of the Process

It is important to stress that the process formalized in the PROMESSE project is not an invented or hypothetical process, but the actual process elaborated and used by ESA and its contractors for building space systems. This process is described in various "standards" documents such as the ESA Software Engineering Standards [2]. Part of the ESSDE project that preceded PROMESSE consisted of an attempt to collate these standards and render them in semi-formal terms [3]. The process covers the overall life-cycle, including both development activities (User Requirements Specification through to Implementation), and operational aspects (Transfer, Operations and Maintenance). Where appropriate, sub-processes common to several phases have been factored out so that they can be described independently. Such sub-processes include: Formal Reviews, Change Control, Sub-Contracting/Contractual Aspects, Project Monitoring, and COTS Management (procurement of commercial off-the-shelf components).

The Process Model Specification consists of three main parts: a product model, a description of process roles, and a description of a set of life-cycle phases and sub-processes.

The product model consists of entity-relationship diagrams identifying the (approximately 200) data element types involved in the process, and the relationships between them.

The description of the process roles identifies and describes a set of 17 types ("roles"), whose instances are process definition variables ("role instances") to which actual participants in a process can be bound ("role occupancies"). For example, instances of the role Product Assurance Engineer (PAE) will be occupied by persons who lead, coordinate and perform product assurance activities in a project. A role description consists of:

- A textual description of the role;

- An identifier enabling to refer to this role;

- A description of which aspects of the process occupants of the role are involved in (e.g., during the Operations and Maintenance phase, a PAE will be involved in monitoring changes);

- A definition of any constraints affecting the performance or occupancy of the role (e.g., in case of critical software, the test engineers must be different from the developers).

The largest part (~70%) of the specification consists of definitions of six life-cycle phases and five sub-processes in terms of activities. Each phase and sub-process is defined using three different, complementary and partially overlapping representations:

1. A textual description of each of the steps involved;

2. A tabular representation listing, for each step, step pre-requisites, activities, roles and resulting artifacts;

3. A graphical representation using a formalism rather like an enhanced form of SADT. This formalism is a development of a formalism previously used by Matra Marconi Space and Cap Gemini Innovation [4], [5].

Fig. 1, 2, and 3 show a fragment of the User Requirements Definition phase specification, expressed in each of these three formalisms.

Fig. 1. Fragment of the User Requirements Definition phase, textual description

---

UR/5. Modification: If RIDs are produced, then the documents are modified by their authors, the RIDs are commented and the documents re-verified (SWPM for SVVP/AT plans, US and/or CL, system PAE[1], and possibly with system SWE for URD (and ICD/UR if any)).
RIDs referring to the URD may also be produced, which will lead to modification without needing a complete Change Control process. The reasons for this are that the Change Control process should be enacted only for products which have been formally approved after a formal review, and this review (UR/R) has not been held yet for the URD.
(return to step UR/4.)

UR/6. Check-in into Master Library: When the UR Outputs (URD, SVVP/AT and SR Plans) are internally approved, its components are checked-in by the CM into the Master Library and the UR/R may be held.

UR/7. *(if the UR/R has already been organised once, and if it has been decided not to re-organise it, go to step UR/9.)*
UR/R: During the UR/R *(apply the process described in "Chapter 13. Formal Reviews")*, the UR outputs are reviewed by SPM, SWPM, PAE, US and/or CL and possibly HWE.

UR/8. If RIDs are produced during the UR/R, then this leads to the modification of the UR outputs. It is also decided whether the UR/R should be re-organised. The documents to be modified shall first be checked-out from the Master Library by CM.
(go to step UR/5.)

UR/9. Check-in into Static Library: Once the UR outputs approved, they are checked-in into the Static Library by the CM.

Fig. 2. Fragment of the User Requirements Definition phase, tabular description

ORIGIN	ACTIVITIES	ROLES	PREREQUISITES	RESULTS
-	- Modification of SVVP/AT plans	- SWPM	- URD, - SOW, - SVVP/AT plans - RIDs	- Updated SVVP/AT plans - [commented RIDs]
-	- Modification of URD [& ICD/UR]	- US and/or CL	- URD, - [ICD/UR] - RIDs	- Updated URD, - [Updated ICD/UR] - Commented RIDs
- R[7]	- Configuration Management: Check-in into Master Library	- CM	- UR outputs	- UR Outputs checked-in into Master Library
- R[1] - R[3]	- UR/Rs Review of User Require- ments Phase Outputs	- SWE (P) - PAE (P), - SPM (R), - SWPM (P) - CL and/or US (P) - [specific domain spe- cialists, e.g. HWE] (C)	- URD - [ICD/UR] - SPMP, SCMP, SVVP, SQAP - [commented RIDs]	- Approval or [RIDs]
- R[1] - R[3]	- UR/R: Approval of User Require- ments Phase Outputs	- SPM (R) - SWPM (P), - US and/or CL (P)	- URD - [ICD/UR] - SPMP, SCMP, SVVP, SQAP	- Decision
- R[7]	- Configuration Management: Check-out from Master Library	- CM	- RIDs	- Addressed UR outputs checked- out from Master Library
- R[7]	- Configuration Management: Check-in into Static Library	- CM	- UR Baseline	- UR Baseline put into configu- ration

Fig. 3. Fragment of the User Requirement definition phase, graphical view

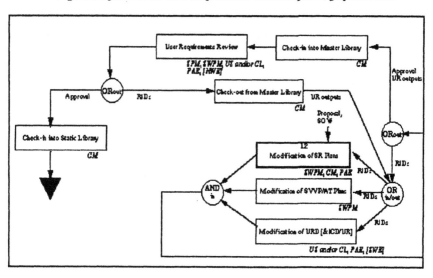

The specification needs to fulfill a number of criteria, including at least:

- It needs to correctly represent the intended process (in this case the overall ESA software development process);

- It needs to meet reasonable standards of internal consistency and completeness;

- It must be appropriate for the needs of its intended audience (which may include managers who want to understand the process at a high level, as well as the implementers of a detailed process model who need a specification of what they are to implement);

- It needs to be easy (or at least possible) to maintain without introducing errors (for example as the process is evolved or improved).

The sheer size of the specification (over 170 A4 pages) made it exceptionally difficult to ensure that these criteria were met, and our attempt to do so taught us a number of important lessons, that we believe will apply to any similar attempt to specify a complete process:

1. Identified difficulty: Generally, a lot of information is spread out all over the document in the processes description. Roles or product description should be quickly presented to the reader. For example, what is the definition of the PAE (Product Assurance Engineer) or the STD (System test document).
Lesson: Purpose built tools are needed for constructing and navigating within a large process specification to help ensure its consistency and completeness. We used a standard document preparation system that allowed hypertext links facilitating automatic cross referencing, but this was far from sufficient. Without tool-supported navigation (and possibly checking) the process of checking e.g. the consistency of textual and graphical representations is tedious and error-prone.

2. Identified difficulty: Some activities are part of the know-how of people from the organization, although their definition cannot be found in the documentation. For instance, this is the case for the Emergency Change Control activity (how to perform quickly changes in critical situations).
Lesson: Systematic "requirements capture" methods are needed to support constructing a process specification from an informal or implicit definition of the process. Informal methods may be adequate for small fragments of processes (such as the ISPW-6 example), but are hard to apply to a more realistic scale. In this project we are using a validation approach (described below) to check the correctness of the specification (and of the models derived from it). However, it would certainly be helpful to have a systematic way to construct a specification with few errors in the first place.

3. Identified difficulty: Having three partially redundant representations of the specification (textual, graphical and tabular) creates a consistency maintenance problem. Any change to the specification has to be made consistently in three places, which risks introducing errors.
Lesson: Although multiple overlapping representations of a process specification may introduce consistency maintenance problems, they are a valuable aid in checking the accuracy and completeness of a specification. Inconsistencies tend to signal that some aspect of the process has not been captured correctly, or that something is missing.

4. Identified difficulty: It is difficult to choose representation formalisms suitable for every kind of user. We found that we would have liked to enhance the graphical formalism to make some synchronization issues clearer for the subsequent model implementers; but we did not want to increase the (already considerable) complexity of the diagrams for, e.g., managerial users.

   Lesson: One solution would be to have additional representation schemes for the needs of these different kinds of users, but this further increases the consistency and maintenance problems. Achieving the right balance seems *very* hard - and will probably take a lot of experimentation in practice.

5. Identified difficulty: Specifying the whole process revealed a number of potential sub-processes that could be factored out. For example, structures very similar to that shown in Fig. 3 appear in the definitions of the Software Requirements Definition and Architectural Design phases. This will later help the organization to improve the homogeneity of its various activities and facilitate the maintenance and the evolution of such sub-processes.

   Lesson: The existing notation does not support the notion of parameterized "chunks" of a specification being reused in several places, but such an extension would be valuable.

3 Implementation

In the scope of the PROMESSE project, the implementation task aimed at:

1. Providing a basis for automated support and guidance of software developers (the "end users") via enactment of the process model.

2. Providing an *enactable model* that could be used to validate both the specification and the standards and methods from which the specification was derived, via simulated enactment (during the validation task described below).

3. Contributing to verifying the completeness and coherence of the specification. The specification has to provide the implementers with *sufficient* information to build a model, and where multiple representations of parts of the specification overlap, *consistent* information.

The implementation task was conducted by Cap Gemini Innovation using *PROCESS* **WEAVER** both for building and for enacting the process model. Six person*months effort over a three month period were required. Approximately 300 activities and 400 work-contexts (task assigned to a user containing the description of what he has to do, the prerequisites - products and tools - and the possible termination states of the task) were implemented using *PROCESS* **WEAVER**.

The implementation task was conducted according to the following life-cycle:

- Identify the connections of the process models with project management activities (actor allocation, activity status);

- Identify the connections of the process models with product management activities (product description, product status, configuration management operations);

- Identify the connections of the process models with tool support (Software Development Environment - SDE);

- Implement the various connections (project management, configuration management, SDE);

- Implement the static aspects of the process model;

- Implement the dynamic aspects of the process model.

The various connections were easily identified and implemented in simulating the different functionalities of a project management, product management and other tools. As *PROCESS* **WEAVER** offers powerful capabilities concerning the invocation of tools, connections with SDEs were parameterized in order to facilitate the integration of the process model with various tool support platforms (currently the model calls "dummy" tools to perform these functions). These and other integration issues will be investigated in more detail in the last part of the project.

The static aspects of the model - structure of the method (see the definition of the Architectural Design plans in the Software Requirements phase, Fig. 4), descriptions of individual activities and of the work-contexts presented to users of the model (see Fig. 5) - proved relatively easy to derive from the specification and implement using *PROCESS* **WEAVER**. We can envisage automatic generation of (at least the skeleton of) the static parts of the model. This would, of course, help ensure close correspondence between the specification and implementation of a model.

Fig. 4. *PROCESS* **WEAVER** method description: Definition of the Architectural Design plans

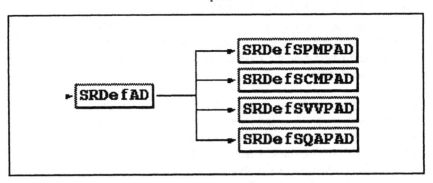

Fig. 5. *PROCESS* **WEAVER** activity description: Definition of the Software Project Management Plan

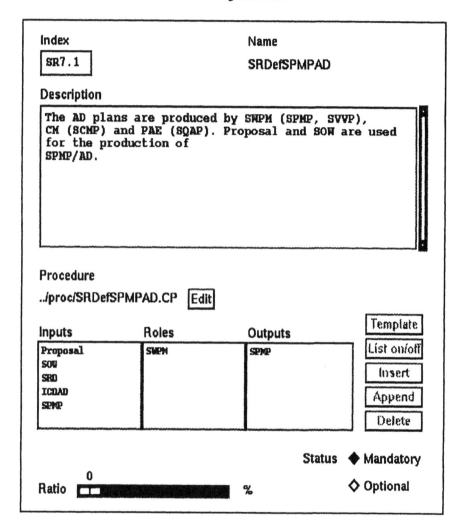

On the other hand, the dynamic aspects of the model - control flow between activities - were more difficult to derive from the specification. A different specification technique, that corresponded better to *PROCESS* **WEAVER**'s way of modeling the dynamics of process, would make this easier, and open the possibility of automatically generating an even larger part of a model. An example of the dynamic description of the activity "Approval of a Software Change Request" as a *PROCESS* WEAVER cooperative procedure is provided Fig. 6.

Fig. 6. *PROCESS* **WEAVER** cooperative procedure: Approval of a Software Change Request

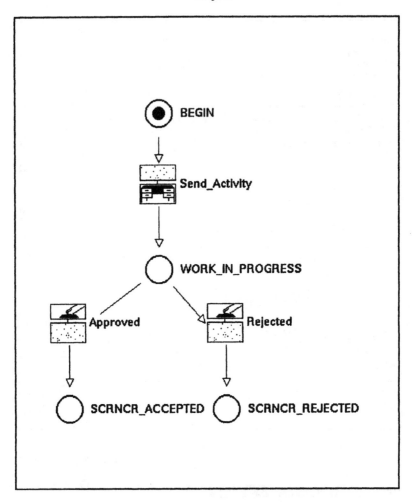

The implementation task also revealed weak points and ambiguities in the process being modeled, mainly in terms of the content of activities being vaguely stated or even not described. This was not acceptable to the implementers, who had to make the decision about what would be presented to the end user when the model was enacted, and led to refinement and enrichment of the specification during the course of the implementation task. (We note that not *all* activities need to be specified in detail - *PROCESS* **WEAVER** allows end users to define their own detailed procedures for some activities where appropriate).

4 Validation

Our approach to the validation of the process model is to exercise it in the simulated environment of a project following a number of pre-defined *scenarios*. These scenarios are in the form of message sequence charts which define a number of roles whose occupants (members of the validation team) interact with the model, stepping through a (scenario defined) path through the process (see Fig. 7).

The PROMESSE validation approach allows us:

- To validate the implementation through the execution of the scenario against the specification by the process model implementers;

- To validate the process model though dry-run execution of the scenarios by operational people against their end user needs;

- To complete the specification during the definition of the scenarios by detection of inconsistencies and incompleteness.

Ultimately, validation of the model can only occur via its use to support real software projects - and this is likely never to be complete because the model will be subject to continual evolution and improvement. Nonetheless, some attempts to validate the model before its actual use are essential.

Fig. 7. Validation Scenario Message Sequence Chart

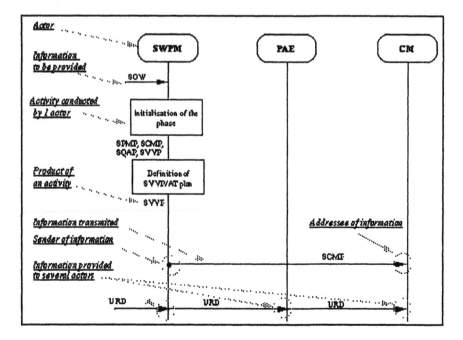

A main scenario was designed to exercise and validate the basic software development life-cycle, while five additional scenarios address specific aspects of the process. Construction of the scenarios required one person*month of effort.

Each participant in a scenario (adopting one or more of the scenario's defined role instances) invokes a *PROCESS* **WEAVER** Agenda for each instance. This serves as the medium for interaction between the role occupant and the enacting model. For example, the main scenario defines ten different role instances (Software Project Manager, Product Assurance Engineer, Configuration Manager, User, System Project Engineer, Test Engineer, Software Review Board, Client, and two Software Engineers). Typically, two or three participants will simulate occupation of these role instances on three or four workstations, carefully following the steps laid out in the scenario as they interact with the *PROCESS* **WEAVER** model.

The six scenarios defined during the project (which occupy approximately 60 pages of Message Sequence Charts similar to Figure 2, plus approximately twenty pages of additional text) cannot be guaranteed to exercise every aspect of the model. Nonetheless, they are sufficiently comprehensive to provide a reasonable degree of confidence that the model represents the intended process accurately.

As noted above, we are only just beginning the validation task (which is planned to occupy one person*month of effort) at the date of writing. Running parts of the scenarios for demonstration purposes etc., however, has already shown us that this is an extremely powerful approach to validation of the model and the specification. Carefully following a scenario allows the participants occupying the scenario roles to quickly pinpoint areas where the implementation differs from the specification, or from an experienced developer's intuition of what is a correct process. Closer investigation of these areas can then lead to corrections to the implementation, the specification, or even to the development standards from which the specification is derived.

5   Conclusions

Formalizing and modeling ESA's complete software process is an ambitious project; certainly, the specification and model developed during the PROMESSE project are the largest we have been involved with (and the largest we know about). We were pleased (and relieved) to discover that our technology and methods did scale up to the problem, and although capable of improvement, can capture a complete industrial software development process.

To a large extent, the process that we followed in performing the project was developed and evolved as the project progressed. Much can be done to systematize and improve that process. For example, it is clear that developing validation scenarios should precede model implementation.

The project brought home to us the importance of support tools in developing large-scale process specifications and models. *PROCESS* **WEAVER** is a powerful tool that proved adequate for model implementation, but provides little or no help with process capture, specification, documentation, analysis, or validation (beyond providing a means of enacting the final model). More tools (some of them quite simple), are urgently needed, including tools to help process engineers construct specification and check them for consistency and tools to automatically generate parts of the process model implementations for their specifications.

New methods are also needed. In particular, we felt the lack of any systematic method for process capture (deriving a process specification from standards documents and other real-world sources of information). We also expect our process specification formalism to undergo evolution and improvement in the longer term.

In spite of the above reservations, we feel that the approach we adopted was fundamentally sound, and the results of the project will be of considerable value, both in terms of the specification and model produced, and in terms of our improved knowledge of how to go about similar projects in the future.

Validation is a critical aspect of process modeling that increases in importance with the size of the process being modeled (i.e., as informal "by inspection" approaches become progressively less adequate). Much more work remains to be done in this area, particularly to find ways in which a generic model can be validated, rather than just a single "instance" of its enactment. Nonetheless, we were impressed at how powerful our approach (separating specification from implementation; multiple representations of the specification; exercise of the resulting model against pre-defined scenarios) was in detecting and correcting errors in the process specification and process model.

References

1 D. Heimbigner, The Process Modelling Example Problem and its Solutions, Proc. 1st International Conference on the Software Process, IEEE Computer Society Press, October 1991.

2 BSSC, ESA Software engineering standards, ESA PSS-05-0, February 1991

3 J. Galle, F. Verlinden, Overall ESA Software Process Model, ESSDE project, ESSDE/STREP/A42, April 1992

4 L. Mangane, JF. Muller, Space FIP Process Models, Eureka/ESF project, D208.D.1.2.2.1, June 1992

5   JM. Aumaitre, F. Bainier, Space FIP Process Models design, Eureka/ESF project, D208.D.1.6.1.1, January 1993

6   C. Fernstrom, *PROCESS* **WEAVER**: Adding Process Support to UNIX, Proc. 2nd International Conference on the Software Process, IEEE Computer Society Press, March 1993.

Acknowledgments

The authors would like to thank the PROMESSE team (Didier Bronisz, Annie Leclerc, Cap Gemini Innovation) for their contribution and for the work carried out up to now.

Applying Process Technology to Hardware Design⋆

Bernd Krämer and Burhan Dinler

FernUniversität, D-58084 Hagen, Germany
GMD, D-53575 Sankt Augustin, Germany

Abstract. We report on a case study of applying a two-tiered approach to model hardware design processes. First we use CCS and tools of the Concurrency Workbench to specify and rigorously analyse the dynamics of design processes. Then we transform the validated abstract process model semi-automatically into Marvel rules, objects and envelopes. The resulting executable model provides a process environment for the public domain collection of design tools, Alliance. The purpose of this experiment was to demonstrate that much of the effort currently spent for research under the headings "CAD frameworks" and "task and session management" could be saved by exploiting software engineering results, in particular the emerging software process technology.

1 Introduction

Hardware designers are not only confronted with an increasing complexity of design objects[2] but also with a growing number of sophisticated design tools. These tools are not easy to use and customise individually, let alone their task specific composition to an integrated support environment. Moreover, design decisions that may have a enormous impact on the cost and time-to-market of new hardware components must be taken early in its development cycle. Therefore we observe a growing awareness in the CAD community to consider product design and development process as a unit. The large number of CAD framework prototypes resembling more and more process-centered software environments provide a distinct sign for this tendency. But, amazingly enough, up to now we observe little activity of both hardware and software communities to leave the grails and join their forces. (Hardware-software codesign provides an adequate heading but no tangible results yet.)

We report on a case study of formalising and enacting VLSI design processes using existing software process technology. We use the public domain collection of hardware design tools Alliance[3] as a carrier of elementary process steps. The

---

⋆ This work was partially funded by the ESPRIT WG 6071 ISCORE and the German Minister of Research and Technology under project number KAN INF 16.
[2] We observe a doubling of complexity every two years.
[3] Alliance runs under Unix and just needs a colour graphics display for presenting the final mask layout [1].

four-bit bipolar microprocessor AMD2901[4] serves as a real-life design object.

The paper is organised as follows: Section 2 sketches the AMD design process and relates selected characteristics of hardware design processes to software processes. In Section 3 the dynamics of the design process is formalised in terms of CCS agent definitions [3]. To check various properties of the abstract model, we rely on the simulation and analysis capabilities of the Concurrency Workbench (CWB)[5]. In Section 4 we sketch how the design flow captured in the CCS model is transformed into a collection of Marvel rules and control objects whose attributes control the chaining of rules according to CCS model. This transformation process can be automated by adapting the method described in [10]. This rule-based design flow model is then manually extended by object classes defining the structure of design objects and other artifacts that occur through a design process. The activities defining the core of the rules are implemented by a suitable subset of Alliance tools. These tools are encapsulated by means of tool envelopes to enable the activation of design tools through the Marvel environment. We conclude with a brief discussion about the suitability of the process paradigm to model hardware design tasks and drive CAD frameworks.

2   Hardware Design Processes

An elaborate description of the AMD design process and the functionality of Alliance tools is given in [5]. Here we leave it at an overview description of the process depicted in Fig. 1. In this figure ellipses denote design documents that are typically stored in files, boxes denote tool functions, solid arrows indicate the design flow, and dashed arrows indicate feedback loops taken in case of errors.

Similar to software development, digital systems development is largely a design process. It typically starts from a description of functional requirements which are manually transformed into a *behaviour specification*. Such specifications are usually given in a hardware description language such as VHDL or Verilog and have much in common with high-level programs. Behaviour specifications are then compiled into executable models (e.g., by a tool like ASIMUT). Together with concurrently specified and compiled *test patterns* the models are simulated to validate the design at a logical level. This step is comparable to module testing in software engineering. High level *synthesis* then comprises the transition from the algorithmic specification of behaviour to a *structural description* (assigned to the register transfer level). It implements behaviour in terms of net lists specifying a collection of predefined components such as registers, adders, multiplexers, or ALUs and their interconnections. The Alliance tool set provides no automatic support for this step. Subsequent down-stream tasks are concerned with the stepwise transformation into a mask layout which concludes

---

[4] The microprocessor is designed as a high-speed cascadable element intended for use in CPU's, peripheral controllers, programmable microprocessors and numerous other applications [2].

[5] CWB was developed by the department of computer science of the University of Edinburgh[11].

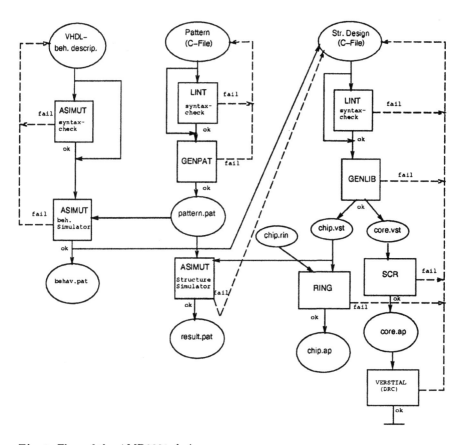

Fig. 1. Flow of the AMD2901 design process

the design task by producing an encoded representation of silicon structures to be fabricated. These process steps include the generation of net lists from the structure specification through GENPAT, their simulation using ASIMUT, the standard cell placing and routing, whose quality is controlled through an option of tool SRC, the chip routing with RING, and a final design rule check with tool VERSTIAL. These steps are constrained by technology-specific restrictions, such as spacing, topology, logic, packaging, routing, or testing.

The design rules and constraints to be observed are usually more rigorous and deterministic than we are used to in software engineering. In simple cases, a circuit can even be specified by a set of constraint rules that can be solved automatically by a computer program. But in most cases such constraints cannot be deterministically optimised but require human skill and experience. This is the place where process technology receives its value by providing automatic tool invocation whenever possible and appropriate, controlled access to design data, and consistent update of process information.

Hardware design processes can be comparably complex as software in terms of components and interconnections. Support for information storage and retrieval as well as configuration management is therefore extremely important. This issue will, however, not be considered here.

Hardware design comprises, of course, not only technical and but also managerial tasks as the size of development teams varies from 3 to hundred developers (e.g., in the design of modern microprocessors). Thus support for team coordination, scheduling, and communication is required. But, as time-to-market and first-time-correct are the key notions to success on the chip market and these qualities are strongly influenced by the design process, it is extremely difficult to obtain real process data from hardware industries. Thus we could focus on tool factors only and had to neglect group and other factors described in [6].

3 Formalising and Analysing Process Dynamics

CCS is a well-known process-algebraic formalisms for specifying concurrency and communication in distributed systems. It underlies the Formal Description Description Technique LOTOS which has been applied to software process modeling in [7]. We chose to use CCS as it is better supported by formal analysis methods and tools, such as the Concurrency Workbench (CWB, [4]).

CCS describes concurrent processes as a system of communicating agents whose behaviour consists of elements of a given set of actions. Each action either represents an interaction with neighbour agents or it denotes an invisible action that can occur concurrently to the actions of other agents. Complex process models can be systematically constructed from simpler models by means of few operators including '+', which denotes the mutual exclusion of two processes, '|' denoting the parallel composition, and '.', which composes an action and a process to a new process. Some simple examples taken from the CCS description of an Alliance based design process are:
Agent

$$AsimutSyntax \stackrel{\text{def}}{=} fBehav?.(failASyntax! + fOkBehav!).AsimutSyntax$$

which represents the syntax checker of tool ASIMUT, receives a behaviour specification $fBehav$ as input, then either communicates a successful or failed syntax check to its environment, and finally behaves like $AsimutSyntax$.
Agent

$$Behav \stackrel{\text{def}}{=} (Input|Designer|EditBehav|AsimutSyntax)\backslash_{\{ed, failASyntax, spBehav, fBehav\}}$$

comprises the actions of task "syntax check of AMD behaviour". It results from a parallel composition of four other agents with the restriction that the channels ed, $failASyntax$, $spBehav$ and $fBehav$ are no longer accessible for communication from the environment of agent $Behav$.

Besides command interpreter, syntax checker and parser, the construction interface of CWB includes a component to produce labeled transition graphs as visual representations of agent behaviour. They represent process states and transitions between states caused by action occurrences. Fig. 2 shows the transition graph of agent *Behav*.

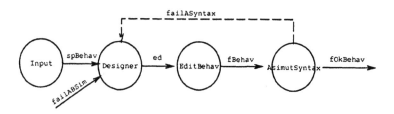

Fig. 2. Transition graph of agent *Behav*

CWB offers different functions to analyse CCS specifications and, thus, to increase the process designer's, project leader's or other responsible persons' confidence in the process model at hand. They are

- simulation,
- equivalence checking, and
- deadlock analysis.

Simulation is performed through interaction with the process model's input channels (cf. Fig. 3). It compares to program testing on the level of specifications. A simulation protocol is recorded automatically.

Equivalence checking determines whether two processes have the same behaviour. This analysis method can be used to verify desired properties of a process by comparing it with a second process which is known to have these properties. Often, the latter is a much simpler process than the former, so that an equivalent minimised process in the sense of having a minimal number of states can be found. It should be obvious that the fine-grain behaviour of a process as shown in Fig. 3, which abstracts from the details of its component agents, can become hard to understand completely. In fact, it took us several iterations over the equivalence check to come up with a satisfactory process definition as depicted in Fig. 3.

Deadlock analysis of our agents revealed several potential deadlock situations. For agent *Behav*, for example, CWB noted a potential deadlock state in case that *AsimutSyntax* attempts to communicate an erroneous syntax check to agent *Designer*, while the latter is involved in an interaction with agent *Input* or *Simulator*. In a concrete design process, however, this construction raises problems only if multiple designs are handled at a time and not enough human resources (i.e., hardware designers) are available. An evaluation of the other deadlocks led to similar results.

It should be noted here that, at the current stage of support, both CCS and the Workbench require more skill and training than can be expected from the average process designer in practice.

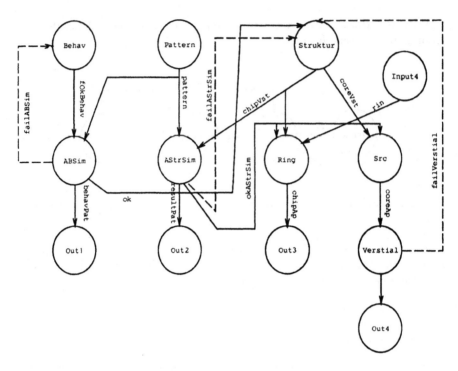

Fig. 3. Design process as transition graph

4 Construction of an Executable Process Model

After an extensive analysis and simulation of the CCS model of the AMD design
process we transformed it manually into an executable model in terms of Marvel
rules, object classes, and tool envelopes. As Marvel and its features have been
discussed extensively in the literature (cf., e.g., [8, 9]) we restrict ourselves to a
brief discussion of the transformation procedure we adapted from [10] and the
role of Marvel as a process environment for Alliance tools.

Each action of the CCS model, except for the actions of pseudo agents
(*Input1*, ..., and *Out1*, ..., *Out4*), was encoded in a rule. As rules have no
hierarchical structure but agent definitions are usually built recursively from
other agents, we had to flatten our process expressions first to obtain a top level
process consisting of actions only. This was achieved by replacing process applications by their corresponding agent expressions and substituting recursion as in
$Input \stackrel{\text{def}}{=} spBehav!.Input$ by an iterative expression like $Input \stackrel{\text{def}}{=} spBehav!+$. As
their is no direct correspondence between the parallel operator of CCS and the
Marvel rule chaining mechanism, expressions of the form $a.b|c$ had to be replaced
by the sum $a.b.c + a.d.b + d.a.b$ of all possible interleavings of parallel actions
according to the semantics of the parallel operator. To obtain a proper chaining
of rules, suitable preconditions and effects had to be designed both from a *con-*

trol and a *product oriented* perspective. The former reflects the semantics of the CCS model and is captured by appropriate status attributes of objects occurring and evolving in the process. The product-oriented view comprises the structure of the design objects and other artifacts relevant to the process as well as tool envelops encapsulating appropriate tool functions to perform the actions. This part of the case study was largely guided by the structure and types of design documents available for the AMD2901 microprocessor and the functionality of Alliance tools.

In principle the control oriented view can be derived automatically from CCS behaviour descriptions using a collection of predefined control objects (for sequence, alterative, iteration) controlling the chaining of rules according to the CCS description. This approach was taken in [10] to implement the model of activity structures, whose control constructs have much in common with CCS, on top of Marvel rules.

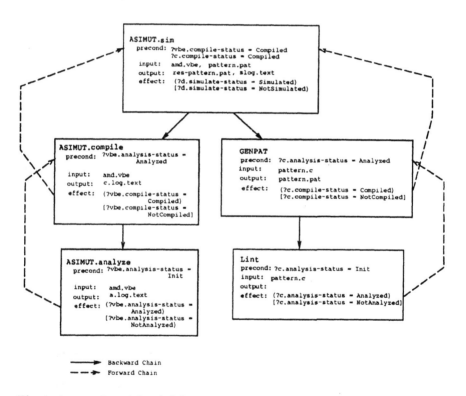

Fig. 4. Automatic activity chaining

As a result we obtained an automatic invocation and execution environment for Alliance tools based on the Marvel rule chaining mechanism. The session protocol presented in the five window panes of Fig. 4 illustrates the history of a design flow controlled by the Marvel process model. It shows, for example, that whenever a designer wants to change a pattern file, which contains information about test patterns to be used in behaviour simulation, the **Marvel** interpreter attempts to form a backward chain by which a lock is set on this file. Upon termination of the edit step the status attribute of the pattern object is redefined which triggers Marvel to build a forward chain of rules activating the tools LINT (which performs a syntax and static semantics check), GENPAT (which compiles the pattern description into an executable form), and ASIMUT's simulation function automatically.

The additional performance overhead introduced by Marvel turned out to be acceptable as opposed to the pain that novice users, for which Alliance was designed, usually suffer when attempting to activate the appropriate tool by hand. In the Unix environment this includes the setting related environment variables directing input and output, the selection of the proper tool options, and the like, let alone a consistent book-keeping of the process state.

A further process quality assurance step would consist in the verification of the behavioural equivalence of both the CCS model and Marvel rule chains. This would require a computation of the set of maximal rule chains and their translation into labeled transition graphs to enable CWB to perform the equivalence check. This work is under investigation.

5 Conclusion

One objective of our case study was to emphasise the idea of process as an important asset of an engineering discipline such as hardware design, which has much in common with software engineering. In particular, we tried to demonstrate that software process technology can be applied successfully for this purpose by illustrating the use of explicit task specifications, including causal or temporal dependencies between tasks, preconditions and effects of individual tasks, design artifacts involved and the role of support tools, for organising and improving design processes, independently of whether they are concerned with software, hardware, or both.

As a byproduct, our simple case study addressed major objectives of CFI's[6] Task and Session Information Model.

- Marvel's tool envelops allowed us to encapsulate tools and thus embed them in the process without requiring modifications to them.
- Based on the data-driven (forward) and goal-driven (backward) chaining mechanism, the process model drives the (automatic) invocation of tools if possible and appropriate.
- Rules, in particular their precondition and effect specifications, provide controlled access to process data as the preconditions may depend on role-specific policies describing responsibilities, obligations, and permissions.

---

[6] CAD Framework Initiative

– Finally, the rule-based process model handles all update of process information consistently.

Further aspects of design process we did not consider here include managerial tasks, configuration management of design objects, and coordination of multiple designers. Our hypothesis is that related results and ongoing experiments in the software process domain will carry over similarly as we demonstrated for technical tasks in the main body of this paper. A major problem for carrying out case studies with an extended focus is, however, access to real process data in this domain, which is driven by the requirements to be quick on the market with the right product.

References

1. A. Greiner; F. Pêcheux. ALLIANCE: A complete Set of CAD Tools for teaching VLSI Design. Technical report, Laboratoire MASI/CAO-VLSI, Institut de Programmation Université et Marie Curie (PARIS VI).
2. A. Greiner; F. Pêcheux. AMD2901-TUTORIAL. Technical report, Laboratoire MASI/CAO-VLSI, Institut de Programmation Université et Marie Curie (PARIS VI).
3. R.A. Milner. *Communication and Concurrency*. Prentice-Hall, 1989.
4. F. Moller *The Edinburgh Concurrency Workbench (Version 6.0)* Department of Computer Science, University of Edinburg, August 15, 1991
5. B. Dinler and B. Krämer. Integrating a CAD Tool Box with a Software Process Environment: A Case Study. In Procs. *Intern. Workshop on Hardware-Software Codesign*, October 1993.
6. I. Sommerville and T. Rodden. Understanding the software process as a social process. In *Software Process Technology*, LNCS 635, pages 55–57, Berlin, Heidelberg, New York, 1992. Springer.
7. M.Saeki and T. Kaneko and M. Sakamoto. A Method for Software Process Modeling and Description using LOTOS. In *First International Conference on the Software Process – Manufacturing Complex Systems*, pages 90–104, October 1991. Computer Society Press.
8. G.E. Kaiser; P.H. Feiler; S.S. Popovich. Intelligent Assistance for Software Development and Maintenance. *IEEE Software*, pages 40–49, May 1988.
9. G.T. Heineman, G.E. Kaiser, N.S. Barghouti, and I.Z. BenShaul. Rule chaining in MARVEL: Dynamic binding of parameters. In *6th Annual Knowledge-Based Software Engineering Conference*, pages 276–287, September 1991.
10. G.E. Kaiser, I.Z. Ben-Shaul, and S.S. Popovich. Implementing Activity Structures Process Modeling on Top of the MARVEL Environment Kernel. Columbia University, Department of Computer SCience, September 1991.
11. F. Moller *The Edinburg Concurrency Workbench (Version 6.0)* Department of Computer Science University of Edinburg, August 15, 1991

Related Domains Session

Vincenzo Ambriola

Università di Pisa, Dipartimento di Informatica

In a software process many activities require the concurrent participation of multiple users, often geographically dispersed. The cost and the complexity of the process are also related to the interactions that occur among them. Controlling, managing, and supporting these interactions are means to improve process quality and to decrease their costs.

The cooperative work theme is assuming a growing relevance in the research community. State-of-the-art technologies are now available at affordable price: significant experiments can be executed and technological transfer can be planned in the short term.

Traditionally, cooperative work has been studied in the areas of information systems and office automation. Process modelling covers some aspects of cooperative work, although its objectives are more in the active guidance of the process rather than in the passive control of a predefined interaction schema. For this reason, process modelling issues are wider and harder to achieve: take, for instance, the intricacy and the challenge of modelling change and evolution in the software process.

This session is dedicated to domains related to the software process. The theme of cooperative work is the strategic goal of the discussion, while the tactics is more on the analysis of cooperative work from the process modelling perspective. Four position papers will give substance to the discussion. Lonchamp focusses on the different aspects of cooperative work showing how process modelling can benefit from the concepts of cooperation, collaboration, and communication. Conradi compares concepts, methods, formalisms, and tools classically exploited in the process modelling community with the needs of information systems. Gruhn describes the similarities between business processes and software processes. Estublier discusses the requirements posed by cooperative work on the data base technology.

Software Process Management and Business Process (Re-)Engineering

Volker Gruhn*
Fraunhofer Institute for Software and Systems Engineering
Baroper Straße 301
44227 Dortmund
Germany

1 Introduction

A *process arena* that has evolved nearly independently from the software process arena over the recent years is that of workflow management and business process (re-)engineering.

While software process management has its roots in software development research and in research on software engineering environments, workflow management and business process (re-)engineering are influenced by business organization [7] and office automation [3, 1].

Software process management and business process engineering both deal with similar subjects. They both focus on managing logically related sets of activities carried by different people (called software processes and business processes). In this position paper some differences and similarities between software process management on the one hand and workflow management and business process (re-)engineering on the other hand are pointed out. This helps to identify where both areas could benefit from each other.

2 Business Process (Re-)Engineering and Workflow Management

Workflow management means to coordinate people who interact to complete a transaction. To manage the workflow in an interpersonal process means to take care of efficient flow of information between process participants. Workflow management means to coordinate process participants, to make required objects accessible to them and to ensure a consistent order of tasks [5].

Workflow management software systems are defined as *pro-active* systems. The term *pro-active* indicates the most important feature which distinguishes workflow management from computer supported cooperative work (CSCW) [4]. While CSCW systems provide mechanism to support cooperative work, workflow management systems are also used to drive processes forward. They are an active element in processes, while CSCW systems are understood as passive enablers.

---

* Current address: LION GmbH, Universitätsstraße 140, 44799 Bochum, Germany

Business Process Engineering is understood as the attempt to define business processes according to logical and organizational demands. *Business Process Reengineering* is similar to business process engineering, but it pays more attention to already existing business processes and their actual implementation [2]. In [6], business process reengineering is understood as the *reinvention* of business processes. Reinvention - instead of improvement - means that basic structures of processes are not necessarily left intact, but may be changed due to new technologies or changed business opportunities. Examples of business process exercises (Kodak, IBM, Aetna Life) are discussed in [6]. For these examples it is claimed that a process reinvention resulted in substantial increases in productivity. Moreover, advantages related to shorter times to market are reported.

In contrast to the promises made by *business process consultants*, most business process engineering[2] tools and environments (such as COSA (from Ley), E.C.H.O. (from DEC), Workparty (from Siemens), Workflo (from Filenet), Staffware (from AIC) do not cover the entire process management life cycle. For most of them only modeling support is available [5]. Others provide enaction support, but they do not support comfortable modeling. Instead of modeling, processes have to be programmed by the tool supplier. Once processes are programmed in such tools, they can only be modified by experts.

3 Software Process Management and Business Process Engineering - Differences and Similarities

First of all, there are some basic similarities between business process engineering and software process management. These similarities cover:

Notion of processes The notions of processes are similar in both communities. A process is understood as a set of logically related activities which have to be executed by different people and in a certain order.

Notion of process management Generally speaking, the notions of process management are similar. In both cases *process management* is meant to cover modeling, evaluation and improvement, and enaction of processes.

Maturity of tool support Another similarity concerns maturity of tool support for process management. Neither in the commercial field of business process engineering, nor in the academic arena of software process management, we find tools that provide comfortable support for the entire management of complex processes.

Some basic differences between business process engineering and software process management are discussed below:

Process reuse Most companies do not want to invent completely new business processes, but they want to improve their existing processes. This requires

---

[2] We use the term *business process reengineering* as general term for business process (re-)engineering and workflow management.

that existing processes have to be captured at first. For that purpose certain types of questionnaires and interview procedures have been developed. This is different from numerous software process modeling efforts, in which processes are designed fore reasons of illustration, but not for enaction purposes. Such modeling exercises do not necessarily have to reflect the actual way of software development. In other words, business process modeling is much more oriented towards the state of the practice than software process modeling. This will certainly change as soon as complex software processes are to be established in companies. At that moment software process models have to reflect what is going on in companies. For the time being, capture of existing processes and reuse of processes is less important for software processes than for business processes.

Process modeling In the software process community there is a *history* of arguing about the best process modeling language (procedural, declarative, prescriptive, descriptive, rule-based, net-based, procedural, etc.). It is generally accepted that process models are subject of communication and that, therefore, comprehensibility of process models is important. There is a different attitude in the area of business process engineering. Business processes are assumed to be well-understood. The focus is on an efficient implementation of business processes, while comprehensibility of process models is considered less important.

Process enaction Software process enaction is understood as critical subject. Careful assistance and guidance may be successful. Any form of strict process control is expected to be not accepted by software developers. The *big-brother*-syndrome has influenced the discussion on software process enaction for years. This discussion is much less important in business process engineering. While software process enaction usually means nothing more than to assign tasks to people, business process enaction support usually provides a set of features, like delegation, replacement in vacation, archiving of processed documents, etc. These details implemented in business process enaction tools show that enaction is accepted as a worthwhile and necessary aspect of business process engineering.

Flexibility Software processes usually are very flexible. This is partially due to the fact that software processes are ill-understood. Another reason for the flexibility of software processes is that circumstances for software processes (requirements for software to be developed, resources available) change frequently. Because of these reasons software process technology considers on-the-fly-modifications of software processes as important feature of software process management. Such modifications are less important for business processes, because they are much more routine. This difference is also due to the fact that software processes are one-of-a-kind. This means, that software processes differ from project to project, while business processes are usually well-established and, therefore, stable. Business processes which are not well-established are as unstable and subject to modifications as software processes are. Such business processes have to be managed in a very flexible way. Because of this difference, it is crucial to distinguish well-understood and stable business processes from others which are less stable.

4 Conclusion

Software process management and business process engineering both deal with similar problems. The emphasis of both has been put on different aspects of process management. A look at solutions developed in both communities helps to benefit from each other.

Business process engineering most of all could benefit from the architectures of software process management tools and from the well-defined process modeling languages. Moreover, it seems worthwhile in business process engineering to pay more attention to comprehensible and adaptable process models.

Software process management could, for example, benefit from the enaction features implemented in business process engineering tools. Moreover, it looks promising to consider the requirements, which actually result from enacting processes with hundreds of process participants. Business processes of that size are actually enacted and their enaction causes many problems for most business process enaction tools. In software process management there is less experience with enacting really large processes. Thus, software process enaction could benefit from analyzing business process enaction problems.

References

1. G. Bracchi and B. Pernici. *The Design Requirements of Office Systems. ACM Transactions on Office Information Systems*, 2(2), April 1984.
2. T.H. Davenport and J.E. Short. *The New Industrial Engineering: Information Technology and Business Process Redesign. Sloan Management Review*, 1990.
3. H. Fleischhack and A. Weber. *Rule Based Programming, Predicate Transition Nets and the Modeling of Office Procedures and Flexible Manufacturing Systems.* In *Proceedings of the 10th Int. Conf. on Application and Theory of Petri Nets*, Bonn, FRG, June 1989.
4. I. Greif, editor. *Computer-Supported Cooperative Work: A Book of Readings*, San Mateo, California, US, 1984. Morgan Kaufmann Publishers.
5. K. Hales and M. Lavery. *Workflow Management Software: the Business Opportunity*. Ovum Ltd., London, UK, 1991.
6. M. Hammer and J. Champy. *Reengineering the Corporation*. Harper Business, New York, US, 1993.
7. P.C. Nystrom and W.H. Starbuck, editors. *Handbook of Organizational Design - Adapting organizations to their environments*. Oxford University Press, 1984.

A Comparison of Modelling Frameworks for Software Processes and Information Systems

Reidar Conradi, Geir Magne Høydalsvik, Guttorm Sindre,
Norwegian Institute of Technology, Trondheim, Norway.

Abstract. This paper takes the position that software process modelling and information systems modelling are closely related in topic — although research is performed by two rather distinct camps and approaches differ. We think that both fields would benefit from more cooperation. The close relationship between the fields is indicated by a modelling example.
Keywords: software process modelling, information systems modelling.

1 Introduction

So far, research in software PM has been rather separate from the related field of information systems (IS) modelling. Although not completely disjoint, there are basically two different groups of people involved — each with their research projects, workshops and conferences. However, the problem domains are actually quite similar — the only difference being a shift in meta-level. Just like an information system supports an organizational information processing activity, a software process tool supports the activity of developing such systems. Indeed, this system (i.e. process support environment) is itself an information system, and software is itself information. Hence it is not surprising that the disciplines should be similar in topic: software process modelling has just narrowed the topic to investigating support for one specific kind of human information processing activity, namely software development. In contrast, information systems engineering considers information processing activities in general.

The purpose of this paper is to illustrate through a simple modelling example that the difference between the two fields is mostly in the approaches chosen, not in the problems which they have to deal with. Thus, a closer coupling between the fields should therefore be fruitful. For this exercise we use the PPP approach for information systems modelling, and the EPOS approach for software process modelling.

2 Examples

2.1 PPP

The PPP (Phenomena, Process and Programs) environment [GLW91] is based on a certain development strategy for IS. A PPP model consists of four sub-models using four different sub-languages: a *Process Model (PrM)* (an "activity model" from the PM view) based on structured analysis and data flow diagrams, a *Phenomenon Model (PhM)* based on the classical Entity–Relationship datamodel with type inheritance, a *Process Life Description (PLD)* (operations) giving an algorithmic sequential description of some behaviour pattern, and a *User Interface Description (UID)* based on a diagrammatic, formal language for specifying any user interface. We will only give a short indication of the PrM sub-language.

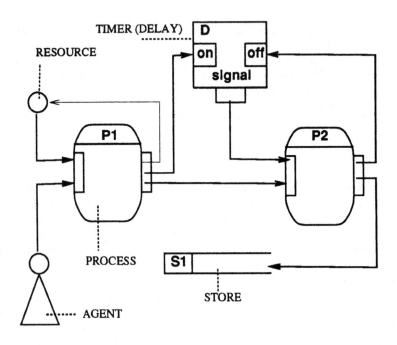

Fig. 1. *Basic concepts of the PrM language.*

The basic concepts in PrM is shown in figure 1. It includes the fundamental concepts of processes, data flow, stores, and external entities. Additional concepts include ports, triggering rules and timers, this to remove vagueness and make the model executable. Graphical symbols for ports include AND, XOR, OR, repeated output and conditional output – or any combination of these.

2.2   EPOS-PM

The EPOS PML or *SPELL* [CJM+92] is used to describe product models (for passive artifacts), activity models (for "active" tasks), tool models (as envelopes), and to some degree role models and project models. SPELL is fully object-oriented data model with explicit relations, meta-types, and where tasks are special objects. We can say that SPELL is a concurrent, reflective and persistent

PML, expressed in Prolog. It is a superset of the DDL/DML of the uniformly versioned EPOSDB.

Process (sub)models in EPOS can be template models (schemas of types), enactable models (instances of such types), or enacting models (active task instances). Process models can be versioned (e.g. customised), and can *evolve* dynamically in a (sub)project context, utilising nested and cooperating transactions. We can define both generic and specific process models, e.g. by subtyping of reusable model libraries.

A project-specific template model is typically instantiated by a Planner and executed by an Execution Manager, our Process Interpreter. Tasks (activities) stand in a task network, and operate on products employing humans and tools – all defined by SPELL types. In this paper we will only consider EPOS-PM and associated Task Networks.

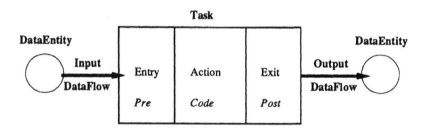

Fig. 2. *Conceptual task model.*

Figure 2 shows a conceptual task model. *Entry* is the pre-condition to be met before *Action* initiation. The task will execute whenever its pre-condition becomes true. A task's *Code* part is responsible for causing its *Post*-condition to become true. A task network is a partially ordered network of tasks (boxes), edges (flows), and denoted data entities (circles). A task can be decomposed into a subtask network.

2.3 The IFIP Working Conference example

The following example is a subset of the IFIP conference example that has been around for about 10 years, serving as a reference example in the information engineering communities. Activities to be undertaken can shortly be described as follows:

1. Prepare a list of persons who will receive information of the conference, and who are invited to contribute papers (call for papers).
2. Record letters of intent.
3. Record papers received.

4. Distribute papers among referees.
5. Record referee-reports and select papers for presentation.
6. Group papers into sessions and appoint chairman for each session.

To keep the example short we will focus on a decomposition of "Distribute papers among referees".

IFIP in PPP The solution depicted in Figure 3 is adopted from [Ber87]. It can briefly be described as follows: When the current date reach the submission deadline, a signal will cause P3.1 to be activated (triggered). Before this process is allowed to execute, items P in S1 must be available. The output from this process consists of unchanged items P, and two signals Num. The processes P3.2 and P3.3 is activated in parallel, but process P3.3 must wait for "Paper Copies" generated by P3.2. The output port in process P3.2 shows a repetition. The original paper is stored in S3 and a number (Num) of copies in S3.1, and is repeated for all papers. Process P3.3 will send each paper to each referee and register this information in S2.

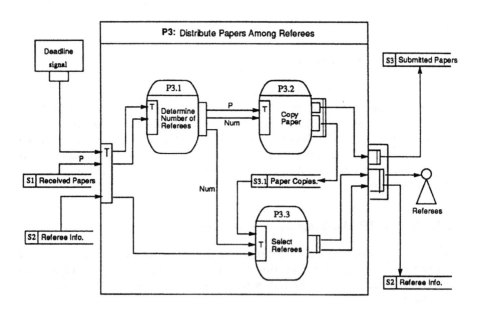

Fig. 3. *PPP: Process Decomposition*

IFIP in EPOS The solution depicted in Figure 4 is based on the PPP solution in the previous section. Only a task network instance is depicted, not the corresponding type specifications and hierarchy.

The task T3 is decomposed into three subtasks, taking as input a subset of T3's input and generating a subset of T3's output. The sequencing among tasks is obtained by dynamic PRE/POST-conditions over the status information of its input/output products. E.g. task T3.1 will execute at a specific point in time (i.e. the pre-condition reads the system clock and compares it to the task's deadline attribute), but only if there exists papers at this point in time. If so, task T3.1 will change the status of "Received Papers" from **exists** to **counted**, and create the entity "Num". A table of pre/post-conditions is outlined in Table 1. An external agent in EPOS is modelled through a task, as we assume that this

TASK	PRE	POST
Det.Numb.of.Ref.	Rec.Pap.status = exists	Rec.Pap.status = counted
		Num.status = created
Copy Paper	Rec.Pap.status = counted	Rec.Pap.status = submitted
	Num.status = created	Pap.Copy.status = created
Select Ref.	Pap.Copy.status = created	Ref.Pac.status = created
	Num.status = created	
	Ref.Info.status = exists	Ref.Info.status = allocated

Table 1. *EPOS: Pre- and Postconditions*

task (sending a referee package) is found elsewhere, and thus we only produce its input.

2.4 Comparing the IFIP solutions

The formalisms found in PPP and EPOS-PM are aimed at different problems: PPP at generating code (CASE-tool) and EPOS-PM at process enactment. However, both have the same building blocks of data entities, data flows, and input/output transformations. Comparing the two solutions results in the observations outlined below.

Diagrammatic language: PPP have an explicit graphical representation of instances, ports, external agents, and time. This facilitates understandability, a prerequisite to conceptual modelling. However, these is no type-editor for PhM types. EPOS-PM is more language-oriented, and has a more primitive and not formalised (and thus user-controllable) graphical representation.

Instances versus Types: PPP do not have explicit types and inheritance for PrM (activities), only for PhM (phenomenons). The PLD operations might also have been expressed by normal object-oriented procedures in the PhM

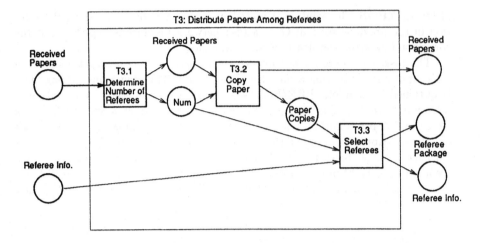

Fig. 4. *EPOS: Task decomposition*

model. Adding these features would — to some degree — have unified three of the four PPP submodels, supporting e.g. reuse of task definitions and added flexibility in the evolutive dimension. While PPP rely on instance specifications, EPOS-PM rely on type specifications. EPOS-PM task networks are incrementally and automatically (re-)generated by the Planner, observing the type specificatons on legal network structure.

Flow among processes: PPP separates between real entities and information entities. Both PPP and EPOS-PM is differentiating between single entities and sets of such. None of the formalisms differentiates between signals and data.

Control among processes: PPP has an explicit representation of sequence, choice, and repetitions (port symbols). In EPOS-PM this is implicitly defined by Pre/Post-conditions, although the flow is more implicit.

Activation and deactivation of processes: PPP differentiates between triggering and non-triggering signals. A PPP task is activated if it receives a triggering signal, then it executes its PLD and terminates when all the required output has been generated. An EPOS task is activated if its pre-condition becomes true, it then sequentially execute its code, generate all outputs, and then terminates (awaits further activation). The pre/post-condition of a task is "AND-concatenated" by the corresponding conditions of its supertypes.

Time: PPP has an explicit representation of time. In EPOS-PM this is modelled in terms of attributes and reading the system clock when evaluating the pre-condition.

Constraints: None of the formalisms can express overall consistency rules.

3 Conclusion

The paper has compared the disciplines of software PM and IS engineering, both with respect to the problems they are addressing and the approaches chosen. All in all, the problem areas are very analogous, but there are notable differences in the approaches. These may partly be attributed to the historical background of the two research camps — the IS field originating from database research and the PM field originating from programming language research.

Whereas the modelling techniques used in IS has had a stronger emphasis on end-user comprehensibility, through diagrammatic representations of the models and various support for validation, PM is maybe using more low-level languages — the research focussing on mechanisms to support system evolution and cooperation between developers. This is also illustrated by our example comparing the environments PPP and EPOS.

Since there are strengths and weaknesses with both approaches, the two camps could have a lot to learn from each other. For instance, EPOS could benefit from providing a more high-level diagrammatic modelling language along the lines of PPP, and PPP could benefit from introducing object-oriented typing of activities and generally from a versioned transaction context, along the lines of EPOS.

This work on comparison will be continued in an upstarting ESPRIT Basic Research Action, PROMOTER, where it will be applied to different scenarios and process management systems.

Acknowledgement

Thanks go to our colleagues, whose research and comments have made this paper possible, in particular Cristina Mazzi and Odd Ivar Lindland.

References

[Ber87]   S. Berdal et al. Modelling an IFIP working conference. Technical Report DAISEE-79, Dept. of electrical engineering and computer science, Norwegian Institute of Technology, 1987.

[CJM+92] Reidar Conradi, M. Letizia Jaccheri, Cristina Mazzi, Amund Aarsten, and Minh Ngoc Nguyen. Design, use, and implementation of SPELL, a language for software process modeling and evolution. In *J.-C. Derniame (ed.): Proc. from EWSPT'92, Sept. 7-8, Trondheim, Norway, Springer Verlag LNCS 635*, pages 167-177, September 1992.

[GLW91]   J. A. Gulla, O. I. Lindland, and G. Willumsen. PPP — an integrated CASE environment. In R. Andersen, J. A. Bubenko jr., and A. Sølvberg, editors, *Advanced Information Systems Engineering, Proc. CAiSE'91, Trondheim*, pages 194-221, Heidelberg, 1991. Springer Verlag (LNCS 498).

A Process-Centered Framework
for Asynchronous Collaborative Work

Jacques Lonchamp

C.R.I.Nancy - Campus scientifique, BP n. 239,
54506 Vandoeuvre les Nancy Cedex, France
jloncham@loria.fr

1 Introduction

Process Modeling (PM) and Process-Centered Software Engineering Environments on the one hand, Computer-Supported Cooperative Work (CSCW) and Groupware on the other hand have attracted much attention in recent years within the Software Engineering community as two distinct areas. An obvious intersection exists, because producing large software systems is a complex cooperative work. But the CSCW community often restricts its scope to specific domains, such as computer-mediated communication, group decision support systems, or coordination systems, and specific groupware products, such as electronic meeting rooms, teleconferencing facilities, desk-top conferencing, shared editors, or electronic mail enhancements. Similarly, the PM community often restricts cooperation to consistent sharing of coarse grain entities between long transactions.

The CPCE (Collaborative Process-Centered Environment) project summarized in this paper aims at applying 'process modeling orientation' and its underlying techniques to various kinds of collaborative applications. Main challenges are to deal with *fine grain interactions*, and to provide *the high level of adaptability and flexibility required by real world collaborative situations*. Not all CSCW applications can take advantage of a process modeling orientation. For instance, a real-time concurrent editing session does not follow usually any predefined process. We have to classify CSCW applications with regard to PM orientation. The time-space matrix is a well known attempt to structure the CSCW field [1]. It centers on the time and location of the cooperation involved, and distinguishes between: local/synchronous applications (i.e. same place, same time), local/asynchronous applications (i.e. same place, different times), remote/synchronous applications (i.e. different places, same time), remote/asynchronous applications (i.e. different places, different times). Asynchronous applications are more likely to be process model driven. They are long term activities, requiring various policies enforcement, and sophisticated assistance: for instance, to 'resynchronize' people working intermittently to the current state of the work through process history and decision rationale. In contrast, synchronous applications are short lived, and rely more on spontaneous reactions of the participants sharing a common view of the ongoing work, than on predefined policies and processes enforcement. Another interesting distinction separates collaboration, communication, and coordination. Collaboration refers to joint work on a common object, communication refers to the exchange of pieces of information, and coordination structures the flow of communication [1]. In what we call 'collaborative work', multiple participants perform consensually a single common task, such as designing or reviewing a given artifact. The overall task is long lived, but the elementary activities to obtain consensus or to evolve a specific aspect of the artifact are generally short lived. The main emphasis is on consensus: most of the decisions about the artifact under consideration must be consensually taken all along the work, through issue resolution processes. Obviously, there exists a continuum of applications regarding the level of collaboration. Even the collective design of a single artifact, can rely more on isolated work than on consensual work: the artifact (or parts of it) can be replicated in multiple work contexts, with merging phases either under the responsibility of a single participant, or more consensually performed.

The paper discusses a prototype of process-centered framework for asynchronous collaborative work. Dedicated environments are built by customizing the framework for a given task and context. The asynchronous collaborative design of a document (which is the first target application), and the asynchronous collaborative review or inspection of an artifact (which will be the second one) are two typical examples of such tasks.

2 Main Requirements and Design Decision

The basic process model orientation of the project means that a set of 'classical' requirements has to be satisfied by the supporting environment, such as: model-based control of user initiatives, model-based automatic execution of some parts of the process, model-based assistance and guidance for users. These aspects have been often discussed for process-centered software engineering environments. However, the project emphasizes *retrospective assistance through design history and rationale* which is of paramount importance for asynchronous work. More specific requirements under consideration here are fine grain interaction modeling, adaptability, and flexibility.

Fine grain interactions shall be modeled as first class concepts within the process model beside classical process entities such as tasks, artifacts, roles, actors, and their relationships. In the collaboration domain currently covered by the project, it means entities for the description of deliberations for consensus. Issues, positions, and arguments are frequently used for modeling such deliberations. More generally, a 'decision-oriented' process modeling is appropriate (terminology of DAIDA and NATURE ESPRIT projects). A detailed description of the internal structure and semantics of the product (which is the topic of most of the deliberations) is also required. Models for design method description and design rationale capture, already merge most of these concepts. CPCE generic model is an extension of Potts'model for describing design methods [2]. In this perspective, process model and process history representation require persistent storage of objects of various granularities. Object oriented repositories are good candidates to fulfill this first requirement.

Adaptability has been extensively studied for process-centered software engineering environments. A software process model is built by customizing a generic model, and instantiating it before its execution. The large variety of asynchronous collaborative tasks, sharing an important set of common features, implies a similar approach: the supporting environment shall be a kernel which can interpret every process model customizing a given generic model. The class specialization concept, with inheritance for both statical and dynamical aspects, reinforce the interest for object orientation. Generic entity types capture the common behavior associated to all their instances: for example, what happens when a user gives an argument, whatever its type is. The specific behavior of every customized type is specified at the sub-type level.

Statical customization is not sufficient. Dynamical change to the running process model has been recognized as a major issue by the process modeling community. For collaborative environments two main reasons can be stated: first, groups often evolve and adapt their way of working to their evolutive contexts; secondly, describing in advance all aspects of a given model is generally very difficult, especially in the case of argumentative entity types such as issues, positions, and arguments. The approach adopted in CPCE distinguishes two aspects. First, the technical point of implementing dynamic evolution of the running model; secondly, the organizational point of managing evolutive environments. For the first aspect dynamic typing, dynamic inheritance, reflectivity, and interpretability provide a sound basis. The second aspect is one of the main originality of CPCE. The point is that the dynamic evolution of a collaborative environment shall be *controlled and consensual*. CPCE solution is to drive process model evolution thanks to another *collaborative process model*, called the 'meta-process model'. The meta process model is obtained by customizing the same generic model which is used to produce the collaborative process model. Both processes are very similar, and participants work in a similar consensual way either to evolve the products or to evolve the model which defines how they work. *This mirrors usual meetings, where people discuss in the same way of the job and of its organization.* The 'full object' orientation of languages such as Smalltalk, where all entities, including classes and methods, are objects, in conjunction with the interpretative, reflective and dynamic nature of these languages, are interesting features to implement easily such a meta level. Therefore, a persistent object store extend-

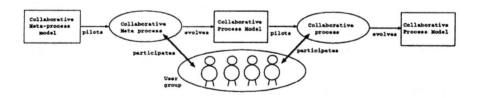

Fig. 1. CPCE logical architecture

ing a Smalltalk environment, and supporting multi-user concurrent access (local or remote), constitutes the core of the CPCE prototype [1]. The object base is used to store the artifacts of the collaborative process, the customized process model, the customized meta process model, the process history and rationale, and the meta process history and rationale. Models are expressed at the schema level, in terms

---

[1] currently Gemstone OODBMS.

of class methods (i.e. methods of metaclasses) and class variables. Histories and rationales are expressed at the instance level. In Smalltalk, methods are inherited dynamically and class variables can change 'on the fly'. Users invoke class methods, either to work (modify the artifacts and create new process history instances), or to evolve the process model (modify the process classes and create new meta process history instances). Model evolution is non-destructive, as the historical instances are immutable. But classes may be 'inhibited', by forbidding new instances creation.

It is worth noticing that *effective meta process modeling implies fine grain modeling* to be able to describe and control the evolution of every fine grained process model component.

3 Current Experiments and Perspectives

A simple customized environment has been developed on top of the first version of the prototype framework. The framework provides a generic process model in terms of generic classes such as 'Step' (specialized into 'ProcessStep' and 'MetaStep'), 'Issue' (Process/Meta), 'Position' (Process/Meta), 'Argument' (Process/Meta), 'Role' (Process/Meta), 'Artifact', and mechanisms to customize the generic model in terms of specific step types, specific role types, specific issue types, and so on, and to instantiate and execute customized models. Generic class methods define the basic behavior of the framework and specific class methods implement the specific behavior of each customized environment. The first customized process model describes the collaborative design of a document. Main ideas are taken from the Cognoter project [3].

In the prototype, when a participant connects to the environment, he can interact through a menu driven and graphical interface. The menu driven part allows participants to take initiatives (raise an issue, give a position, give and remove an argument, solve an issue, perform a step) and to obtain various assistance and guidance information (e.g. ongoing steps and issues, 'raisable' issues and 'performable' steps in the current process state and according to the participant's role). Apart the initial step, every step is either automatically triggered or made ready for invocation by an issue resolution. The interface is used in the latter case, when a participant take the initiative to perform a step. A set of model-based prescriptions are controlled for each user initiative. Dynamically built menus are extensively used and mirror the process state and the participant's role. The user can also obtain graphical information about the process model and about the process history and rationale (a complete picture of all generic and customized types, three partially overlapping views covering all the model because a single representation would be awfully complex - step view, issue view, role view -, similar views on the process history, the current state of the artifact and all previous states.

The meta process is a collaborative process very similar to the design one. The meta process model is statically customized for every application. Participants plays meta roles such as model manager or model performer, which define their rights and obligations. The menu-based interface and the graphical interface are roughly similar to those of the collaborative design process. Each participant can switch freely between the process and the meta process. Changing a software system is always possible, but at very different costs. Here, we aim at providing dynamic consensual evolution at *low cost*: just by manipulating menus and typing values, without any programming.

For instance, the resolution protocol of a given issue can be easily changed, among pre-existing protocols, just by changing a class variable value. The generic issue resolution class method has been written to cope with all pre-existing protocols. In contrast, creating a new resolution protocol is more costly: a non trivial piece of code has to be written. The prototype has been designed to permit *a large number of low cost consensual evolutions, under the control of the meta process.* For instance: add a customized class and its methods or inhibit it, add/suppress a customized model link (e.g. add/suppress a trigger through a 'ToTrigger' link between a position class and a step class, or add/suppress some issue type for a given phase of a process through a 'ToRaise' link between a step class and an issue class), add/change a class attribute (e.g. the precondition of a step or issue class, or a resolution protocol through the 'IssueType' variable of an issue class). On the contrary, the generic model cannot easily change: the kernel part of the framework heavily rely on its generic classes. *Different process model evolution policies can be enforced, through the meta model definition*: who may deliberate about process model changes and who may perform the modification job? (meta role definition), how consensual decisions are taken? (meta issue definition), and so on.

In the application under consideration here, all activities, such as participating to issue resolutions or modifying a given aspect of the document, are short lived. These activities can proceed in parallel and their results are committed into the repository when they finish if no read/write or write/write conflict has occurred between them. In the case of a conflict, a rollback is performed. As people work asynchronously within small groups, an optimistic concurrency control scheme is thought to be adequate: the number of conflicts should remain low. Obviously this optimistic scheme is not sufficient. In the next future we plan to enrich the kernel with other schemes. Mixing asynchronous and synchronous work is another prerequisite, for instance to be able to negotiate how conflicts have to be solved. We plan to rely mainly on user consensus to solve conflicts, and to assist them by tracking all dependencies and commitments resulting from their interactions.

References

1. C.A. Ellis, S.J. Gibbs, G.L. Rein: Groupware: Some Issues and Experiences. CACM, 34, 1, pp 38–58, 1991.
2. C. Potts: A Generic Model for Representing Design Methods. Proc. 11th ICSE, pp 217–220, 1989.
3. M. Stefik, G. Foster, D. Bobrow, K. Kahn, S. Lanning, L. Suchman: Beyond the Chalkboard-Computer Support for Collaboration and Problem Solving in Meetings. CACM, 30, 1, pp 32–47, 1987.

Appendix

The following snapshots exemplify the interleaving of process and meta process activities. As they take place asynchronously on several user workstations we show their effects mainly through graphical representations of process and meta process histories. The scenario is part of the Cognoter-like document design process.

In Fig.2 the 'Step view model' window gives the overall organization of the document design process with several sequential phases. The 'Step graph' window details the 'BrainstormingPhase' when participants individually propose their ideas for the document. The 'Issue view model' window gives the position and the argument class related to the 'AddIdeaIssue' (there is only one position type because the issue is individually solved). The purpose of the scenario is to exemplify the dynamical and consensual creation of a new argument class ('RelevantIdea') supporting 'AddIdea-Position'. The 'Step view history' window presents the current history of the process: two ideas have been proposed. 'Issue view history' windows detail the corresponding individual issue resolutions. 'Idea graph' window displays the resulting document design state.

In Fig.3 we have similar windows showing the meta process model with only one phase ('ChangeProcessModel') and several issue types within it for evolving the process model. The 'AddArgumentTypeIssue' model is detailed in the 'Meta issue view model' window. The meta process history shows the dynamical creation of the new argument type. The issue has been solved consensually by the two model performers each giving a 'UsefullType' argument. The 'inspect' windows displays the textual definition of 'AddArgumentTypeIsue#1'. In the TEXT field the parameters for creating the argument class and its methods appear. This exemplifies what we have called a 'low cost evolution'.

Fig.4 demonstrates the use of this new argument class for creating, through the menu based interface of one participant, the third idea in the document. The pop-up menus for process execution and process assistance are pinned up on the low part of the picture. The graphical representation of the new 'AddIdeaIssue' resolution and the new document design state are depicted on the right part of the screen.

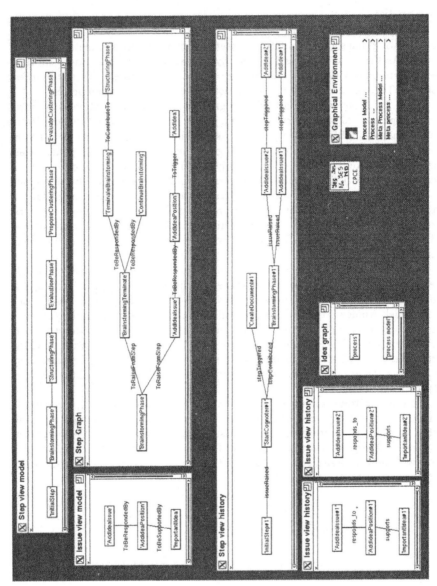

Fig. 2. The process model and process history.

268

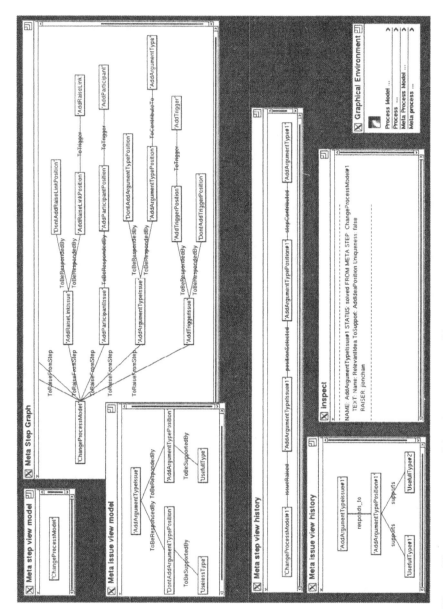

Fig. 3. The meta process model and meta process history.

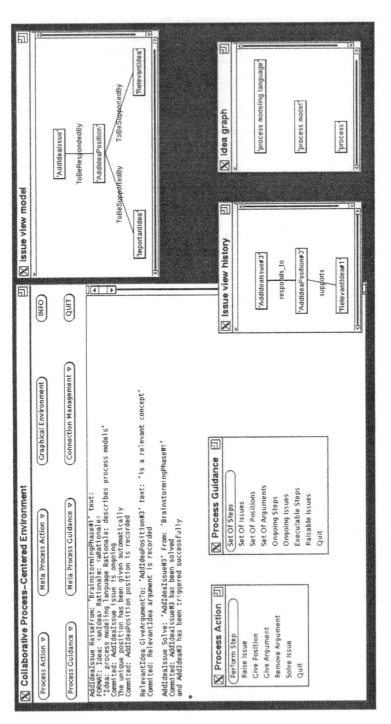

Fig. 4. A participant menu based interface.

What Process Technology needs from Databases

Jacky Estublier

L.G.I. BP 53X 38041 Grenoble FRANCE

Abstract. It is now accepted by most of the Process Community, that a database is needed to store not only the software artifacts but also to provide modelling power for all the resources involved in the process, including process models and instances themselves. The specific problems of process modelling give rise to the question of: what would be the "ideal" data base for the support of software processes. In this article we put forward what are, in our view, the specific features such a DBMS should provide.

1 Data modelling

Software Process managers are designed to support agents in their effort to reach a common goal: the development and maintenance of a software product. The entities they operate upon are thus all the resources involved. They include software objects, documents, tools, agents, teams, schedules, meetings, and processes. Some of these entities are composite entities (complex documents, configurations), may contain files of different kinds and have complex relationships with one other.

Clearly we need a data base with high modelling capability, one which is able to model easily and to deal with arbitrary complex objects (which may or may not contain files) and complex interrelationships between entities. In SEE users think in term of these relationships, and thus I do think explicit relationships are needed for clear modelling.

One controversial issue is that of granularity. It has been claimed [Emmerich93] that abstract syntax trees must be supported; we think this is not a major requirement for process management, and should come last in our list of requirements. Versionning is an important topic since, in SEE environments, software entities are usually versioned. The data base should support most versioning paradigms, since it is not independent of the process model. For instance, the consistency constraints when changing an object may differs depending on whether it is the current underway version or an old release. I do think one of the major roles of an SEE data base (and Process support DBMS) is its ability to hide as much as possible the versioning dimension, while still following rules related to versioning.

2 Cooperative work, Sub-databases and Transactions

Many agents are working towards a common goal and share objects whilst performing their tasks. This is the difficult problem of cooperative work. It is clear that the data base should provide a broad ranging support to the different cooperation strategies, instead of imposing one. Each process works on certains entities (a sub-set of all available entities), using some tools (a sub-set of all available tools), and a specific schema (a sub-schema). The union of a sub-set of instances along with a sub-schema and some properties constitute the usual definition of a sub-database. If sub DBs are provided, a large number of problems are solved. For that, a number of requirements must be satisfied.

A sub-DB must enable an arbitrary sub set of entities to be contained, and arbitrary schemas (not just a sub-schema of a unique overall schema). Furthermore, the relationships between sub-DBs must be highly customizable. It is not acceptable to have only visibility on commit, and only a tree-like sub-database. I think a sub DB must not (always) be seen as a transaction, but the place where a process performs. Arbitrary cooperation protocols between arbitrary sub DBs should be formally described.

If a DBMS provides these functionalities, the process formalism is in charge of defining and controlling the inter-process behaviour, in a high level formalism, then translated into sub-DB relationships fully supported by the DBMS. Most problems of collaborative work are solved. However since most concepts are only under elaboration [Godart93, Belkhatir91, Belkhatir93], it is not surprising that no DBMS yet provides such functionalities. I suspect that it will be a mandatory feature for effective and comfortable support of collaborative work. State of the art is currently far from meeting this requirement. PCTE provides a concept of sub schema (SDS) but not sub-DB, Orion [Kim91] a sub DB, but only a tree-like one with synchro on commit. Most other DBMS do not provide any help.

3   Evolution and Flexibility

Evolution is recognized as a fundamental requirement for software processes. The reason for this have been repeatedly emphasised: long time duration of processes in conjunction with multiple evolutions (product, organisation and methods), the unpredictability due to the nature of some processes (fixing a bug), and to any process involving multiple human interactions. The evolution problem is essentially due to the fact it must be performed without stopping current processes, and thus without DB restructuring.

This evolution, from the DBMS point of view, materialises in the following ways:

1 Adding and removing types: easy.

2 Changing types of existing instances: not easy.

3 Modifying types and adding views of existing instances: hard.

4 Modifying only a view of a type independently of the other views: pretty hard.

5 Changing type of some instance only for some views, not for others: very hard.

Most DBMSs offer only feature 1,; Adele supports features 1 to 4. I do think a very flexible type management from the DB is a mandatory feature for supporting process evolution, and probably one which is very difficult to offer from a DBMS point of view. This is because it impacts deeply on the DBMS implementation, and has negative consequences on efficiency since more computation must be done dynamically (the internal format of entities is not known statically).

4 History, Traceability and Measure

The definition and customising of corporate wide processes will become a major task for most companies, and will mobilise substential resources. It will become increasingly important to be able to measure and assess process models, in order to tune, customize and enhance process models during their execution in a given project and to store them, along with information about their context [Basili93] for later use in other projects.

This aspect will require, that the underlying DBMS have the ability to provide pertinent information about the performance of current and past processes. Since processes may have a long duration (weeks and months), queries have to work on past facts, objects in their past state, objects now deleted, past relationships and consumption of past resources, i.e. temporal queries. Here we differentiate from usual temporal databases where the aim is to "retrieve" a full data base "slice" at a given point in time [Snodgrass87]; we need instead to perform traceability over long periods of time, but on a sub set of stored information; this is a more generalised traceability and history mechanism than that of a temporal database.

Suppose a given design change D is performed in a design process. We must be able to answer the following questions: "what are all the actions (processes) performed as consequences of D?", "who decided to accept D?", "which changes in which processes to which objects have been performed to satisfy D?", "how long did it take?", "who was involved, when and for how much time?", "how expensive it was?".

5 Viewpoints and Contextual Behaviour.

There is an increasing interest in the software process community in considering multi viewpoint approaches. In the development of any large and complex system by multiple agents, each agent holds an overlapping and partial view of the total process. Each agent has a specific view of the total process in terms of knowledge, representation, and process.

It looks appealing to respect and even enforce this fact: the process governing the behaviour of each agent class should be described independently, allowing each agent to have only a limited knowledge of the global process, to modularise the total model, to allow extension (by adding viewpoints), and to simplify evolution (a viewpoint change propagation is limited to that viewpoint). Unfortunately, supporting this approach raises numerous difficulties for the underlying DBMS. Each entity may have different descriptions (static and dynamic) depending on viewpoints. Entities can be shared by different activities and consequently the data base must support multiple simultaneous description of entities. Furthermore, each viewpoint may have its own consistency constraints, raising the problem of managing local (to a given viewpoint) and global (to the total process) constraint management [Finkelstein93].

In reality it is not only viewpoints we need but "contextual behaviour" [Belkhatir93]. It means that since an object O pertains to a process instance P with a given point of view, O behaviour is not only changed in P but may be changed in all processes. For instance if P requires the global constraints "cannot be deleted" all processes (view points) using O will be affected. The behaviour of an object depends on the context.

The concept a sub-DB, with a different schema per sub-DB provides the viewpoint approach, but usually not contextual behaviour. PCTE offers viewpoint services with SDS (more or less sub-schema), but does not provide any contextual behaviour and no sub DB. Adele offers both multiple schemes and contextual behaviour, but sub DBs are only partial and some features are already missing for supporting a generalized role approach (feature number 5 described previously).

6 Enaction support, Active DBMS

I think the enaction support is a very difficult and controversial topic. It seems to be accepted that the data base must be active; it means the data base must react to some events (actions in the database, time, or even arbitrary external events) which wake up the process machine. The event manager can be external [Krishnamurthy93], a simple notifier in the database (PCTE+), or a complete event manager in the data base[Belkhatir91].

Clearly the last possibility is the most appealing, since events, data model and database transaction can be integrated. The provision of this kind of feature appears to be a widely-held goal. Whatever the case may be, I feel that the help of an external event manager for the detection of external events, may be helpful. It is my belief that the data base must provide a full event manager closely integrated with the transaction mechanism and with a computationaly complete language i.e. a basic process engine.

7 Conclusion

I have tried to show that process support and process engines must rely on many features of the underlying database; and that the ideal DBMS is currently a dream. More fundamental perhaps, is the fact that the ideal DBMS, as presented here, overlaps substantially with the process engine, possibly at the expense of DBMS efficiency and generality. It is probably a fundamental architectural issue to define boundaries and relationships between the event manager, transaction manager, database manager, data model, computational language, process engine and process formalisms. I feel all the above requirements must essentially be satisfied by the DBMS, thus providing a general basic process engine. On top of this engine just about any other process engine and process formalismes can be implemented.

Most of these requirements have arisen from the experiments on implementing a demanding process formalism (Tempo) on the Adele DBMS kernel. We expect Adele to satisfy all the above requirements in the future; work in this direction is under way.

Basili93 The experience Factory and its relationship to other
        Improvement Paradigms.
        Vic Basili, Proc ESEC'93, Garmish September 1993, Germany.
Belkhatir93 Software Process Control and Work Space Control in the Adele System.

N. Belkhatir, J. Estublier, W.L. Melo

Proc. Proc. First Int'l conf. on the software Process (ICSP2)

Berlin, February 93, Germany.

Belkhatir92 Adele2: A support to large software development process.

N. Belkhatir, J. Estublier, W.L. Melo.

Proc. First It'l conf. on the software Process (ICSP1).

Redondo Beach, CA, USA, October 1991.

Emmerich93 Databases for Software Engineering Environments -

The goal has not been Attained.

W. Emmerich W. Schafer, J. Welsh

Proc ESEC'93, Garmish September 1993, Germany.

Finkelstein93 Inconsistency Handling in Multi-perspective Specifications.

A. Finkelstein, D. Gabbay, A. Hunter, J. Kramer, B. Nuseibeh

Proc ESEC'93, Garmish September 1993, Germany.

Godart93 A Transaction Model to Support COOperative Software Developers

COOrdination.

C. Godart.

Proc ESEC'93, Garmish September 1993, Germany.

Kim91 A Distributed Object-Oriented Database System Supporting Shared

and reference Private Databases.

W. Kim, N. Ballou, J. Garza, D. Woelk

ACM Transactions on Information Systems. January 1991.

Krishnamurthy93 Provence: A Process Visualisation and Enactment Environment.

B. Krishnamurthy, N.S. Barghouti

Proc ESEC'93, Garmish September 1993, Germany.

Snodgrass87 The Temporal Query Language TQUEL.

R. Snodgrass.

ACM Transactions on Database Systems. 12,2 (June 12 1987).

Author Index

Lecture Notes in Computer Science

For information about Vols. 1–693
please contact your bookseller or Springer-Verlag

Vol. 729: L. Donatiello, R. Nelson (Eds.), Performance Evaluation of Computer and Communication Systems. Proceedings, 1993. VIII, 675 pages. 1993.

Vol. 730: D. B. Lomet (Ed.), Foundations of Data Organization and Algorithms. Proceedings, 1993. XII, 412 pages. 1993.

Vol. 731: A. Schill (Ed.), DCE – The OSF Distributed Computing Environment. Proceedings, 1993. VIII, 285 pages. 1993.

Vol. 732: A. Bode, M. Dal Cin (Eds.), Parallel Computer Architectures. IX, 311 pages. 1993.

Vol. 733: Th. Grechenig, M. Tscheligi (Eds.), Human Computer Interaction. Proceedings, 1993. XIV, 450 pages. 1993.

Vol. 734: J. Volkert (Ed.), Parallel Computation. Proceedings, 1993. VIII, 248 pages. 1993.

Vol. 735: D. Bjørner, M. Broy, I. V. Pottosin (Eds.), Formal Methods in Programming and Their Applications. Proceedings, 1993. IX, 434 pages. 1993.

Vol. 736: R. L. Grossman, A. Nerode, A. P. Ravn, H. Rischel (Eds.), Hybrid Systems. VIII, 474 pages. 1993.

Vol. 737: J. Calmet, J. A. Campbell (Eds.), Artificial Intelligence and Symbolic Mathematical Computing. Proceedings, 1992. VIII, 305 pages. 1993.

Vol. 738: M. Weber, M. Simons, Ch. Lafontaine, The Generic Development Language Deva. XI, 246 pages. 1993.

Vol. 739: H. Imai, R. L. Rivest, T. Matsumoto (Eds.), Advances in Cryptology – ASIACRYPT '91. X, 499 pages. 1993.

Vol. 740: E. F. Brickell (Ed.), Advances in Cryptology – CRYPTO '92. Proceedings, 1992. X, 593 pages. 1993.

Vol. 741: B. Preneel, R. Govaerts, J. Vandewalle (Eds.), Computer Security and Industrial Cryptography. Proceedings, 1991. VIII, 275 pages. 1993.

Vol. 742: S. Nishio, A. Yonezawa (Eds.), Object Technologies for Advanced Software. Proceedings, 1993. X, 543 pages. 1993.

Vol. 743: S. Doshita, K. Furukawa, K. P. Jantke, T. Nishida (Eds.), Algorithmic Learning Theory. Proceedings, 1992. X, 260 pages. 1993. (Subseries LNAI)

Vol. 744: K. P. Jantke, T. Yokomori, S. Kobayashi, E. Tomita (Eds.), Algorithmic Learning Theory. Proceedings, 1993. XI, 423 pages. 1993. (Subseries LNAI)

Vol. 745: V. Roberto (Ed.), Intelligent Perceptual Systems. VIII, 378 pages. 1993. (Subseries LNAI)

Vol. 746: A. S. Tanguiane, Artificial Perception and Music Recognition. XV, 210 pages. 1993. (Subseries LNAI).

Vol. 747: M. Clarke, R. Kruse, S. Moral (Eds.), Symbolic and Quantitative Approaches to Reasoning and Uncertainty. Proceedings, 1993. X, 390 pages. 1993.

Vol. 748: R. H. Halstead Jr., T. Ito (Eds.), Parallel Symbolic Computing: Languages, Systems, and Applications. Proceedings, 1992. X, 419 pages. 1993.

Vol. 749: P. A. Fritzson (Ed.), Automated and Algorithmic Debugging. Proceedings, 1993. VIII, 369 pages. 1993.

Vol. 750: J. L. Díaz-Herrera (Ed.), Software Engineering Education. Proceedings, 1994. XII, 601 pages. 1994.

Vol. 751: B. Jähne, Spatio-Temporal Image Processing. XII, 208 pages. 1993.

Vol. 752: T. W. Finin, C. K. Nicholas, Y. Yesha (Eds.), Information and Knowledge Management. Proceedings, 1992. VII, 142 pages. 1993.

Vol. 753: L. J. Bass, J. Gornostaev, C. Unger (Eds.), Human-Computer Interaction. Proceedings, 1993. X, 388 pages. 1993.

Vol. 754: H. D. Pfeiffer, T. E. Nagle (Eds.), Conceptual Structures: Theory and Implementation. Proceedings, 1992. IX, 327 pages. 1993. (Subseries LNAI).

Vol. 755: B. Möller, H. Partsch, S. Schuman (Eds.), Formal Program Development. Proceedings. VII, 371 pages. 1993.

Vol. 756: J. Pieprzyk, B. Sadeghiyan, Design of Hashing Algorithms. XV, 194 pages. 1993.

Vol. 757: U. Banerjee, D. Gelernter, A. Nicolau, D. Padua (Eds.), Languages and Compilers for Parallel Computing. Proceedings, 1992. X, 576 pages. 1993.

Vol. 758: M. Teillaud, Towards Dynamic Randomized Algorithms in Computational Geometry. IX, 157 pages. 1993.

Vol. 759: N. R. Adam, B. K. Bhargava (Eds.), Advanced Database Systems. XV, 451 pages. 1993.

Vol. 760: S. Ceri, K. Tanaka, S. Tsur (Eds.), Deductive and Object-Oriented Databases. Proceedings, 1993. XII, 488 pages. 1993.

Vol. 761: R. K. Shyamasundar (Ed.), Foundations of Software Technology and Theoretical Computer Science. Proceedings, 1993. XIV, 456 pages. 1993.

Vol. 762: K. W. Ng, P. Raghavan, N. V. Balasubramanian, F. Y. L. Chin (Eds.), Algorithms and Computation. Proceedings, 1993. XIII, 542 pages. 1993.

Vol. 763: F. Pichler, R. Moreno Díaz (Eds.), Computer Aided Systems Theory – EUROCAST '93. Proceedings, 1993. IX, 451 pages. 1994.

Vol. 764: G. Wagner, Vivid Logic. XII, 148 pages. 1994. (Subseries LNAI).

Vol. 765: T. Helleseth (Ed.), Advances in Cryptology – EUROCRYPT '93. Proceedings, 1993. X, 467 pages. 1994.

Vol. 766: P. R. Van Loocke, The Dynamics of Concepts. XI, 340 pages. 1994. (Subseries LNAI).

Vol. 767: M. Gogolla, An Extended Entity-Relationship Model. X, 136 pages. 1994.

Vol. 768: U. Banerjee, D. Gelernter, A. Nicolau, D. Padua (Eds.), Languages and Compilers for Parallel Computing. Proceedings, 1993. XI, 655 pages. 1994.

Vol. 769: J. L. Nazareth, The Newton-Cauchy Framework. XII, 101 pages. 1994.

Vol. 770: P. Haddawy (Representing Plans Under Uncertainty. X, 129 pages. 1994. (Subseries LNAI).

Vol. 771: G. Tomas, C. W. Ueberhuber, Visualization of Scientific Parallel Programs. XI, 310 pages. 1994.

Vol. 772: B. C. Warboys (Ed.),Software Process Technology. Proceedings, 1994. IX, 275 pages. 1994.

Vol. 773: D. R. Stinson (Ed.), Advances in Cryptology – CRYPTO '93. Proceedings, 1993. X, 492 pages. 1994.